D0982986

THE PERILS OF GLOBAL LEGALISM

The Perils of Global Legalism

Eric A. Posner

The University of Chicago Press ‡ CHICAGO AND LONDON

ERIC A. POSNER is the Kirkland and Ellis Professor of Law at the University of Chicago Law School. He is an editor of the *Journal of Legal Studies* and the author or coauthor of several books, including *Law and Social Norms*; *Cost-Benefit Analysis: Legal, Economic, and Philosophical Perspectives*; *New Foundations of Cost-Benefit Analysis*; *Terror in the Balance: Security, Liberty, and the Courts*; and *The Limits of International Law*.

The University of Chicago Press, Chicago 60637
The University of Chicago Press, Ltd., London
© 2009 by The University of Chicago
All rights reserved. Published 2009
Printed in the United States of America

18 17 16 15 14 13 12 11 10 09   1 2 3 4 5

ISBN-13: 978-0-226-67574-9 (cloth)
ISBN-10: 0-226-67574-2 (cloth)

Library of Congress Cataloging-in-Publication Data
Posner, Eric A.
    The perils of global legalism / Eric A. Posner.
        p.   cm.
    Includes bibliographical references and index.
    ISBN-13: 978-0-226-67574-9 (cloth : alk. paper)
    ISBN-10: 0-226-67574-2 (cloth : alk. paper) 1. International law —
Philosophy. 2. International relations. 3. International and municipal
law. I. Title.
    KZ3160.P67P47   2009
    341.01 — dc22

                                                         2008054849

♾ The paper used in this publication meets the minimum requirements
of the American National Standard for Information Sciences —
Permanence of Paper for Printed Library Materials, ANSI Z39.48–1992.

For Emlyn

CONTENTS

———————

Is international law anything more than the sum of states' interests, a useful instrument for cooperation but nothing more? In earlier work, I argued that international law reflects norms of cooperation that emerge when states act in their self-interest.[1] It followed from that conception that when a state considers whether to obey international law that conflicts with what it perceives to be good policy, it should weigh the costs and benefits and act accordingly. The usual cost of violation of international law is that another state will object or retaliate, and valuable cooperative opportunities could be lost. This cost can be high, so states do not violate international law lightly. But when circumstances change, so can the payoffs from complying with a particular norm of international law, in which case it may make sense for the state in question to violate the law. It may do so on the sly or it may do so explicitly. States refuse to admit that they violate international law and instead simply advance an "interpretation" of the law that more closely aligns that law with that state's interest, in some cases hollowing it out completely. Sometimes, they insist on renegotiating international agreements that stand in their way.

Consider, for example, the decision of the United States and its NATO allies to launch a military intervention in Serbia in 1999. Serbian forces had begun to put pressure on the mainly ethnic Albanian population of Kosovo, which supported an insurgency that sought to achieve autonomy for that region. Atrocities multiplied, and the foreign governments feared a recurrence of the violence and instability of the Yugoslavian civil war that had occurred earlier in that decade, which had killed many thousands, sent refugees spilling over borders, and destabilized the region. The problem was that under the UN charter, Serbia's conflict with its insurgency was an internal matter, and foreign countries could not intervene without the approval of the Security Council. Neither Russia nor China would withhold their veto, which meant that such approval would not be forthcoming. If NATO invaded, it would break international law. But if it did not, then it would have to stand by and watch a genocide unfold.

NATO broke international law and intervened. NATO countries did not admit to breaking the law, but they also did not try very hard to drum up a legal rationale. Some commentators bruited about the idea that international law really ought to, or maybe already does, have an implicit exception to the UN charter, one that allows uses of force for humanitarian purposes. However, this idea never gained traction.[2] The only way to explain this episode is to admit that the relevant nations believed that they had a stronger interest in violating international law than in complying with it. Russia and China were too weak at the time for their opposition to matter.

The benefits of the intervention were clear; what of the costs? Was there a cost to "international law" or to the "rule of international law" that can be distinguished from the apparently tolerable cost of Chinese and Russian opposition? It may be that the force of the UN rule eroded as a consequence of the intervention; whether in fact it did or not is hard to say. It is possible, but unlikely, that the weakening of the UN rule contributed to the intervention in Iraq in 2003, which also lacked Security Council authorization, at least under the most plausible reading of earlier resolutions, or to Russia's incursion in Georgia in 2008, which was clearly unauthorized. After all, the Kosovo intervention was hardly the first use of military force that violated the UN charter.[3] So it is hard to say whether the Kosovo intervention weakened the charter. Even if it did, it is unclear whether this weakening was beneficial or not. Suppose, for example, that the effect of the intervention was to carve out an exception for humanitarian interventions. Such a rule could very well be desirable; or it might not—everything depends on how that exception was subsequently interpreted.

Violating international law has identifiable short-term costs and benefits relating to the particular course of action, and it has much more speculative long-term costs and benefits touching on the legitimacy or robustness of international law in general. In public discussion in the United States, popular and elite opinion think of international law in a straightforward cost-benefit sense. The main divide between liberals and conservatives is over the long-term costs and benefits. Liberals believe that the long-term costs for the United States from breaking international law are high, while conservatives think they are low. But, although the two groups have different ideas about what the national interest requires, they agree that the national interest may justify violating or working against international law—for liberals, when international trade threatens environmental standards and working conditions; for conservatives, when human rights treaties and international criminal law interfere with security.[4] The result is a pattern of American international lawbreaking that long predates the years of the Bush administration.[5]

This type of instrumental thinking about international law offends Europeans, especially European intellectuals, who argue that international law—and especially certain core norms of international law—cannot be put into a cost-benefit analysis but simply must be obeyed. Whether this view actually influences European governments is another question, as the Kosovo case illustrates. The European Union has also authorized illegal trade practices when pressures from European industry or public sentiment were great enough, and many commentators see European attitudes about international law as an instrumental effort to promote European values and interests.[6] As for the rest of the world, no serious observer contends that countries like China, Russia, India, Brazil, and Japan think of international law in other than instrumental terms.

In the United States, conventional legal-academic thinking about international law hovers somewhere between the European view and the liberal popular-press view in the United States. American legal scholars typically argue that preserving and enhancing international law is in the long-term interest of the United States even if particular short-term costs are high. However, it is increasingly rare for an American legal scholar to acknowledge that any particular illegal act on the part of the United States could be justified on national interest grounds, and there seems to be movement toward the view that the real justification for international law is cosmopolitan, the implication being that the United States should incur costs for the sake of international law in some abstract sense—perhaps for the sake of the international community, but this is always left a little obscure.

The conflation of America's interests and the world's interests is a typically American stance, and so it is no surprise that American legal scholars have fallen into this trap. In American legal scholarship, it has led to a view of international law that I will call "global legalism." Most European scholars are global legalists as well. Global legalism is an excessive faith in the efficacy of international law. For some (mainly American) global legalists, the very high value of international law creates a presumption against violating it that is so strong that, for all practical purposes, it may never be violated. For others (mainly Europeans), international law has value for its own sake — it does not have merely instrumental value for the states that it governs — and therefore it is wrong for states to evaluate potentially illegal conduct with a cost-benefit analysis that uses national interest as the metric. Indeed, global legalists have long since dropped the conventional view that international law is based on the consent of states; international law transcends the interests of states and holds them in its grasp. I will argue that global legalism is not just a scholarly fashion; in fact, it has deep roots in American thinking, which explains why it exerts so much power in scholarly and, sometimes but to a lesser extent, in popular discussion.

The premise of this book is that law and legal institutions can obtain prestige among the public when they function in a highly effective manner, especially when they function more effectively than political institutions do. The prestige of the law often leads to *legalism*, which is a view that loses sight of the social function of law and sees it as an end in itself, one that thinks of moral and political problems in legal categories and asks lawyers and judges rather than politicians to solve them. In the United States, legalism has been a powerful way of thinking for almost two hundred years. Legalistic thinking has favorably disposed Americans to international law where, however, legal institutions have always been extremely weak and unreliable, despite the many efforts (since World War I, led by the United States) to construct and strengthen them.

The weakness of international law, by contrast to domestic law in the United States and many other advanced democracies, can be traced to the absence of robust international political and legal institutions — legislatures, executives, courts — which can in turn be traced to the extreme heterogeneity of the global population and the vastness of the globe. Although there are some recognized global values and interests, virtually everyone around the world owes his or her primary loyalty to a state, which delivers goods such as security that promote local values and interests. Even in poorly run and authoritarian states, people trust and defer to conationals in their governments in ways that would never happen for an international government, which would have to draw its staff from all around the world and could not be monitored or even understood by ordinary people. It can hardly be exaggerated how important the supporting institutions of law are for making the law work in a way that advances people's interests; without those institutions, law is more like social norms or customary norms or norms of etiquette — free-floating rules that emerge somehow from the maelstrom of human behavior that people only vaguely understand, that are rarely clear, that can't be easily changed, and that have an obscure relationship with human well-being.

So international law is a peculiar type of law that exists but lacks effective legal institutions to manage it. Legalism has its global counterpart, *global legalism*, which is a contradictory faith that both acknowledges this problem — in a phrase, the problem of "law without government" — but also believes that international law can nonetheless carry out its functions and deserves loyalty beyond national interest–based cost-benefit calculations. The reasoning is as follows. True, world government does not exist, and the reason is that nations refuse to yield authority to supranational institutions that they cannot trust. But nations can yield that authority to international law that, after all, they have agreed to. If the authority of international law merely rests on nations' consent, then why shouldn't a nation withdraw its consent if it believes that it can do better by violating the law? The answer is that if states do that, international law will lose its authority, and thus its ability to constrain nations to act in the general interest. International law is effective because states defer to it; they defer to it because it is effective.

This book is about this circularity, its implications for international institutions, and attempts to break out of it. Chapter 1 defines global legalism by comparing it to other utopian approaches to solving global problems like war and environmental degradation — problems that states cannot solve unilaterally because the behavior responsible for them extends across multiple borders. These other approaches — setting up a world government, for example — no longer seem plausible and few people take them seriously anymore. But the problems remain, and global legalism presents itself as a more realistic method for approaching them. It does not require as dramatic a change in human nature or the organization of the world, and it presents itself as a simple extension of the domestic version of legalism that prevails in the most successful states, preeminently, the United States and the quasi-state European Union. The prestige of domestic legalism underlies the faith in global legalism. But I argue that the two kinds of legalism are fundamentally different: domestic legalism flourishes because governments support it; global legalism has no government to turn to. Chapter 2 spells out this problem in detail. Law cannot control behavior unless legal institutions support it; without legal institutions—legislatures, enforcers, courts—international law is unavoidably weak.

In chapter 3, I consider various defenses of global legalism in the academic literature. Scholars have argued that only a "state-centered" view of international law would insist that it is weak. If one disaggregates the state and looks at its component parts, one discovers reasons for believing that international law transcends the interests of states. I argue that none of the intrastate components that advocates identify—interest groups and civil society, the consciences of citizens or government officials, democratic processes or judicial review—provide a theoretical basis for global legalism or evidence that global legalism provides an accurate description of the world, nor do trends such as the fragmentation of states (chapter 4) or the increasing incorporation of international law in domestic law (chapter 5), as is sometimes argued. The efforts of advocates to persuade national courts around the world to take international law more seriously than they have in the past are likely to be futile.

In part II, I focus on international courts. One might think that the proliferation of international tribunals provides evidence for global legalism, and it is true that international courts have fared much better than international legislative and executive institutions, which are virtually nonexistent. The courts do provide evidence of legalistic thinking—the prestige of the judge has always been a central element of legalism—but not of the accuracy of that worldview. Chapter 6 explains the limited power of international tribunals to resolve disputes, and chapter 7 explains what happens when those tribunals' ambitions exceed their limited grasp—states work around them, constructing new tribunals that they can more tightly control. Chapter 8 examines international tribunals that have jurisdiction over individuals and argues that the legalistic ambitions for international criminal adjudication do not reflect their roots in security policy, and its continued vitality depends on a return to those roots. Chapter 9 examines domestic courts and their relationship with global legalism and shows that domestic adjudication that seeks to advance international law can do little to address the global problems that one should care about.

The proliferation of courts does need to be explained, however; and part II argues that international courts have fared better than international legislatures and executives because courts have real but limited instrumental value for states and can be controlled and worked around. In this way, they have little in common with domestic courts, which have mandatory jurisdiction. Legalists seek more than that from the international judge—a person who stands outside international politics and turns away the lances of state interest with the shield of justice. On such a mirage do they try to construct the international order.

This book follows a long line of warnings about excessive reliance on international law and international institutions for solving problems of global conflict. Its predecessors include E. H. Carr's *The Twenty Years' Crisis* and Hans Morgenthau's *Politics Among Nations*, whose diagnoses I update with the help of the intervening literature on legalism and judicialization. These authors are sometimes misunderstood as pessimists about all forms of international cooperation. In fact, they did believe that ideals matter and that international law can solve certain problems, but because they did not provide a constructive account of international law—that is, a theory that explains its existence—their skepticism is their defining legacy. The challenge for today is explaining when international law works and what its limits are.

Some political scientists have accepted this challenge and their most convincing work uses rational choice theory to explain the conditions under which states can cooperate.[7] Law professors, by contrast, have largely ignored the challenge, having instead succumbed to the lure of global legalism. Building on an earlier book that I wrote with Jack Goldsmith,[8] in this book I have two aims: to refute global legalism and to further develop the rational choice account of international law. As in the earlier book, it is most definitely not my claim that international law does not exist or does not matter. The argument is instead that international law exists and matters when it serves nation-states' interests in international cooperation. Understanding when those conditions exist and do not exist should be on every international law professor's academic agenda.

If this book has a single theme, it is that politics, idealism, and careless thinking conspire to produce a picture of international law that bears little resemblance to reality. This picture emphasizes universalism (the rules apply to all states), sovereign equality, and human rights; the reality is one of bilateralism (states typically cooperate in pairs), heterogeneity (states frequently have opposing interests), and power. While refuting the picture, I try to suggest ways in which appreciation of reality allows for more effective forms of cooperation than those that prevail when states yield to idealistic agendas. For states do, from time to time, construct idealistic institutions — they can agree to anything they want, after all, and under the influence of popular enthusiasm, they sometimes do. But under the pressure of events, these institutions always either crumble or are put to other uses more consistent with international realities.

ACKNOWLEDGMENTS

Thanks to Daniel Abebe, Ken Anderson, Anu Bradford, Rosalind Dixon, Jake Gersen, Tom Ginsburg, Michael Glennon, Jack Goldsmith, and Adrian Vermeule, for their helpful comments on parts or all of the manuscript, and to audiences at Northwestern Law School, Harvard Law School, and the European University Institute in Florence. I received very helpful comments from several anonymous reviewers. In addition to correcting errors, they persuaded me to reorganize the book and modify aspects of my argument. David Pervin, my editor, also gave me helpful organizational and thematic suggestions.

Several of the chapters have their origin in previously published work that I have heavily revised in light of comments and criticisms, in some cases preserving only a few paragraphs or a stray passage. This work includes: *The Decline of the International Court of Justice*, International Conflict Resolution 111 (Stefan Voigt, Max Albert, and Dieter Schmidtchen eds., 2006); *Judicial Independence in International Tribunals*, 93 Calif. L. Rev. 1 (2005) (with John Yoo); *International Law and the Disaggregated State*, 32 Fla. St. U. L. Rev. 797 (2005); *International Law: A Welfarist Approach*, 73 U. Chi. L. Rev. 487 (2006); *Political Trials in Domestic and International Law*, 55 Duke L. J. 75 (2005); Review of Robert E. Scott and Paul B. Stephan, *The Limits of Leviathan: Contract Theory and the Enforcement of International Law*, 101 Amer. J. Int'l L. 509 (2007); *Law without Nations? Why Constitutional Government Requires Sovereign States*, 4 Perspectives on Politics 432 (2006) (book review); *Climate Change and International Human Rights Litigation: A Critical Appraisal*, 155 U. Pa. L. Rev. 1925 (2007); Boumediene *and the Uncertain March of Judicial Cosmopolitanism*, Cato Supreme Court Review: 2007–2008, p. 23 (2008). I thank these publications for the right to reprint my earlier work.

— PART I —

Global Legalism

Global legalism reconciles an old utopian impulse to solve the world's real and very serious problems through world government and a modernist skepticism about the feasibility of world government. The reconciliation generates a paradoxical commitment to, and faith in the capacity of, international law without government. However, law relies on institutions if it is to function effectively. Global legalists have therefore sought to improve international institutions even while arguing that they are not really necessary.

I describe the utopian impulse behind global legalism in chapter 1 and lay out the case against global legalism in chapter 2. In chapter 3, I describe academic defenses of global legalism and attempt to refute them. Chapters 4 and 5 discuss the impotence of global legalism in the face of one of the most striking trends of international relations — the fragmentation of states — and its troubled relationship with domestic law.

The Utopian Impulse in International Relations

——— CHAPTER ONE ———

People around the world have always faced serious problems of a global scope, problems that could be solved only if governments cooperate. For a long time, the chief such problem was that of war, but there were many others—the international slave trade, beggar-thy-neighbor trade policies, and the spread of disease. In modern terms, these are problems of collective action, and the logic of collective action explains why these problems are so hard to solve.

GLOBAL COLLECTIVE ACTION PROBLEMS

Economists call the various essential goods and services that cannot be supplied privately—including defense against external aggression, law enforcement, a currency, a social safety net, enforcement of property rights and contracts, environmental protection, a transportation infrastructure, basic education, and so forth—public or collective goods.[1] These goods are those that are most efficiently supplied at a scale beyond that available to individuals or corporations: they are solutions to collective action problems. Yet governments fail to supply their populations with public goods that exist at a scale that transcends national borders—what I will call global public goods. Global collective action problems pose the most significant challenges of our time.[2]

War. Two states go to war. Not all wars have spillover effects—many remain the affair of just two belligerents—but most do. The war produces refugees who seek shelter in neighboring states, causing turmoil there, too. Meanwhile, the belligerents make trouble with their neighbors, trying to enlist others in their cause. Trade is disrupted, and war and destruction spread as previously neutral states are drawn in. It would be much better if war had been prevented from starting in the first place or could have been confined to the initial belligerents. An internationally enforced rule that prohibits war and requires states to resolve their disputes peacefully would be an enormous benefit to humanity. But such a system is not in place. Rules against war exist, but states often ignore them, and interstate war remains a problem today as in the past.

Pollution. Pollution does not stop at national boundaries, and states have long struggled to resolve disputes where a polluting state harms the people in another state. By and large, states could resolve these disputes through negotiations and ad hoc agreements. In recent years, however, technological changes have made interstate pollution problems more severe. Chlorofluorocarbons and other emissions have created a hole in the ozone layer over Antarctica. This hole has spread over populated areas, where individuals are at heightened risk of skin cancer. The Chernobyl nuclear disaster of 1986 spread radioactive debris over not just the Soviet Union, where the accident occurred, but over much of Europe, as well. The burning of forests to clear land for farming in Indonesia creates smog over China and other countries in that region. Most important, industrial activity has created the problem of global warming. Yet there is no international environmental law to speak of. A single treaty regime, the Montreal Protocol on Substances that Deplete the Ozone Layer, has to date effectively addressed the problem of the ozone hole, but for every such success, dozens of other problems only get worse.[3]

Overfishing. The oceans' fish stocks have been seriously depleted, with some scientific studies claiming that if current practices are not modified, many fisheries could eventually be destroyed. Fisheries are classic public goods. If they are overfished, they will disappear. Thus, it is in everyone's collective interest to maintain fishing levels at sustainable levels. However, this is not in any individual's personal interest, because most of the harm one inflicts by pursuing one's own personal interest will be absorbed by others. Within their jurisdictions, governments can solve this collective action problem, but states have a hard time cooperating to preserve ocean fish and whales outside their own territorial waters. Many treaties and other agreements attest to the importance of the issue: everyone sees that states have to cooperate to preserve fisheries. But states nonetheless cooperate very poorly, which has led to the depletion of the world's fish and whales.

Disease. Disease has always crossed borders. Just as the great plagues of the past spread via merchants and other travelers, today many experts fear the rapid transmission of a virulent strain of avian influenza over the modern transportation network might soon cause a worldwide pandemic. The SARS outbreak of 2002–2003 killed several hundred and severely disrupted travel. Quick detection and quarantine in a state of origin would benefit victim states—but an originating state has few incentives to be vigilant on behalf of other states, since it does not bear the full cost of the pandemic. States of origin may in fact have an incentive to hide the outbreak, so as not to scare off foreign investment and tourism, until the pandemic becomes uncontrollable and can no longer be hidden in any event. China covered up the SARS outbreak at first. Sharing of early evidence of an outbreak would clearly be collectively beneficial, but individual state interests are in conflict.

Terror. Before 9/11, states dealt with terrorism mostly as a crime problem, as much of it is domestic. International terrorists often aim to draw other states into their struggles, adding this external pressure upon their enemy. Palestinian terrorists, for example, disrupted international travel in order to isolate Israel and deprive it of tourism, hoping that foreign states would pressure it to make concessions to the Palestinians. Today, Osama bin Laden believes that by attacking the United States and other Western countries, he can force the West to exit the Middle East, thereby causing apostate governments to crumble. International terrorists seek support and shelter everywhere, and combating international terrorism is an immensely difficult cooperative endeavor. The United States understands this. It has put great pressure on other nations to combat terror and tried to coordinate counterterrorism efforts by treaties, but many states have been reluctant to ratify these treaties, and enforcement is difficult.

Others. Other international collective action problems include macroeconomic shocks in one country spreading rapidly to other countries, causing regional or even global economic downturns; uncontrolled migration, including refugee flows, which disrupts communities, spreads crime, and leads to political backlashes or even war. Ordinary transnational crime, as opposed to terrorism, remains an entrenched problem. Only international cooperation can address drug smuggling, money laundering, the sex trade, and piracy of intellectual property, such as films, books, computer programs, and video games—the list of problems that require greater international cooperation is long. Yet international cooperation in all these areas has been rudimentary.

To say that cooperation is limited or rudimentary is not to say that it does not exist. And, of course, it is difficult to quantify the amount of cooperative activity, so optimists can point to successes even while pessimists point to the failures. But one thing is clear: most states, and certainly all developed states, can solve the domestic versions of these collective action problems, or at least deal with them far more effectively than states as a group can handle global collective action problems. Most developed states can keep crime at an acceptable level, repress violent challenges to government authority, maintain renewable resources by regulating users, keep pollution at an acceptable level, and so forth. The question is, if states can do this domestically, why can't they do the same thing, as effectively, at the international level?

There is no clear answer to this question, but a few observations are familiar. States have governments, which have a monopoly on force and the loyalty of most citizens or subjects. Governments are complex institutions that obtain information about the interests, values, and concerns of citizens; enact rules that restrain people's behavior; monitor people's behavior for violations of the rules; and impose sanctions. Crucially, governments have institutional mechanisms, such as majority rule, that enable them to implement policy that benefits most people, and prevent individuals or small groups from blocking needed reform. As long as governments perform their functions adequately, people will for the most part obey the rules, participate in government (as voters, as employees), and in other ways maintain their loyalty. Governments are often unable to exercise authority over people who see themselves as a distinct group within a larger society, a group separated by ethnic, linguistic, cultural, historical, or geographic peculiarities. At the extreme, "failed states" are those where the government cannot exert control over a large portion of the population that nonetheless is unable, or unwilling, to separate itself into an independent state.

At the international level, no world government exists, and so no entity has the power to tax and regulate states, or the individuals who live in them, in order to ensure that collective goods are produced. The problem seems to be the extraordinary diversity of the world population as well as the extremely difficult problems of scale. When people are sufficiently diverse, there are few or no public goods that benefit most people or nearly everyone; instead, government policies can only have highly unequal effects. Arranging transfers so as to mollify the losers is also highly difficult, because it is so hard to determine the real effect of policies on highly diverse people. And when the scale of government is large enough, it becomes difficult for the government to monitor people, and for the people to monitor the government.

One can thus draw a crisp analytic distinction between intrastate cooperation, which is capable of solving major nation-level collective action problems, and interstate cooperation, which is itself subject to collective action problems and thus cannot solve them, except in a very rudimentary fashion. Within states, governments overcome collective action problems by applying force to individuals. Between states, governments must cooperate with each other—government to government—and, with occasional exceptions, the cooperation takes the form of agreements that are enforced with bribes or threats of retaliation. This type of "spontaneous cooperation," as it is sometimes called, is certainly possible, but it is very difficult, and it becomes more and more difficult as the number of participants increase, their time horizons shorten, and information asymmetries worsen. If spontaneous cooperation were really effective, there would be no reason for states to have governments in the first place, as citizens could simply cooperate directly with each other in order to produce national or subnational collective goods.

This analytic distinction does not perfectly describe the real world, of course. Political scientists distinguish between "international" or "intergovernmental" cooperation and "supranational" cooperation, in which individuals owe loyalty to multiple levels of government authority. The European Union is the supreme example of supranational cooperation today, but there are other examples as well.

It seems plausible that global collective action problems cannot be solved—or not very well. If it is true that national governments are needed to solve national collective action problems, then it seems that it would follow that a world government would be needed to solve global collective action problems. If a world government is not possible, then solving global collective action problems is also not possible. Or so one would think.

However, there is currently a project to escape this dilemma—a project that I will call "global legalism," one that can be summarized with the slogan, "law without government." To understand this project, we must first back up and see why the more traditional methods of escaping this dilemma—including that of creating a world government—no longer have any serious adherents.

POLITICAL, ECONOMIC, AND IDEOLOGICAL INTEGRATION

History does not so much repeat itself as play variations on a theme. The theme is the likely or inevitable solution of the world's problems—what I have called global collective action problems—through institutional or ideological development. The three main variations have been political integration, or the creation of a world government; economic integration, or the creation of a world market in which collective action problems melt away; and ideological integration, or the universal adoption of a set of beliefs that define collective action problems out of existence. I will also say a few words about a variant of political integration—hegemony.

Political Integration

One solution to global collective action problems would be to integrate the existing 190 or so states into a single world state. The world government would use its powers to tax and regulate in order to solve collective action problems just as national governments do today. The oceans would be like inland lakes, and the world government could maintain fisheries with the type of licensing systems that states use to maintain fisheries that fall within their jurisdictions. War and terrorism would be internal crime problems (or perhaps civil war), and the world government would use law enforcement and the criminal justice system to address them. Global warming and other pollution problems would similarly be treated as internal problems that could be solved in the same way that acid rain is dealt with in the United States.

A world government is an old dream, and it is no nearer to realization today than it was hundreds of years ago. Indeed, the trend over the past one hundred years has been in the opposite direction: states have been multiplying rather than merging. The problem with a world government is that the global population is far too heterogeneous to govern. People living in different parts of the world have different values, interests, loyalties, and ideas about governance. Heterogeneity frustrates world governance, and the plausibility of world government is receding with the passage of time.

A few people still imagine that a world government is possible. Some philosophers imagine that a federation of some sort might come into existence, but they fail to provide a plausible account of how this might happen.[4] The political scientist Alexander Wendt does supply a mechanism: he argues that the struggle among individuals for recognition must inevitably lead to a world state in, he thinks, one or two hundred years.[5] Wendt thinks that individuals have an inbred psychological desire to be recognized subjects, and this leads them to demand such recognition from others. As long as the battle for recognition leads to hierarchical relations like the master-slave relationship, the social system will be unstable because the hierarchical inferiors will, unless temporarily paralyzed by false consciousness, eventually demand a greater degree of recognition, as autonomous human beings. Within the state, the struggle leads to liberal democracy, which is the only system in which all individuals are recognized as equals. But the struggle for recognition persists at the international level, as weak states demand greater recognition from stronger states and citizens within weaker states demand greater recognition from the citizens of stronger states. Wendt insists that a stable world system cannot exist as long as people are divided among states, because even if the states take relatively peaceful attitudes toward each other, there is always the possibility that disputes will lead strong states to fall back on their greater power, resulting in the use of force. Such instability must eventually give way to a world state, where all individuals enjoy legal equality and liberal rights—the point at which they will finally stop struggling for recognition.

Wendt's argument depends on some contentious empirical assumptions. Although at times he seems to acknowledge that he must make strong empirical assumptions, the tenor of his argument, with the notion of the inevitability of the world state, is either that, in fact, such assumptions are unnecessary and his argument is analytic, or that they are obviously correct. Clearly the first cannot be true. Wendt himself admits that the people's desire for recognition must be stronger than their desire for security for his story to be correct. He points out that people do, from time to time, take risks and even voluntarily die for the sake of recognition of themselves or their group, but this hardly settles the matter. If enough people care more about security than recognition, then his contraption cannot get started. He also acknowledges that nationalism and other urges to form collectivities below the global level are in tension with evolution toward the world state. Although he takes nationalism as evidence for his theory—proof of the power of struggle for recognition—and enthusiastically notes that nationalisms will enjoy stability only when they themselves embrace reciprocal recognition, he ignores the possibility that nationalism is simply a stronger force—again, an empirical question. Other moving parts in his theory—the destructiveness of technology has made war more unattractive, the role of collective memories of past bloodlettings spurs integration—are also empirical conjectures that are not particularly plausible and indeed could have made with equal force one hundred years ago.

One cannot disprove Wendt's style of utopianism, but it provides a flimsy foundation for policy. More parsimonious and plausible accounts of recent world history are available. At least for the foreseeable future, we cannot depend on a world government to solve global collective action problems.

Economic Integration

On the eve of World War I, the British intellectual Norman Angell published *The Great Illusion*, an instantly famous book that made arguments that were both ingenious and (with hindsight) wrong.[6] Although Angell has been misinterpreted as saying that war was no longer possible, in fact his argument was that war was no longer in the interest of any state. A state that went to war would end up harming itself because it would merely disrupt its own economic relationships, from which it benefited far more than it could benefit from conquest. He acknowledged that many people believed that war could be advantageous for a state, and for that reason war remained possible and Britain should not discard its military;

but he also believed that with time everyone would see that this belief was erroneous and so eventually war would no longer occur.

Angell argued that the then-modern economic integration of different countries made war a losing proposition even for the winner. Suppose, for example, that Germany defeated Great Britain in a war. Then what would happen? The German army could cart off all British valuables from the homeland and enslave the population. It could seize Britain's colonies and claim them as its own. But Britain's valuables were not worth all that much. Much more important would be the disruption of Germany's financial and trade relationships with Britain. German-owned factories in Britain would lose their workers, and German firms in Germany would lose a source of inputs and a market for their goods. British debtors would be unable to repay their loans to German creditors, which would fold, and British creditors would call in their loans. The subjects of Britain's colonies would still need to be mollified, and Germany would quickly realize that it had to treat those subjects as well as Britain did (which Angell thought was quite well). In short, a country like Germany does much better by maintaining friendly economic relations with Britain than by invading it and reducing it to a colony or wasteland. This can be interpreted as a claim that even if a world government is not possible, the kinds of problems that we would hope the world government could solve — chiefly, war — can nonetheless be solved in a decentralized fashion, as states voluntarily, without being forced by a world government, refrain from going to war simply because they have no interest in doing so.

Although badly timed, Angell's argument was insightful. It anticipated America's policies toward Germany and Japan after World War II, as well as the decolonization movement of the 1950s and 1960s. The United States realized that it was better off if Germany and Japan were wealthy and democratic than if they were not, and invested a great deal of resources into ensuring that this would happen. No major figure believed that they should be turned into colonies, and those like the secretary of state Henry Morgenthau, who believed that Germany would always remain dangerous unless converted into an agrarian society, were proved wrong. Later, Britain, France, and the other imperial powers would realize that, quite apart from the difficulty of maintaining control over restless populations, decolonization was not necessarily an economically unsatisfactory policy. The newly independent states would remain economic partners in much the same way as they had prior to colonization, supplying raw materials to the former imperial master, receiving manufactured goods in return, and more or less willingly maintaining friendly political relations.

But Angell was excessively optimistic. States can prosper by cooperating with other states, but they can also gain advantages by preying on other states. Predation need not take the form of conquest and devastation or looting; the modern form could simply be insistence on advantageous economic relations. In modern terms, the fact that states would all benefit in the aggregate if they could resolve their disputes peacefully does not mean that states will resolve their disputes peacefully. Peaceful settlement of disputes is, except in narrow cases, a global public good, given the ways that conflicts create trade and refugee problems for uninvolved countries, and states have an incentive to free ride rather than contribute to its production, which in many instances would mean refraining from engaging in an advantageous war.

The problem with Angell's view is even more apparent as we turn our focus from war to the other collective action problems. Consider global warming. Nearly all states recognize global warming as a problem, but states have so far failed to cooperate to solve this problem, even though the eventual losses to states may well exceed those that would be caused by any war. The increasing economic integration of the world does not solve global collective action problems; it simply creates a new set of them. To be sure, Angell did not believe—nor do his modern-day followers—that economic integration would solve all the world's problems. The point, for present purposes, is that even if some global problems can be solved with little or no cooperation, others cannot.

Ideological Integration

The theory of economic integration does not purport to solve global collective action problems; it is instead a theory that at least some such problems do not really exist because they, or some of them, will disappear as long as states act in their self-interest. By contrast, the theory of political integration recognizes that global collective action problems exist as long as the state system exists, and thus advocates or predicts the development of a world state, for which the collective action problems would be merely domestic problems, resolvable with taxation and regulation and the other instruments of government. The third approach combines elements of the first two. Ideological integration means that states develop similar or identical beliefs, commitments, and institutions, and as a result, the global collective action problems can be solved or simply melt away.

The most important modern advocate of this view is Francis Fukuyama, whose famous 1989 essay, "The End of History?" argued that history had ended because all ideological conflict had been resolved.[7] Fukuyama, like Wendt, is inspired by Hegel, and his theory is similarly motivated by the assumption that the struggle for recognition is central to human existence and that technological advance favors equality. But where Wendt foresees a world state, Fukuyama foresees a continuation of the state system, but with the qualification that all states, in the future, will be liberal democracies. Fukuyama believes that the collapse of the Soviet Union ended the last major ideological battle, between Communism on the one hand and market-based liberal democracy on the other. Everyone now, more or less, recognizes that the only viable organization of a state is along liberal, democratic, and market-based lines.

Fukuyama's theory is too optimistic. There will always be people with grievances, real or imagined, and these people will turn to ideologies that make sense of their grievances and provide a basis for action. In the past, such ideologies included anarchism, Fascism, nationalism, Communism, and — liberalism. Today, certain strains of Islam have taken on this role for many people and authoritarianism enjoys a revival. But whether Fukuyama is right or wrong in his diagnosis, the question of interest here is whether ideological integration could solve global collective action problems.

The affirmative answer draws on the democratic peace literature, which argues that democracies do not go to war with other democracies. The literature rests on an undeniable factual pattern: for the last two hundred years, there are many examples of democracies fighting nondemocracies and nondemocracies fighting other nondemocracies, but there are few examples of democracies fighting other democracies, and these are generally ambiguous anyway.[8] The most plausible explanation for why democracies do not go to war with each other is that democracies, being relatively open, cannot keep secrets and so can more credibly commit to war during a crisis — with less likelihood of bluffing leading to war.[9] War occurs most often when states misjudge the capacities and interests of other states; when this does not happen, states appease or settle rather than incur the costs and risks of war.

But greater information does not solve collective action problems — the problems exist even with perfect information — nor does the capacity to make credible commitments. It may be that, on the margin, democracies can solve global collective action problems more effectively than nondemocracies can. Because their interests and capacities are more visible, bargaining costs are lower, and thus negotiations are less likely to fail. But the advantages of democracies are limited. They remain independent actors, and so they will have trouble cooperating with each other. This means that they cannot solve global collective action problems, though they may make more progress than authoritarian states do.

Hegemony

A fourth solution to global collective action should be mentioned, although it does not have the advocates that the first three do. This solution involves the hegemony of a single state or, in some versions, a system of cooperation among a small number of dominant states — "regional hegemons" — which in turn enforce order among the small states within their respective spheres of influence.

The clearest modern precedent of a hegemon is the British Empire, which maintained order on the high seas during much of the nineteenth century, and which also controlled many smaller states by virtue of its financial and economic dominance. All or nearly all states benefited from freedom of the seas, which Britain protected by defeating pirates and deterring states that sought to exert greater control over the seas. Britain could also prevent some small states from starting regional wars and took the leading role in the abolition of the international slave trade.

But Britain could not prevent war between great powers, and it could not solve numerous other global problems. Today, the most powerful state, the United States, is far too weak to be a global hegemon. The United States could not, for example, solve the problem of global warming by simply threatening other states with a military intervention unless they reduce greenhouse gas emissions. The United States has had some success in deterring interstate wars, reversing aggression (the Gulf War), and settling regional conflicts (Yugoslavia's civil war). It helps maintain freedom of the seas, and it takes the lead in many kinds of international cooperation, but the United States does not have enough power to resolve global pollution problems, save fisheries, suppress many conflicts around the world, and solve the various other global collective action problems.

Even if the United States could serve as a hegemon, and therefore had the means and the incentives to solve global collective action problems, many people would find troubling the distributional implications of such a system. The reason that the hegemon has an incentive to solve global collective action problems is that it can capture the value of the public good — and will, if it is self-interested. Consider, for example, the problem of global warming. As a hegemon, the United States could solve this problem by threatening to bomb states that exceed their share of the globally optimal level of greenhouse gas emissions. As a result, the United States would reap the benefits from climate change mitigation without having to pay any costs, aside from those of maintaining the credible military threat, which may well be a fixed cost — a cost that would be incurred in any event because of security needs. U.S. industry would not be restricted, or not as much; and, in addition, the United States could demand (or extort) monetary compensation from the world. Indeed, it is hard to see why the United States would not extract all the rents that the rest of the world obtains from American-enforced peace and prosperity.

To be sure, the hegemon does not always have the power to extract rents. During the cold war, the United States frequently complained that western Europe did not pay its fair share of the cost of the nuclear umbrella because the United States could not credibly threaten to close that umbrella for nonpayment.[10] But the possibility of this type of strategic behavior also weakens the incentive of the hegemon to supply global public goods in the first place. Either a state is so powerful that it can capture the gains from solving a global action problem or it is not. In the first case, it has the incentive to solve the collective action problem but no incentive to share the gains. In the second case, it has no incentive to solve the collective action problem.

Nor does a system of regional hegemons hold out much hope. In the nineteenth century, the major western powers — Britain, Russia, France, Prussia/Germany, the Austro-Hungarian Empire — would sometimes cooperate in useful ways. They could settle disputes among each other and suppress violence in smaller states. But cooperation did not go much beyond preventing war, and did not always succeed at that. Today, one sees a similar configuration, with the United States, Japan, China, Russia, the European Union (or its major members), and other states taking the main roles. But these countries do not seem capable of solving global collective action problems except in special circumstances.

LEGALISM

There is yet one more approach. This last approach to solving the problem of global collective action can be called "global legalism." Global legalists believe that a world government is not possible in the foreseeable future, but that international law, without a world government, can nonetheless solve or greatly ameliorate global collective action problems. International law, normally thought to be an object of government interest, becomes a subject: it develops, it expands, it constrains. And it develops in a certain way, enveloping states within its embrace, compelling them to act outside their interests, pushing them to greater and greater levels of cooperation, and hence to solving the global collective action problems.

Global legalism is not a doctrine or theory. It is akin to an attitude or posture—a set of beliefs about how the world works, one that, in various forms, dominates the thinking of academic international lawyers, as well as practicing international lawyers and some government officials.[11] Global legalism has popular appeal and it affects government policies: many international institutions bear its imprint. Rather than defining it immediately, let me begin by describing "legalism" in general—as opposed to its global variant.

Legalism in America

Legalism is a set of assumptions about how the world works. It places great faith in the power of law and legal institutions to solve problems. The dominance of legalistic thinking in the United States is an old theme, first discussed by Alexis de Tocqueville in *Democracy in America*.[12] Tocqueville was not concerned about the role of legalism in international relations; his discussion of legalism was focused on its domestic variant. About this version of legalism as it then existed in the United States, he famously said: "There is almost no political question in the United States that is not resolved sooner or later into a judicial question."[13] He meant that Americans expected law and legal institutions to resolve moral and policy disagreements that in other countries would be resolved by political, religious, or communal institutions. Tocqueville captured an important truth and seems to have uncannily predicted the future.

Legalism in the United States is due to several factors.

The common law tradition. American judges, like British judges, have the authority to develop the common law, which is essentially a kind of constrained policymaking. The common law governs chiefly disputes between individuals — property disputes, breach of contract, accidents, and so forth — and in the course of developing the common law in the United States judges have resolved numerous policy questions concerning these subjects. By and large, Americans have been satisfied with common law development, and judges' authority to make law in this domain is unquestioned. It is also subject to correction by state legislatures, and this has ensured that the common law has not deviated too far from the values and interests of the people.

The constitution. American judges claimed early on the power to nullify state laws that violate state constitutions, as well as state and federal laws that violate the federal constitution. Judicial review is more controversial than common law development, but it is just as entrenched. Because the U.S. Constitution is a short and ambiguous document, judges have been able to use it to advance policy goals, which they have done very aggressively. As a result, in the United States, all kinds of policy choices — regarding slavery, abortion, contraception, the minimum wage, taxation, voting districts, and much else — have been made, or heavily influenced, by judges.

Legal institutions and the legal profession. Tocqueville noted the dominant role of lawyers in American society and politics, likening them to aristocrats in Europe. Lawyers constituted a kind of ruling class. Aside from arguing cases and serving as judges, they also dominated political institutions such as legislatures. Lawyers share certain interests and ways of seeing the world — one that emphasizes the ever-present possibility of resolving conflicting interests rather than the inevitable struggle of entrenched classes or ideologies. This made them highly useful to everyone who has a problem—businesses, unions, repressed minorities and religious groups, anyone with a grievance—and possibly enabled them to be the glue that held together a society that lacked a common religion or religious establishment and was highly individualistic and disinclined to defer to authority. In exchange for their aristocratic position, lawyers must practice *noblesse oblige*.[14] As professionals, lawyers see themselves as serving the public interest, and so, at least in principle, they recognize that certain kinds of behavior are off-limits because they exacerbate rather than resolve conflict.

The love of order. Tocqueville argued that lawyers love order more than liberty—a claim that would raise hackles in law schools today—but it remains as true now as it did in the nineteenth century. A few exceptions aside,[15] lawyers distrust democracy, fearing that it will lead to chaos or (more commonly, today) the domination of either unjust majorities, who abuse racial and other minorities, or the domination of the wealthy, who use their money to influence elections. For American lawyers, *Brown v. Board of Education* is an unshakeable testament to the heroic judiciary facing down popular passions. For European lawyers, democracy is associated with the excesses of nationalism; by contrast, supranational legal structures, operated by bureaucrats and judges, are Europe's highest postwar achievement.

The heterogeneity of American society. The United States has always been a heterogeneous society. The earliest citizens came mainly from British stock, but there were also Germans, Dutch, and others—not to mention American Indians, who had to be dealt with in one way or another, and Africans, who were mostly slaves. Even among the British, there were great and sometimes violently divisive religious differences, and people who traced their ancestry from different parts of Britain had highly different cultures.[16] Sectional differences were also significant and, indeed, in the greatest failure of legalism in U.S. history, led to the Civil War. Meanwhile, additional migrants came from China, Japan, Italy, Ireland, and many other countries, and by the early twentieth century, the United States had become the highly multiracial society that we know today. The importance of this development for legalism cannot be exaggerated. When people cannot resolve their differences by appealing to common religious beliefs, or common ethnic norms, or common historic memories, or tribal elders, they can at least appeal to the law — to constitutional law, which they implicitly accepted when they migrated, to the common law that has continually proved its worth, and to statutes that have been passed by officials who have been elected by them.

And so Americans argue about policy by appealing to the law. They say that the constitution, rightly understood, endorses this or that policy choice. They bring lawsuits whenever they disagree with elected officials' policy choices. And thus judges continue to play a dominant role in setting policy. This development has not been smooth and uniform, to be sure. The rise of the administrative state of the twentieth century can be described as a repudiation of legalistic thinking, which had failed America during the Great Depression, when legalistic Supreme Court justices prevented the implementation of New Deal reforms. But America's regulatory agencies are themselves highly legalistic, and although courts defer to their decisions in many settings, this is largely because the agencies themselves have adopted legalistic procedures.

What Is Legalism?

As should be clear from the previous discussion, legalism is a complicated and ambiguous concept, and any attempt to reduce it to a definition is hazardous. Still, one can identify several common elements.[17]

Rules. Laws are rules that are issued in advance of the behavior they regulate. They are not always precise, though legalism favors precision over vague standards. But the key point is that the rules are set out in advance so that people have notice. The rules prevail over power. Thus, for the legalistic mind, abortion rights are settled by the U.S. Constitution and are not to be determined by religious and political forces slugging it out in the political arena. Smoking policy, similarly, is better determined by courts applying common law tort principles than by legislative horse trading.

Judges. One could imagine a rule-bound society that was not legalistic; for example, the rules could come from a religious text. A crucial element of legalism is the powerful role of the judge. Judges, by ideological reputation, lie outside politics; they resolve cases impartially by appealing to the rules. This gives them immense prestige.[18] The legalistic mentality implicitly assumes that existing rules can resolve every problem. Actual judges know better. Like priests in an ancient society who know that their magic is just an illusion, judges purport to find law—that is, apply the rules—even as they make it. They make law by appealing to vague or conflicting rules that do not indicate a determinate outcome while making a policy choice on the sly. The trick works because like the ancient priests, judges use common sense and share the dominant values of society, and so can usually make cases work out in a manner that seems broadly fair. When judges dominate policymaking, a society becomes litigious: people seek to affect policy by bringing lawsuits.[19]

Procedures and the adversarial system. Legalism loves procedures. In the ideal, a case is resolved fairly because neither side has a procedural advantage—thus, the substance of the law determines the outcome, and not the wealth of one party or the skill of his lawyer. Procedures ensure that both sides have access to all the evidence, have time to prepare their cases, are not surprised by revelations, are not disadvantaged by the judge or jury's prejudices, predilections, or interests. Of special importance is the institution of review. The judge reviews the jury's verdict, and an appellate panel reviews the judge's decisions, and a high court may review the appellate panel's views. Along the way, there are many opportunities for rehearings by the same judge or by a larger or different panel, and there may be additional opportunities for collateral challenges—in criminal cases especially, where defendants may get a second chance by filing a habeas petition in state court and a third chance by filing a habeas petition in federal court, and each time with additional layers of review.

Liberal legalism. There are other elements of legalism but the discussion so far should suffice to give its flavor. But one should recognize one other aspect of legalism which is important, and that is its longtime association with liberalism—in the classical sense that emphasizes individual freedom. The rule of law, for example, is thought to be a liberal virtue as well as a legalist virtue: it refers to the idea that people should not be subject to the whims of rulers, as this is inconsistent with freedom and autonomy. Although it is true that legalism bans arbitrary governance, it does not literally ban illiberal laws—such as laws against freedom of conscience and speech. But in practice legalists tend to be liberals and, at least in the United States, liberals tend to be legalists. Legalists do not believe that laws issued by dictators are truly consistent with legalism, and so they generally insist on democratic institutions, and for democratic institutions to work, there must also be open debate, freedom of speech, and so forth. Liberals could possibly endorse an unconstrained direct democracy, where everything would be determined by politics, as long as the public was itself liberal in thinking. But in practice liberals insist that judges must guard the liberal order on the basis of a largely liberal constitution, at least as those judges have interpreted it. So legalism tends to be liberal, but it need not be so.

In sum, legalism defined broadly is the view that law and legal institutions can keep order and solve policy disputes. It manifests itself in powerful courts, a dominant class of lawyers, and reliance on legalistic procedures in policymaking bodies.

Why Legalism?

To understand the appeal of legalism, one needs to understand the appeal of the judge. Why would people place so much confidence in judges to resolve their disputes, rather than looking to traditional authorities such as religious figures, or to political authorities such as legislatures and executives?

Several answers suggest themselves.[20] When a population is highly diverse, different groups will appeal to different traditional authorities — different religious figures, or charismatic figures, or tribal leaders, or what have you. Thus, the authorities cannot resolve disputes involving people from different groups, at least not without the difficult process of bargaining over differences. We might attribute the early growth of legalism in the United States to the diversity of the population. Many (but not all) empires with diverse populations — the Roman Empire, the Austro-Hungarian Empire, the British Empire — have also been legalistic.

But why not rely on political authorities? The answer may be that legalism becomes more attractive when regular government is weak, fragmented, unpopular, or otherwise incapacitated, while the courts themselves are effective and enjoy a good reputation.[21] As noted above, American courts inherited power and authority from the British system, and their appeal in the nineteenth century must have been enhanced by the weakness and remoteness of the national government; state legislatures were also widely distrusted. In Europe today, a legalistic mentality has taken hold in part because of the success of the European Court of Justice in knitting together sovereign states that had otherwise refused (until recently) to give much power to Europe's major political institutions, which were hampered by strict voting rules and featured other weaknesses.

Further, it may be that elites and the power holders fear mass democracy and see judges, who are by training and temperament more likely to identify with the elites than with the masses, as a bulwark against the people.[22] This is similar to Tocqueville's argument that the legal profession serves as a governing aristocracy, although where Tocqueville saw the legal profession as relatively benign and crucial for maintaining order, one might also see a class defending its interests.

Finally, one needs to explain why judges would be willing to take on the burden of policymaking, when they might believe that doing so would undermine their reputation for impartiality and weaken public support for the judiciary. One possible answer is that individual judges have policy preferences and, all else being equal, would like to impose those preferences on others.[23] And because the public seeks policy guidance from judges, *failure* to engage in policymaking might weaken public support for the judiciary.

Legalism is not just faith in the judges; it also involves faith in the law—for example, the belief that a vague document written in another era, like the U.S. Constitution, can provide guidance for policy today, or that the common law provides a basis from which one can derive right answers, or that statutes have inherent meanings. These views have been under furious assault in the legal academy for almost a century, but the public seems to hold them as strongly as ever. It may be that people have internalized the self-conception of the legal profession—illustrated by such mantras as "judges discover law rather than make it"—because legalistic nations have been relatively free and prosperous. It may be that legalistic thinking appeals to ordinary habits of mind. Or it may be that people prefer the rule of judges to that of politicians but have been unable to reconcile this preference with the ideological appeal of democracy. Whatever the case, legalism is a powerful force.

Legalism Spreads Across the World

The legalism I have described is the specifically American version with which I am most familiar, and the American version seems to be its purest manifestation anywhere in the world.[24] But legalism has spread and plays an increasing role in other countries, especially the Western democracies.

There are many reasons for the spread of legalism. As I noted before, legalism has existed in other countries aside from America, though usually in a more diluted form. Britain's traditions of judicial independence influenced all of its former colonies, not just the United States. Fascism and Communism subordinated the courts to party rule; the collapse of those systems in major states from the end of World War II to 1991 gave a boost to liberal democracy and judicial independence. And the institutions of the United States are widely admired and imitated. In recent years, legalism has made further gains. Governments grant new powers to judges, judicially enforceable bills of rights become more popular, the number of lawyers increases around the world, and issues of politics increasingly move to the courts.[25] As noted above, Europe presents an important case. The European Court of Justice has played an important role in entrenching European law by persuading the national courts of European countries to defer, in many instances, to the European Court's judgments and interpretations.[26] The spreading appeal of legalism worldwide can be attributed to the same factors that explain the appeal of legalism in the United States: increasing effort at cross-border governance of highly diverse populations, the weakness and fragmentation of national governments, and efforts by political elites to entrench themselves or their values or interests against their own populations.[27] That the United States and, increasingly, other legalistic Western democracies are prosperous, powerful, and free must suggest to foreign observers that, in fact, legalism has some merit; governance by judges may be superior to plausible alternatives.

GLOBAL LEGALISM IN INTERNATIONAL RELATIONS

Whether legalism can take hold and do well for people in countries without legalistic traditions remains to be seen. If one confines one's attention to the vast developing world, there is perhaps nothing as impressive as the distance between their legalistic ideals and the behavior of governments. Many countries have ambitious, generous constitutions that grant significant rights — to education, to health care — that are simply not enforced. Judges may write well and impressively about the importance of these rights and the government's obligation to respect them, but they cannot enforce their judgments. More often, the judiciary is corrupt or incompetent or controlled by the government; people can queue up to the courts but not expect a judgment for a decade or more.

Even in the West, legalism has always had its critics. In the United States, critics argue that legalism and especially an obsession with rights has corrupted national debate,[28] interfered with democratic self-governance,[29] burdened judges with decision-making for which they are ill-suited,[30] and led to excessive litigiousness.[31] In Europe, justified pride in the development of effective supranational institutions has been accompanied with deep uneasiness about the so-called democratic deficit — the evident lack of interest of European publics in European politics, and a distrust for the supranational institutions over which they have little control.[32]

Meanwhile, however, legalism seeks to conquer new realms. Having infiltrated many national polities, and one regional polity, it now seeks to govern the world.

Global legalism is the extension of legalism to international relations. It is most easily understood as an alternative to the other approaches to solving global collective action problems. According to global legalism, international law will solve these problems. Global legalism is the world government approach except without the government. Legalists recognize that a world government is not likely in the near future, but they believe that law without government can nonetheless solve global problems. Like economic integrationists, global legalists believe that states will solve global collective action problems because it is in their interest do so, but global legalists, as we will see, do not put as much faith in decentralized action: global legalism is an odd mixture of top-down and bottom-up institutionalization, with states both creating international law and finding themselves caught in its snares against their will. Like ideological integrationists, global legalists believe that states are converging toward ideological agreement, but the ideological agreement is not so much about liberal democracy as about the value of legalism. Global legalists also emphasize institutions to a greater extent than ideological integrationists do.

First, global legalists believe that international political disputes should, as much as possible, be resolved according to law and by legal institutions. Wars should not be fought without the approval of the United Nations; disputes should be submitted to international courts. Increasingly, people argue that customary international law binds states that object to it, and thus political and moral disagreements—for example, over the use of the death penalty—can be resolved by appeal to the law, even when the law cannot be traced to state consent.

Second, states should enter more treaties, especially multilateral treaties, and treaties should be as specific, detailed, and comprehensive as possible. As noted, global legalists also believe that customary international law—international law that evolves outside of treaty making—should be interpreted robustly. Jus cogens norms should evolve and expand.

Third, international courts should have jurisdiction over a broad array of disputes, jurisdiction should be compulsory, and judges should be independent of the governments of states. Judges should not be the pawns of powerful states; they should be highly qualified and selected through a fair procedure.

Fourth, other types of international legal institutions—legislative and executive—should be promoted to the extent possible, though global legalists acknowledge that a full-fledged world government is not possible in the near term.

Fifth, global legalists believe that domestic political institutions should be bound by international legal obligations. In the United States, legalists believe that courts should use customary international law and treaties as sources of law, even without the approval of the political branches.

Sixth, many global legalists see the growth of international law as inevitable, a byproduct of larger historical forces that no state can control. In some work, international law takes on a life of its own—expanding, ramifying, weaving itself among the states and their institutions. Sometimes, this type of thinking comes across as a Whig history–style conviction that international law has always advanced (to be sure, with temporary setbacks) and will always continue to advance.

Global legalism should be distinguished from the views of political scientists and lawyers who believe that international law can serve the interests of states and that the extent to which an area of international relations is subject to international legal regulation should (in normative scholarship) or does (in positive scholarship) reflect cost-benefit tradeoffs. In the political science literature, for example, a group of scholars has been debating the advantages and disadvantages of legal forms in international relations, focusing on the precision of rules, the existence of legal as opposed to political obligation, reliance on third-party dispute resolution mechanisms, the availability of standing for individuals as opposed to states, and so on.[33] With its emphasis on the specific (and changeable) interests of states, on considering the costs as well as the benefits of law, and on empirical verification, this research program diverges from the assumptions underlying global legalism.

The difference between these scholars (with whom I agree) and the global legalist can sometimes be obscure. Many international legal regimes — such as those that solve coordination problems involving communication and transportation — are robust and desirable from the perspective both of the rational choice theorist and the global legalist.[34] The camps diverge with respect to the question of whether such "law without government" can solve more significant global problems, such as global collective action problems. The rational-choice theorist is skeptical. The global legalist is not, or is less so. These differences stem from a methodological choice as well as a general view of the world. Rational choice theorists believe that compliance with international law must be in the rational self-interest of governments, or of the individuals and groups that compel governments to act. Global legalists have no such methodological commitment. Most American international law scholarship simply takes compliance for granted; only a few scholars have tried to explain why states would comply with international law.[35]

What explains the rise of global legalism? The simple demand-side explanation is that the implausibility and failure of the world government, economic integration, ideological integration, and hegemony approaches to global collective action problems have left a gap that global legalism has filled. The world needs institutions that will solve global collective action problems and, if these other approaches have failed, international law itself has not been directly refuted.

Moreover, the view that law without government can solve global collective action problems can point to some successes. It received a boost from the Nuremberg trials, which demonstrated — however imperfectly — that international trials could take place and result in convictions that seemed less arbitrary and more legitimate than traditional alternatives such as summary execution or immunity.[36] International tribunals are proliferating. The international trade system has worked well. The United Nations has not fulfilled the ambitions of its founders, but it has earned a measure of respect. Other ambitious legal regimes, such as the Law of the Sea Convention, have come into effect. If world government seems as distant as ever, international law offers some real hope.

So isn't it churlish to criticize global legalism? To that question we now turn.

The Flaws of Global Legalism

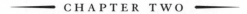

CHAPTER TWO

If the rule of law has flourished in the United States and many (though not most) other states, why can't it flourish internationally? The global legalist might point out that individuals overcome *domestic* collective action problems by consenting to a domestic government that has the power to pass laws and punish those who violate them. If individuals can overcome collective action problems in this way, why can't states? Or, why can't individuals, acting through their states, solve global as well as within-state collective action problems? Further, it is well known that some states have had law without government, and in many states law prevails even though the government is weak. William Ian Miller has written of a quasi-legal system in early Iceland, one that lacked sophisticated legal institutions but seemed to keep a degree of order.[1] Robert Ellickson has also described various settings in which people maintain complex cooperative relationship without relying on legal institutions.[2] Why can't the same occur at the global level?

THE INSTITUTIONAL WEAKNESS OF INTERNATIONAL LAW

Initially, we need to be clear about just how limited international legal institutions are, compared to domestic legal institutions. This point is familiar to international lawyers and political scientists, but it bears emphasis.

Legislation without legislatures. In the United States and all other countries, most law is made through legislation. The public becomes aware of some problem—acid rain or spousal abuse or inadequate schooling or overdevelopment—and brings it to the attention of legislators. Interest groups and other intermediary groups—churches, environmental organizations, businesses—play a facilitating role. A legislator or governor or president proposes a bill and, if all goes well, the bill is voted on and enacted. Usually, votes occur by majority rule; in practice, because of bicameralism, a president's veto power, or the influence of money on politics, a supermajority will need to agree to the bill (or some watered down version of it). But, except in special circumstances, small groups of people will not be able to block it. The whole institutional structure—formal votes, hearings, elections, and so forth—ensures that proposed laws are publicly debated and that affected people can make their voices heard so that the final product will enjoy a fair amount of support, even if not unanimous, and so will not be immediately overturned after the next election. At the same time, the existence of majority rule—or some level of de facto supermajority rule that nonetheless falls well below a requirement of consensus—ensures that the existing law can be revisited and amended if it turns out not to have the desired effect.

At the international level, no such system exists. There is no international legislature with general jurisdiction. The United Nations General Assembly lacks the power to enact legally binding rules. The Security Council does have the power to issue legally binding orders, but its power is limited. It does not have the power to issue legislation; its power is more in the nature of executive and adjudicative—it can evaluate breaches of peace and order an international response.[3] Because the Security Council can act only with the consent of its five permanent members—Britain, China, France, Russia, and the United States—and the interests of those members rarely converge, the Security Council can rarely act effectively. And because most states have only a limited and indirect role in the Security Council—they rotate onto the council occasionally, and they can depend on patrons to protect their interest—the Security Council lacks the democratic legitimacy enjoyed by an ordinary domestic legislature.

So how is international law made? Some international law emerges spontaneously, as custom, but when states seek to solve global collective action problems, they can do so only by creating treaties. A state can be bound by a treaty only if it consents to it; thus, a treaty that will solve a global collective action problem requires the consent of all states, or all states that contribute to that problem. The unanimity rule is much more strict than the voting rules of legislatures, and the result is that treaties are much harder to create than domestic law is, and usually end up imposing weak obligations. A significant disadvantage for treaty making is the absence of settled infrastructure for monitoring treaty behavior and revising treaty obligations when treaties turn out to have unintended consequences. Amendment of a treaty requires unanimous consent, which again is always hard to secure. The difficulty of amending treaties makes states cautious about entering them in the first place, lest they be bound to obligations that rapidly turn out to be onerous and of limited value.

For a narrow range of issues, states have attempted to overcome these problems by creating permanent institutions. The WTO (World Trade Organization), for example, provides institutional support for negotiations over tariffs and other trade restrictions. But "policy" changes — tariff levels, for example — require unanimity. Various international agencies — the World Bank, the International Monetary Fund, and so forth — have voting structures that do not require unanimous consent. But states remain free to withdraw from these institutions if they do not serve their interests. By contrast, no one can "withdraw" from a domestic legislature.

In light of these problems, it might seem miraculous that international law exists at all. And tens of thousands of treaties exist. Most of these treaties, however, are bilateral. Two states that seek to cooperate over a discrete issue of importance to them — the location of a border, the construction of an embassy, extradition of criminals, treatment of tourists, and so forth — can easily do so, and their agreements are embodied in bilateral treaties. These treaties cannot solve global action problems; they can only solve bilateral cooperation problems such as prisoners' dilemmas. A relatively small number of multilateral treaties exist, and most of these are regional. NAFTA (the North American Free Trade Agreement) is an example. These treaties facilitate cooperation among a small number of states over trade, regional pollution, regional security, and so forth.[4]

Only a few hundred true multilateral treaties exist. In an earlier book, Jack Goldsmith and I argued that most of these treaties solve coordination problems rather than global collective action problems. Many have had no effect, in part because states could not agree to sufficiently strict obligations, and in part because the collective action problem undermines enforcement of such obligations.[5] But even if we were excessively skeptical about their effectiveness, as our critics have argued, few people will deny that treaty making that requires unanimous consent of all states in the world is an extremely crude way to make global law and falls far short of what is routine and implicitly acknowledged to be essential for domestic policymaking. Effective lawmaking at the global level requires a legislature, just as effective lawmaking at a national level requires a legislature. No such international legislature exists, nor is the creation of one on the horizon.

Enforcement without enforcers. Many people seem to have the impression that enforcement of the law is a straightforward and uncomplicated business in well-functioning nation-states. Police have guns; they arrest people; after a trial and conviction, people go to prison. To avoid prison, people refrain from violating the law in the first place, except in unusual circumstances. Many academics have pointed out that people comply with the law to a greater extent than would be predicted on the basis of a simple rational actor model where individuals weigh the gains from crime against the expected cost of punishment.[6]

The truth is more complex. In both well-functioning and poorly functioning nation-states, a vast institutional apparatus enforces the law. Police act through the criminal justice system and are subject to a web of constraints. They undergo training, they are encouraged to take account of local norms, they have enormous discretionary power *not* to arrest people, they must obtain permission from magistrates and judges before engaging in many searches and arrests, and when they do arrest someone, more actors — prosecutors, judges, juries, and many others — must agree that the person in question ought to go to jail or pay a fine. Even in poorly functioning countries, police face these constraints — indeed, to such an extent that sometimes they cannot enforce the law without breaking the law themselves, and they resort to extralegal tactics such as intimidation and even execution. In the process, they lose their legitimacy and are regarded as armed gangs by citizens who then are reluctant to cooperate with them.

Economies can function only if contract and property rights are respected. People try to enforce these rights in civil courts. Again, they face a vast array of restrictions; defendants enjoy procedural protections that slow down and sometimes undermine enforcement. In many countries, it is quite difficult to enforce a judgment. One must eventually persuade a sheriff or other local official to seize and auction off assets, a complex process that also can be subverted by canny defendants.

Why do such rules exist? If they did not, it would be too easy for the state to abuse its citizens, and for some citizens to use the state to abuse other citizens. Well-run countries incorporate stringent checks and balances in their law enforcement system in order to retain the loyalty of citizens who know that at any time they can be subject to it, but also benefit because others are subject to it.

The distance between domestic and international enforcement systems is even more vast than the distance between domestic and international legislative systems. There is indeed only one enforcement system in international law, and that is the Security Council, whose many defects were described above. Even when the Security Council can agree to approve some action, it cannot call upon an army or police force to carry out its will. It can only authorize or order states to call upon *their* armies to carry out the Security Council's will, but the states have ample reason not to participate, and few do. The WTO system produces judgments for states who are victims of trade violations, but it authorizes these states merely to engage in self-help—to engage in protectionist behavior against the state that initially injured them.

Why haven't states constructed more effective enforcement systems—systems that can keep up with the thousands of treaties they have entered? The most plausible reason—and one that will be explored in subsequent chapters—is that an enforcement agency must be independent of the control of the states against which it will, on occasion, have to act. Such an agency would need an army or police force armed with guns, and if it would be effective against powerful states, the agency itself would have to have a powerful army. But what would prevent that agency from using its power to obtain geopolitical ends of its own—or those of its staff or whoever controls it, including, possibly, influential other countries? The answer is: nothing. And that is why a real international enforcement agency does not exist.

Adjudication without courts. The conceptual landscape of international adjudication is as different from that of international legislation and enforcement as a jungle is to a desert. Where before we saw virtually no institutions, we now see a profusion of them. In addition to the International Court of Justice (ICJ), which is the judicial organ of the United Nations, and the International Criminal Court, which has jurisdiction over certain international crimes, there are courts or court-like institutions associated with the trade system, various human rights treaties, and the Law of the Sea convention; there are also countless ad hoc systems set up to address specific disputes. In its most limited form — as arbitration — international adjudication goes back centuries. The International Court of Justice is more than sixty years old. International adjudication, unlike international legislation and enforcement, is an accepted part of international relations.

The sharp contrast between the flourishing of international adjudication and the barrenness of international legislation and enforcement has received little comment in the literature, and will be a theme of later chapters. For now, the important point is that this contrast can be easily exaggerated. International adjudication, however impressive in outward appearance, lacks an essential feature of adjudication that occurs *within* states: the absence of mandatory jurisdiction. If an individual brings a complaint against another individual in a domestic court, or if a prosecutor files charges, and the defendant purports to withdraw from the court's jurisdiction, she will quickly find out that she can do no such thing. A defendant who fails to appear will find herself subject to a default judgment in civil litigation; a criminal defendant will be compelled to appear.

In most types of international adjudication, a state must consent to jurisdiction. For an arbitration to occur, a state must consent, by treaty, to the jurisdiction of the arbitral panel. For some types of international adjudication, this is also the case. The founders of the International Court of Justice sought to create a type of "mandatory" jurisdiction by giving states the option to submit to any claims brought against them, or a subset of those claims, or claims associated with particular treaties. But states can, and frequently have, withdrawn from jurisdiction when it has served their interests — and, unlike the domestic case, no one has found a way to prevent states from doing this. So, although international law does recognize mandatory jurisdiction in name, mandatory jurisdiction does not exist in practice.

In practice, then, albeit with narrow exceptions, international courts cannot claim jurisdiction over states that refuse consent. Even worse, when international courts issue judgments, they have no means to enforce them.

In this respect, they do not differ much from domestic courts. But domestic courts depend on enforcement by the executive branch or enforcement arm of the government; as we have seen, there is no such international enforcement agency on which courts can depend, with the limited exception of the Security Council, which has never shown any inclination to enforce a judgment of the International Court of Justice. States may voluntarily comply with judgments, and they sometimes do. But they need not. And, in some cases, the weakness of enforcement is overtly recognized by the judicial system. As we saw above, the WTO's dispute mechanism can authorize a state to exercise a self-help remedy against the other state. If the prevailing state is weak, and the losing state is strong, this remedy amounts to very little.

CONSEQUENCES

Most global legalists acknowledge that international law is created and enforced by states. They believe that states are willing to expand international law along legalistic lines because states' long-term interests lie in solving global collective action problems. In the absence of a world government or other forms of integration, international law seems like the only way for states to solve these problems. The great difficulty for the global legalist is explaining why, if states create and maintain international law, they will also not break it when they prefer to free ride. In the absence of an enforcement mechanism, what ensures that states that create law and legal institutions that are supposed to solve global collective action problems will not ignore them?

For the rational choice theorist, the answer is plain: states cannot solve global collective action problems by creating institutions that themselves depend on global collective action. This is not to say that international law is not possible at all. Certainly, states can cooperate by threatening to retaliate against cheaters, and where international problems are matters of coordination rather than conflict, international law can go far, indeed.[7] But if states (or the individuals who control states) cannot create a global government or quasi-government institutions, then it seems unlikely that they can solve, in spontaneous fashion, the types of problems that, at the national level, require the action of governments.

Global legalists are not enthusiasts for rational choice theory and have grappled with this problem in other ways.[8] I will criticize their attempts in chapter 3. Here I want to focus on one approach, which is to insist that just as individuals can be loyal to government, so too can individuals (and their governments) be loyal to international law and be willing to defer to its requirements even when self-interest does not strictly demand that they do so. International law has force because (or to the extent that) it is legitimate.[9]

What makes governance or law legitimate? This is a complicated question best left to philosophers, but a simple and adequate point for present purposes is that no system of law will be perceived as legitimate unless those governed by that law believe that the law does good — serves their interests or respects and enforces their values. Perhaps more is required than this — such as political participation, for example — but we can treat the first condition as necessary if not sufficient. If individuals believe that a system of law does not advance their interests and respect their values, that instead it advances the interests of others or is dysfunctional and helps no one at all, they will not believe that the law is legitimate and will not voluntarily submit to its authority.

Unfortunately, international law does not satisfy this condition, mainly because of its institutional weaknesses; but of course, its institutional weaknesses stem from the state system — states are not willing to tolerate powerful international agencies. In classic international law, states enjoy sovereign equality, which means that international law cannot be created unless all agree, and that international law binds all states equally. What this means is that if nearly everyone in the world agrees that some global legal instrument would be beneficial (a climate treaty, the UN charter), it can be blocked by a tiny country like Iceland (population 300,000) or a dictatorship like North Korea. What is the attraction of a system that puts a tiny country like Iceland on equal footing with China? When then attorney general Robert Jackson tried to justify American aid for Britain at the onset of World War II on the grounds that the Nazi Germany was the aggressor, international lawyers complained that the United States could not claim neutrality while providing aid to a belligerent — there was no such thing as an aggressor in international law.[10] Nazi Germany had not agreed to such a rule of international law; therefore, such a rule could not exist. Only through the destruction of Nazi Germany could international law be changed; East and West Germany could reenter international society only on other people's terms. How could such a system be perceived to be legitimate?

There is, of course, a reason why international law works in this fashion. Because no world government can compel states to comply with international law, states will comply with international law only when doing so is in their interest. In this way, international law always depends on state consent. So international law must take states as they are, which means that little states, big states, good states, and bad states, all exist on a plane of equality.

Global legalists have tried to soften the sharp edges of the international system in three ways. First, international lawyers, especially in Europe, have emphasized human rights treaties as the moral center of the international system.[11] The doctrinal basis of this claim consists of the widespread ratifications of human rights treaties and a very small number of cases, treaties, and other materials that acknowledge that certain human rights norms, called jus cogens norms, supersede all other international law, and that states may not opt out of or change these norms. The UN charter is also often thought to be fundamental in this sense, and hence, a constitutional document. State consent, then, must yield to morally appealing constraints on human rights abuses and aggression. The problem with this view is that states, including leading states like the United States, the European states, and China, do from time to time violate these norms.[12] In practice, the norms yield when states do not consent to them. It is an important and interesting fact that states have not, for the most part, repudiated these norms in official declarations. But, while agreeing that jus cogens norms exist, states have not been able to agree on what the content of these norms are, for the most part, or to their application in specific settings, so the category is largely empty. States claim exceptions and argue by redefinition, and so the basis for the proposition that these norms have constitutional status remains unclear.[13]

Second, international lawyers, especially in the United States, have tried to give international law a democratic pedigree.[14] Some scholars have argued that democracies should have higher status in international law than authoritarian states should; for example, perhaps authoritarian states (but not democracies) should be subject to military intervention. But this approach of pretending that international law is something that it is not cannot succeed. International law can exist only as long as states cooperate in creating and enforcing it, and as long as authoritarian states make up a substantial portion of the globe, wishing them away can only weaken international law.

These tensions burst into the open from time to time, the most famous recent example being the military intervention in Kosovo by NATO forces in 1999. The military intervention violated the UN charter and was clearly illegal. Yet the implication of this view was that the world had to sit by and watch a possible genocide unfold in Kosovo without doing anything about it. Many international lawyers cut the Gordian knot by declaring the war "illegal but legitimate."[15] But this is only to say that states can depart from international law when they have good reasons—a view that threatens to unravel international law and render it indistinguishable from international morality. It was predictable that the Kosovo precedent would be used in future wars, and indeed, the Bush administration cited humanitarian concerns as one of the justifications for invading Iraq. Now the "illegal but legitimate" rationale looks less appealing, and international lawyers are backpedaling.[16]

The problem cannot be avoided, however. The problem with global legalism is that because international law reflects the interests of governments, it will not always be consistent with the moral sense or legitimate interests of populations, so it will lack the authority that law needs to command general assent among individuals. This is not to say that populations will reject all international law; many people will benefit from specific treaties and support them accordingly. Rather, it is to say that international law will always be more appealing in theory than in practice.

The tension is illustrated by the debates even among international lawyers who have accepted the idea of global constitutionalism—that is, a set of international legal rules that apply even to states that reject them. As I noted above, many Europeans argue that these rules are embodied in human rights norms, in particular, those human rights norms that have been embraced by Europeans.[17] On the European view, the death penalty violates international law or is on the verge of doing so, even though it remains on the books in the United States, China, Japan, and many other countries. The human rights norms that are peculiar to the United States—in particular, the United States' unusually expansive notion of freedom of speech—is not one of the constitutional norms. On the American view, if a global constitution exists, it must include a commitment to democracy—a system that does not exist in much of the world, including China, of course, and about which the Europeans, who cannot forget the contribution of popular movements to Nazism and World War II, are not quite as enthusiastic. Meanwhile, developing countries such as China and India claim a "right to development" that gives priority to economic growth on the grounds that alleviating poverty must take precedence over political reform and hence (implicitly) compliance with human rights norms that bind developed states, and in general justifies limiting the international legal burdens of developing states. Run-of-the-mill disagreement, albeit at the level of values rather than of interests, dooms the prospects of global constitutionalism.

Third, international lawyers have increasingly put their faith in international judges and in domestic judges who apply international law.[18] Here we see the connection between domestic legalism and international legalism. People turn to judges when they lose confidence in other instruments of government—because government cannot serve compelling public needs and interests. But domestic legalism can prevail in some countries because nonjudicial institutions remain robust and curb judges who go too far, and judges themselves share the values of the public, and in fact enjoy the confidence of the public because the judicial system has long functioned in a satisfactory way. At the international level, we find no such parallel: the global population feels no particular loyalty to international judges and to other international legal bodies.

THE CHALLENGE

Global legalism has advanced in recent years because problems of global collective action have multiplied and increased in seriousness, and alternative mechanisms for solving them, such as world government, are no more plausible today than they ever have been in the past. Creating international law to solve collective action problems makes good sense, as long as states can enforce the law, but the claim that the decentralized system of international law can do the things for which one would normally think a government would be necessary is puzzling. To be sure, states are able to cooperate, and legal forms can help cooperation and especially coordination, but theory suggests that cooperation to solve global collective action problems will be limited.

The optimism of the global legalist rests on an article of faith: that ordinary people or elites, including government officials, will cause governments to comply with international law beyond what is in the government's narrow self-interest. This faith feeds off the success of domestic legalism in some countries and the proven usefulness of international law in some contexts, but it stubbornly ignores evidence to the contrary. International law, as it currently exists, is a useful device for international cooperation, but it does not have the capacity to command respect as domestic law (in some countries) does, because it is not backed by a world government that has the support of a global community. It rests on and confirms existing power imbalances and ugly political realities that exist in most states, and, lacking strong institutional support structures that can modify and interpret it as circumstances change, it is brittle. The challenge facing international law scholars today is to explain how much of international relations can be successfully and appropriately legalized, and how much cannot.

Defending Global Legalism

As we have seen, global legalism depends on the assumption that states comply with international law routinely or habitually, but it is hard to make sense of this assumption with traditional international relations methodologies that emphasize state interest. Many scholars have risen to this challenge and argued that international legal compliance of states is due to substate processes — processes that involve the interests, incentives, and values of people who operate the government or pressure the government.[1] Disaggregate the state, find out what makes it work, and you will see that routine compliance with international law, and hence global legalism itself, is not hard to understand.[2] Or so the legalists argue. This chapter examines and rejects this argument.

To understand the difference between the unitary state assumption and the disaggregated state assumption, consider the case of sovereign debt. States frequently take on debt, and they usually pay their debt, though not always. The question is: what determines whether a state pays its debt?

The unitary state hypothesis is that a state pays its debt when the state has an interest in doing so. One reason a state might pay its debt is that it fears that if it does not, it will not be able to borrow money in the future because creditors will not trust it. On the other hand, a state might prefer to use funds for other purposes in the present, such as to fight a war that, if it lost, would destroy it. Thus, a state pays its debts if the (discounted) benefit from being able to borrow money in the future exceeds the (current) benefit from using funds in the present. Then one might predict, for example, that the default rate increases during times of crisis such as war.[3]

Disaggregating the state permits richer hypotheses. We might distinguish a state that has stable domestic political institutions and a state that does not. When political leadership changes hands rapidly, a leader may have a stronger interest in defaulting on debt because he does not expect to hold office (or even be alive) in the future when creditors refuse to lend. Thus, holding other things equal, a state with stable political institutions is less likely to default on debt than a state without such institutions. We can test this prediction by finding a variable for stable political institutions (say, democracy or constitutional democracy) and seeing whether it correlates with debt repayment.

The problem with disaggregating the state is that greater accuracy is purchased at the price of complexity. There are many intrastate actors, and it is not clear which ones will matter for the decision of whether to comply with international law. Further, it is rarely clear whether actors care about international law as opposed to particular policies that happen to coincide with the requirements of international law. Do treasury department bureaucrats urge the president and Congress to repay debts in order to comply with international law or in order to ensure that the government can borrow again in the future?

To understand these problems, consider Yale Law School dean Harold Koh's theory of "transnational legal process."[4] According to Koh, states comply with international law because internal actors—including bureaucrats, citizens, politicians, and businesses—and external actors—including other states, NGOs (nongovernmental organizations), and international legal institutions—pressure them to comply with international law. But Koh never explains systematically why these various entities expend resources to force states to comply with international law. Sometimes, he seems to think that interest alone provides them with an incentive; often, it is ideology or "habit" or sympathy. Anne-Marie Slaughter's theory of networking[5] is similarly vague. She describes the many ways in which nonstate actors forge links with each other, but she does not describe a mechanism through which this activity results in international cooperation. Both authors describe foreign policy decisions in terms of the many individuals and entities that make them and influence them—rather than positing, following the unitary state model, a state making a decision as though it were a conscious being—but one cannot derive from their discussions any clear predictions about how and when nonstate actors[6] cause compliance with international law or generate other forms of international cooperation.

Complicating the discussion is ambiguity about the dependent variable. I have so far taken it to be compliance with international law, and that will be the focus of this chapter. An alternative view, however, is that formal compliance with positive international law is not what matters; what matters is international cooperation. Koh does not always mean international law, per se, in the traditional positivist sense. Often he means that nonstate interactions generate understandings or common norms across states about how states should act; these understandings are then internalized in domestic law, even if they are not formalized as a part of a treaty. Thus, Koh's point is apparently that one will notice a greater degree of international cooperation if one observes the interaction of nonstate actors than if one looks for formal agreements between states. Similarly, Slaughter's focus is not so much nonstate actors forcing states to comply with international law; it is about nonstate actors interacting in such a way that results in greater international cooperation than is required by positive international law. The problem with this argument is that it is extremely difficult to determine what counts as international cooperation other than formal compliance with international law. I will return to this problem later.

This chapter discusses the way that nonstate actors may cause states to comply with or violate international law. The theme is that nonstate actors in the aggregate do not have a clear incentive to pressure governments to comply with international law, per se. In some cases, people may want their government to comply with particular treaties, but they often want their government to violate these treaties when conditions change.

A NOTE ON METHODOLOGY

Most international legal scholars believe that states comply with international law as a matter of routine.[7] This view holds that when a state is confronted with an international law that blocks a desired action, the state more often than not defers to the law, and violating it only in unusual circumstances.

This view has two problems. First, no theory provides an adequate explanation for why states would comply with international law. Several theories have been proposed, but none enjoy a consensus. Second, the evidence is ambiguous and, more importantly, given the ambiguity of the theoretical literature, it is not clear what would count as evidence for compliance with international law.

To see why these problems are important, start with the assumption — which no one would contest — that states do sometimes comply with international law but also do sometimes violate international law. For concreteness, suppose that international law says that a state may not send troops across borders with other states (without the other state's permission, but we will leave this and similar qualifications unstated henceforth). Suppose that over a fifty-year period, Big State sends its troops into Small State's territory only once, and Small State never sends its troops into Big State's territory. What could explain this pattern of near compliance by Big State and full compliance by Small State?

As for Small State, suppose that Small State is much weaker than Big State (for example, Small State is Mexico and Big State is the United States). Small State complies with international law but only because it fears retaliation from Big State for violating it. It seems likely that Small State would not have acted differently, even if there was no law against sending troops across borders. International law, then, plays no causal role in Small State's behavior.

If Big State is stronger than Small State, one might be tempted to assume that the law must have prevented Big State from invading Small State except for the one time, where, perhaps, special circumstances intervened. However, this assumption would be hazardous. Big State might have refrained from invading Small State because it anticipated retaliation from other states that feared a shift in the balance of power. Weak states (like Belgium) survived the chaotic international politics of the nineteenth century because some strong states (Britain) feared that other strong states (Germany or France) would upset the balance of the power if they conquered Belgium. Britain guaranteed Belgium's neutrality not because international law required it to respect Belgium's border but because Britain's own interest lay in guaranteeing Belgium's neutrality. Britain did not guarantee the neutrality of other states, and those other states (including Poland, the Ottoman Empire, and China) were frequently invaded.[8]

More important, states often have no interest in invading other states, either because the cost of invasion exceeds the benefits or because they can acquire whatever they want through other means. Big State might not invade Small State just because of the cost of occupation, which history shows can often be extremely high (Iraq is only the most recent example). To the extent that Big State wants something or someone on Small State's territory (resources or terrorist suspects, for example), it may be cheaper to buy them (resources) or bribe or cajole the state (terrorist suspects) or use force below the level of invasion (kidnapping) than to launch a full-scale invasion. In these circumstances, self-interest—with no special deference to the law—may be sufficient to explain various patterns of compliance with the law, from full to none.

These observations do not prove that states *only* obey international law when doing so is consistent with their interests, and that therefore international law has no causal force whatsoever. But they show how difficult it is to evaluate the evidence.

To evaluate the evidence in a systematic way, one must develop a test. There are many possibilities, but let me mention just one. Begin with a theory that states act rationally in their national interest, which may be understood as a combination of security, wealth, and similar goods. In this theory, states comply with international law when doing so enhances their security and wealth, but not otherwise. We might predict some compliance but not full compliance; let's call this level of compliance "C." If it turns out that observed compliance exceeds C by some nontrivial amount, a plausible explanation is that international law plays a causal role in state policy. Otherwise, the baseline theory is more likely to be correct.

To return to our example above, our baseline theory might predict that, given their power difference, Big State would comply with the rule against use of force 50 percent of the time and Small State would comply with the rule 90 percent of the time. Then if we observed that Big State complied with the rule 70 percent of the time and Small State complied with the rule 95 percent of time, we would have some evidence that international law plays a causal role. The problem with this kind of test, however, is that quantifying compliance is extremely hard; even in our simple case, a story about Big State's and Small State's interests is unlikely to give us much of a sense of what the baseline compliance rate would be.

Fortunately, the disaggregated state model provides another way of testing the view that states comply with international law. Because that model holds that individuals cause states to comply with or violate international law, it suggests that information about individuals will be relevant for answering the compliance question. In particular, we might look at the decisionmakers and ask what causes them to decide whether the state should violate international law or not. If we find correlations between their choices and factors that are not closely tied to traditional state interests, we may have evidence that states comply with international law routinely rather than only when self-interest dictates. This is the focus of the next part.

NONSTATE ACTORS

How might nonstate actors cause states to comply with international law? To keep the discussion manageable, I focus on the nonstate actors emphasized by the literature. These include courts, government officials, interest groups, NGOs, and citizens. The question is whether there are theoretical and empirical grounds for believing that these actors cause states to comply with international law more often than would be predicted under the unitary state model.

Courts

One view is that a state complies with a treaty because its courts force it to comply with treaties.[9] This view is popular but puzzling. In the United States, courts do not enforce treaties unless the political branches authorize them.[10] So courts can play a role in the first place only if the treaty in question is either self-executing or non–self-executing but accompanied by implementing legislation.[11] Thus, the court theory does not apply to the numerous non–self-executing treaties in existence.

But even if we focus on self-executing treaties, it is well understood that the political branches can avoid judicial enforcement of such treaties by passing new legislation — that is, domestic legislation, not a new treaty requiring the consent of the other state — that contradicts the treaty.[12] Thus, if the treaty requires X, the state can refrain from X simply by passing a statute that permits it to refrain from X. Courts cannot force the American government to comply with a treaty for the simple reason that the government has the constitutional authority to withdraw from or violate treaties either through the unilateral action of the president or the joint action of president and Congress.

The view that courts enforce treaties rests on a misunderstanding of their role. Consider a typical case: a foreign national suspected of a crime is captured by the police, and his government seeks to extradite him. The U.S. government approves the extradition, but the defendant files a motion opposing the extradition. The court grants the motion on the grounds that the extradition would not be permitted under the relevant extradition treaty. The court thus appears to defy the will of the U.S. government; is this not a case of a court "enforcing" a treaty?

To understand the flaw in this argument, distinguish the state and its various agents and instrumentalities, such as courts and prosecutors. The state itself can decide to violate the treaty simply by repudiating it or enacting inconsistent domestic legislation. Typically, the state does these things through the president and Congress. Thus, the state is in no way bound by the treaty. If the president and Congress have not repudiated the treaty, then the court assumes that the treaty remains in force, just as a court assumes that an ordinary statute remains in force until it is repealed. Until the president and Congress speak in the constitutionally approved way, the court assumes that the prosecutor or executive department that supports the foreign government's motion for extradition is expressing an interpretation of the treaty that is not necessarily the same as that of the president and Congress speaking jointly. For that reason, the court can defy some of the state's agents without defying the state itself.

A clean example of the court forcing the state to comply with international law would involve different circumstances. Suppose, for example, that the U.S. government (the president alone or with Congress) announced that it was withdrawing from the UN charter and a court issued an injunction prohibiting this withdrawal on the grounds that the UN charter does not allow withdrawal. Here, the individuals who are normally thought to control the state's decision whether to comply with international law are being deprived of that power by the court. If the courts did this, and governments obeyed them, then it would be true that courts force governments to comply with treaties. But courts do not do this.

The confusion about this issue probably results from the failure to distinguish between two phenomena: a state committing itself by entering a treaty, and one part of the government committing another part of the government by entering a treaty. I have argued that in the U.S. system, courts do not in any way cause the state to commit itself. Courts do play other functions; for example, they may enable Congress to restrain the president. Put differently, suppose the president wants to commit himself to some other foreign leader, so that he cannot break a promise to reduce trade barriers. One way for the president to enhance the credibility of his promise is to enter a treaty involving Senate consent. If he does that, he may make it legally (under domestic law) or politically difficult to break his commitment.[13] But not impossible: he merely needs senate consent (in our example). So the state remains uncommitted even if particular actors within the state are committed.

In some areas of the law, the federal courts have incorporated international law into federal common law. Prize is the usual example; the federal courts asserted jurisdiction over prize cases and have allowed international prize law to influence their development of federal common law.[14] However, as is always the case with the common law, federal prize law could always be modified or eliminated by statutory law—or even by a declaration by the executive, according to the Supreme Court.[15] So prize law never bound the U.S. government to international law, let alone to any particular treaty.

None of this is to say that courts couldn't bind the state to treaties if they wanted to. Suppose, as is sometimes proposed, that courts refused to enforce subsequent domestic legislation that contradicts a prior treaty.[16] If courts did this, the political branches might have some trouble shaking off a treaty. Of course, they could still repudiate the treaty; but one could imagine a court preventing that as well, as noted above. Why don't courts do this? No one knows for sure, but the answer is probably that courts want to avoid making complex political judgments about when treaty partners have violated their obligations so that the state is justified in withdrawing from the treaty. It is hard to imagine courts taking these steps, for, with the passage of time, as more and more treaties accumulate, the foreign affairs of a state would pass from the hands of the political branches to those of the courts. Courts do not have the legitimacy or the competence to handle the foreign affairs of a state, and it is hard to imagine them acquiring this power.[17]

What does the evidence show? Confining ourselves to the U.S. experience for the moment, it is difficult to find a single example of a U.S. court forcing the government to comply with international law against its will. Again, we must be clear what we mean here. When a court enforces the Alien Tort Statute despite the objections of the executive branch, the court is enforcing Congress' will against the president.[18] The government does not have any clear attitude about international law; it is split. The courts have never prohibited the president from withdrawing from a treaty or violating it,[19] nor have they prevented the political branches jointly from

withdrawing from or violating a treaty. And even when there is a presi-
dent/Congress split, the courts usually refuse to intervene. Probably the
clearest example of the courts compelling the government to comply with
international law against its will occurred in the recent Hamdan case,
where the Supreme Court held that military commissions established to
try Al-Qaeda suspects violated common Article 3 of the Geneva Conventions. Even this case is not a clear. The court claimed only to be interpreting a statute that incorporated international law, thus again enforcing the
will of an earlier Congress, at least in theory, and leaving Congress the
option of repudiating the decision by enacting a new statute, which it did.
It is certainly possible, however, that the court's decision erected an in-
surmountable political constraint for Congress, which could not overtly
repudiate the Geneva Conventions themselves.[20]

Anne-Marie Slaughter claims that courts are "constructing a global legal system"; this claim sounds as if it had something to do with forcing
states to comply with their international obligations, but she provides little
evidence that American courts do this.[21] True, judges meet with their foreign counterparts in conferences in the Alps, but that hardly amounts to
the creation of a global legal system. Judges also cite foreign courts in dicta
sometimes. And today, as in the past, judges must make decisions about
whether to enforce foreign judgments against assets under their jurisdiction; sometimes they do and sometimes they don't, depending on their
assessment of the quality and fairness of the foreign legal system. It may
be that through their interactions judges influence each other, and as a
result, to the extent that they have the freedom to do so, they may produce
similar rules across legal systems. But none of this is evidence that courts
force their own governments to comply with international law.

Nor is it clear that this interaction among judges results in meaningful cooperation between states. Suppose that a plaintiff who is injured in
Canada wants to enforce his judgment against the defendant's assets in
the United States. It's far from clear that a state that permits such enforcement of judgments is more "cooperative" than a state that does not; perhaps for each state it is a matter of indifference as long as court fees are
paid. But even assuming that states that permit the enforcement of foreign
judgments are more cooperative than states that do not, it does not follow
that increasing contacts between judges results in more such cooperation.
Suppose, for example, that during their interactions judges learn that for-

eign law is "unfair" by their lights. As a result, they become *less* willing to enforce foreign judgments.[22] Now, this may be good or bad from a normative perspective, but it surely cannot be counted as an enhancement of international cooperation.

The strongest evidence for a judicial role in the enforcement of international law comes from the European experience, where national courts have in several cases compelled national governments to comply with European law.[23] These events are of considerable interest but have limited relevance for international law. Europe is a quasi-confederation and has been undergoing a process of unification for several decades. Economic, commercial, military, and political integration were all underway long before national courts began enforcing European law. The problem for international law is that most states are not integrated in this way, and that is why national courts are usually not willing to force their own governments to comply with international law.

Government Officials

A second view is that states comply with international law because government officials "internalize" international law.[24] We can distinguish two separate theories for why government officials would seek to comply with — that is, cause the state to comply with — international law. First, the government officials fear that if they violate international law, they will suffer some kind of sanction. The sanction in rare cases might be a formal sanction by an international tribunal or a domestic tribunal enforcing international law; more likely, the sanction would be reputational. Second, the government officials internalize international law in the sense that they believe that they have a moral duty to comply with international law, just as they have a moral duty to comply with relevant domestic law.

External sanctions. The first theory depends on external sanctions. External sanctions do exist, but they are applied with exceedingly low probability. Let us discuss some examples.

Soldiers who commit war crimes face the risk that they will be tried and punished.[25] Trying and punishing soldiers for war crimes has a long history, but mainly enemy soldiers are tried for war crimes — and (of course) only if they are captured in the first place. Most wars do not end the way World War II ended, with an unconditional surrender, and access by the victor to the vanquished state's territory. In these rare cases, the victor may pursue and capture war criminals.[26] In the usual case, the two sides sign a peace treaty that, among other things, provides for the return of POWs (if there are any). In these cases, war crimes are rarely prosecuted.[27]

In another set of cases, third parties demand that war criminals (or other international criminals) be prosecuted in international tribunals. Examples include the various tribunals established to try the people responsible for crimes in the former Yugoslavia, Rwanda, Sierra Leone, and a few other places.[28] However, these tribunals are rare, and have tried few people relative to the number who have committed crimes. The establishment of the International Criminal Court may change this, but it is too soon to tell, and there is ample reason for skepticism—not least being the refusal of the United States to participate.[29]

A final set of cases involves domestic prosecutions of international crimes or domestic civil litigation based on international criminal law. There have been a few attempts to assert domestic jurisdiction over war criminals who have no connection with the state in which the court sits.[30] There have been occasional calls for war crimes trials of people like Henry Kissinger.[31] And, in the United States, the Alien Tort Statute permits aliens to sue people for committing torts against them in violation of international law.[32] I will say more about these lawsuits in chapter 9; their effect has been marginal and limited mostly to cases where American foreign policy is not at issue.

All in all, external legal sanctions for violating international law are extremely weak and unlikely to provide rational officials with an incentive to comply with international law. I have not discussed possible reputational sanctions. Because reputational sanctions are imposed, if at all, by other people, such as the general public, I will address this argument later in this chapter.

Internal sanctions. Do officials internalize international law? The claim here is that they believe they have a moral duty to comply with international law; if they violate that duty, they will feel guilty.[33] To avoid unpleasant feelings of guilt, officials comply with international law.[34]

We cannot peer into the consciences of individuals, so how would we evaluate this claim? One possibility is to evaluate it on its merits: do individuals actually have a moral duty to comply with international law? If not, then it is hard to believe that they would feel guilty for violating it.

Another possibility is to draw on discussions of domestic law. The view that people comply with domestic law out of a sense of moral duty has its adherents, and there have been some efforts to test it.[35] So we can see whether the approach taken in the domestic context can be applied to international law.

As to the first claim, I have argued elsewhere that states have no moral obligation to comply with international law, nor do leaders or officials.[36] The argument is, briefly, that international law has none of the normal sources of moral legitimacy. People may owe allegiance to a domestic government either because the government is good or because the government has democratic legitimacy. As there is no international government, people cannot similarly owe allegiance to what does not exist. There are international laws, but these are negotiated by the various governments, and many of the governments that create international law are bad — authoritarian, corrupt, or just committed to bad policy. International law is a series of compromises between somewhat better governments, mediocre governments, and bad governments. It is not a reflection of the will or interests of a political community in the way that law created by democratic governments may be.[37]

Some people might argue that government officials have a moral duty to comply with international law because their own government is subject to it. But this argument makes the official's duty to comply derivative of the government's duty to comply. If the government repudiates a treaty, the loyal government official has no duty to try to constrain the government and force it to comply with the treaty. A government official's moral duty to his own government cannot be a source of compliance with international law on the part of the government.

Scholars have argued that compliance with domestic law can be explained, in part, by moral duty. One piece of evidence is that compliance rates appear to be higher than what one would predict if people were motivated solely by formal legal sanctions and reputational costs.[38] Although cognitive biases may explain the gap, moral duty is equally plausible. Evidence also suggests that the level of compliance turns on morally relevant factors, such as the perceived fairness or legitimacy of the law, suggesting again that formal legal sanctions and (possibly) reputational sanctions do not fully explain compliance.[39]

In theory, a similar approach could be taken with international law, and it would surely be illuminating.[40] However, no one has yet tried to test this idea empirically, so it remains in the realm of speculation. In addition, because the effect, if it exists, remains controversial in the domestic setting where moral duties are stronger, it would be premature to conclude that they exist at the international level as well.

Other theories have been proposed. Koh suggests that bureaucrats operate out of habit, and once habituated into international law, they cannot stop complying with it.[41] But as Koh does not explain how this habituation process operates and how one would prove or disprove his theory of its existence, it is hard to see how one could evaluate this argument.

A note on bureaucracies. The literature has made much of the possibility that regulatory agencies may care about international law.[42] This view is compatible with the external and internal sanctions arguments: bureaucrats may cause a state to comply with international law because they fear external or internal sanctions. There may be other reasons why international law could become part of the mission or culture of an agency. The U.S. State Department, for example, often acts as if its mission were, in part, to ensure that the United States and other countries comply with international law. And various agencies may care about the enforcement of specific treaties that bear on their domestic functions.

I will discuss this argument shortly. For now, it is sufficient to observe that the evidence for this claim, so far, consists of narrative descriptions of agencies from different states interacting with each other. It is not clear what to make of this evidence. Such interagency cooperation may show that states are, in some sense, cooperating with each other more than is required by positive international law, but no one disputes that this may happen. Such interagency cooperation may make it easier for governments to cooperate or easier for governments to comply with international law. But it also may merely be a result of governments wanting to cooperate with each other and directing their agencies to implement legal or nonlegal agreements. Further, even if agencies are acting on their own, it is not clear that in doing so they promote the joint interests of their governments or the states of which they are a part. As is well-known in the bureaucracy literature, agencies may develop missions that diverge, slightly or greatly, from the desires of elected officials and the interests of the public. If so, much transborder cooperation between agencies should be classified not as cooperation between states but as regrettable but unavoidable friction that results from governments acting, as they must, through bureaucracies. But even on the most charitable reading of the evidence, the role of regulatory agencies in ensuring that nation states comply with international law is marginal.

Interest Groups

Some authors have argued that interest groups force states to comply with international law.[43] We can distinguish a few possibilities. Public interest groups might pressure states to comply with international law because they approve of international law in general or certain treaties in particular. However, we will put off the discussion of public interest groups to the next section, when we talk about NGOs. The other kind of interest group that takes an interest in international law is the trade group of profit-making businesses. This type of interest group is the focus of this section.

The most sustained analysis of the role of interest groups in enforcing international law can be found in the international trade literature. I will discuss some ideas from this literature and then the extent to which they may be applied to international law in general.

International trade law is sometimes conceptualized as resulting from deals between competing interest groups, with the governments acting as mediators. Suppose that state X and state Y both have high trade barriers and do not trade with each other. Each state has two relevant interest groups: import-competers and exporters. Import-competers are firms that would lose business if imports were permitted. For example, the steel industry in X enjoys the high level of protection and would lose profits if trade were permitted, because the steel industry in Y is more efficient and transportation costs are low. Exporters are firms that currently do not export, given the high level of protection but would be able to export and therefore earn higher profits if the barriers were reduced. Y's steel industry thus is a (potential) exporter.

Trade law provides a device by which the exporters in each state can obtain access to the markets in the other state. X's exporters pressure the government to enter trade agreements with Y, so that X's exporters may export to Y; the price of this right is likely to be granting Y's exporters the right to export to X. Once an agreement is reached, the exporters in each state will pressure their governments to comply with the agreement rather than violate it or withdraw from it. Thus, the interest group—the exporting group—forces the state to comply with its international treaty obligation.[44]

There is a further factor. Once the states enter the treaty, each state's exporters will become wealthier, and each state's import-competers will become poorer—just because foreign trade benefits exporters and hurts import-competers. As a result, the political pressure in favor of complying with the treaty is ratcheted up, and compliance is that much more likely to occur.

On the other side, observe that the import-competers retain their interest in pressuring their government to repudiate or, if that fails, unilaterally violate the treaty. So the level of compliance with the treaty depends on the balance of power between exporters and import-competers. When exogenous shocks occur that change the balance of power, then the level of compliance should change accordingly. For example, if a recession hits the import-competers, resulting in the layoffs of organized workers, who in turn pressure the government to violate the treaty, the interest group theory would predict that compliance would decline. The key point here is that in theory interest groups can both enhance the probability of compliance with a treaty and reduce the probability of compliance; their net empirical effect is unknown.

We can make an analogous argument about non-trade treaties. Consider, for example, an arms control treaty. Imagine a setting in which two states, A and B, face each other as potential belligerents. We might imagine that in each state there is an interest group—call it the military-industrial complex—that benefits from wars or international tension, because war and tension increase the demand for weapons. The government balances the interests of this group and the interests of other groups that benefit from peace; the latter groups include ordinary industries. For simplicity, let's distinguish a "war group" and a "peace group" in each state. In a state with a strong war group, the probability that it will go to war in the future is relatively high; the war group, unlike the peace group, creates an externality that harms other states. Weapons are valuable only if they are used; but when they are used, they destroy people and property in other states.

Analogous to the trade story, we can imagine that state A and state B will agree not to go to war—or to go to war less often, or only under special conditions—because A's and B's peace groups will benefit more from the reduction of the probability of war than A's and B's war groups will lose. More precisely, a peace or arms control treaty will, like trade barriers, create an intermediate probability of war where the marginal benefits of war for the war groups equal the marginal costs to the peace groups. On this view, states with big economies and small military-industrial complexes will agree to more restrictive rules than other states. Perhaps this is an explanation for why the United States endorses an expansive interpretation of self-defense, while European states prefer a narrow interpretation.

This hypothesis reflects intuitions about how interest groups could play a role in creating and sustaining a treaty. However, it does not provide any guidance for developing a general theory of how interest groups may cause states to comply with international law. If the exporters and peace groups will lobby states to comply with trade and peace treaties, they have no commitment to international law, per se, and are indifferent to whether the state violates or obeys its other international commitments. Indeed, as we have seen, exporters and peace groups may lobby states to violate treaties that restrict trade and peace. And the import-competers and the war groups will lobby the state to violate international obligations that promote trade and peace. There is no reason to believe that any interest group believes that international law must be followed simply because it is international law. In sum, there is no reason to think that interest groups propel states toward compliance with international law: their effect on compliance is ambiguous.

Nongovernmental Organizations

An increasingly popular view holds that international NGOs encourage states to comply with international law.[45] NGOs can monitor compliance, publicize noncompliance, and take political action against governments that fail to comply with international law. For example, the International Red Cross monitors compliance with the Geneva Convention. Red Cross officials visit prison camps where POWs are held and issue reports to governments that describe the conditions that are observed. The Red Cross does not usually publicize noncompliance, but instead brings noncompliance to the attention of the government or its military authorities and pressures them to change their practices.[46] Other NGOs try to shame governments into action by broadcasting their failure to comply with international law. Amnesty International, Human Rights Watch, and Freedom House monitor human rights in many countries and issue reports. Amnesty International frequently sponsors letter writing campaigns in support of dissidents.[47] NGOs also finance research, lobby for changes in government policy, sponsor conferences, and assist in drafting treaties.

There are two problems with the theory that NGOs encourage compliance with international law. The first is simply that NGOs play no role—or a very minor one—in most areas of international law. It is only in the context of human rights law that the NGO theory has surface plausibility; here, NGOs are numerous, passionate, and well-funded from donations by individuals and groups. There are no comparable NGOs that monitor compliance with the law of consular relations. To be sure, there are groups that care about these issues, but they often consist of regulated firms and other entities—in other words, the interest groups discussed above.

The second problem is that it is not clear that even the human rights NGOs have much power. They do attract the attention of media, raise money, and send staffers to meet with government officials. All this, as noted above, suggests that they do have *some* power. But—with a partial exception discussed below—there is no systematic evidence that they actually influence states. And, even if they do, one must not forget that the power of NGOs will be countered by the power of other groups. Military suppliers will lobby governments to buy weapons that NGOs believe are illegal, for example. And NGOs may find themselves on the opposite side of the same issue.[48] The net effect of these forces is ambiguous.

The third problem is that the agendas of the NGOs and the content of international law differ significantly. The NGOs do not try to enforce international human rights law; they try to enforce those aspects of it that converge with their own agendas and ignore the rest. Many NGOs vigorously oppose the death penalty and expend resources documenting its use and urging states to abolish it. For the states that have not ratified treaties prohibiting the death penalty, or have done so subject to reservations that preserve their right to impose the death penalty, the NGOs serve as advocates rather than law enforcers.[49] Similarly, NGOs focus much of their effort on states that have not ratified human rights laws rather than ensuring that states that have ratified these laws are in compliance with them. Thus, even if NGOs have influence over the behavior of states, it is not clear that they exercise their influence by encouraging states to comply with international law rather than by encouraging states to improve their human rights records generally.

The evidence supports this view rather than the view that NGOs contribute to compliance with international law. I will discuss the evidence later in this chapter.

Citizens

A government might also comply with international law because it fears that citizens will withdraw support if it does not. Why would citizens care if their government violates international law? A number of possibilities suggest themselves. First, citizens might believe that the government should comply with international law because international law is good, either for their nation or for the world generally. Second, citizens might take international law compliance as an indicator of their government's trustworthiness, competence, or reliability; a government that does not comply with international law, like a government that does not comply with domestic constitutional rules, may be unreliable even if the policies it chooses are generally unobjectionable.

American public opinion is largely favorable toward international law. In a 1992 Roper poll, 65 percent of respondents stated that the US should comply with ICJ decisions (21 percent did not know, and only 14 percent disagreed).[50] A 2002 Chicago Council on Foreign Relations (CCFR) survey found that 76 percent of Americans are ready to put American troops at risk to "uphold international law."[51] The CCFR survey also found that 88 percent of Americans favored working through the UN to strengthen international laws to fight terrorism.[52] A report by the Program on International Policy Attitudes found that majorities of those surveyed believed that the United States should strengthen various international institutions such as the United Nations.[53]

These data are interesting, but they do not tell us how much Americans pressure their government to strengthen international institutions and comply with international law. The CCFR survey found that only 43 percent of Americans considered "strengthening international law" a "very important" foreign policy goal; it ranked sixteenth out of the twenty policy goals listed, well below combating international terrorism, preventing nuclear proliferation, somewhat below protecting the jobs of

American workers, and even below maintaining superior military power and protecting American business interests abroad.[54] If any of these goals conflict with an international treaty or ICJ decision, politicians driven by public opinion polls ought to violate international law.

An additional reason for skepticism is the lack of examples where the U.S. government clearly violated international law and was punished by voters or their representatives in Congress for this violation, rather than for the policy itself. Consider as a useful analogy the Iran-Contra scandal. This scandal hurt the Reagan administration not because the public believed that the policy was a bad one (though people may have certainly thought that), but because the public believed that the Reagan administration violated domestic law. But it is hard to think of an international law version of this scandal, even though we can easily think of cases where the United States violated or weakened international law and leaders suffered no political repercussions. These include NATO's intervention in Kosovo; the American invasions of Grenada[55] and Panama;[56] and countless WTO/GATT violations. Even the unpopular Iraq war does not provide an example. Its unpopularity derived from the policy failure, not the illegality—though in other countries, notably Britain, the lack of a Security Council authorization may well have contributed to opposition to the war.

In sum, Americans—and people elsewhere in the world[57]—appear to care about international law and think that, all things being equal, governments should try to comply with international law. But it seems unlikely that they care enough about international law to punish governments that violate international law in order to advance other goals—security, national wealth—that citizens care about. Without evidence, it is premature to conclude that public opinion is the key to understanding when and why states comply with international law.

SOME EXAMPLES

Above, I provided some theoretical reasons for doubting that nonstate factors systematically cause states to comply with international law; I also discussed evidence or (more often) the lack of evidence that these factors do have this effect, or suggest that nonstate factors can push in both directions—in favor of law compliance and law-breaking. The discussions of the evidence were necessarily abstract. In this part, I look at the evidence from a different perspective, focusing on specific incidents in which non-state factors may have caused states to comply with international law.

Given the large number of international incidents, the choice of which ones to discuss is necessarily arbitrary. To avoid charges of selection bias, I have, with one exception, chosen to discuss examples used by proponents of the disaggregated state model. Most of my examples are taken from articles written by Harold Koh, an energetic defender of this model. One example is taken from the work of some political scientists.

ABM

The ABM (anti-ballistic missile) treaty of 1972 prohibited the United States and Russia from, among other things, creating missile defense systems located in outer space.[58] The treaty reflected the contemporary wisdom that the doctrine of mutually assured destruction kept the peace, and if one state developed a successful ABM system, it would thenceforth not be deterred from military action against the other state. To prevent being placed at a disadvantage, the other state would either create its own ABM system—contributing to the ruinous arms race—or else be tempted to engage in an anticipatory strike. The ABM treaty seemed to work well: for more than a decade, both sides complied with it.

In the 1980s, the Reagan administration announced the Strategic Defense Initiative (SDI), a project involving the development of exactly the sort of ABM system prohibited by the treaty. The source of the Reagan administration's enthusiasm for SDI remains obscure: it may have been a fantasy of Reagan's, or it may have been a sophisticated effort to ratchet up the arms race and threaten the Soviet Union by exploiting America's technology superiority in a highly visible way. Critics of SDI argued that the system would not work and would destabilize relations with the USSR; they also argued that SDI would violate the ABM treaty. Nonetheless, the Reagan administration forged ahead with the program.

Koh notes that "had one stopped tracing the process of the dispute in 1987, one might have concluded that the United States breached the treaty and gotten away with it."[59] But, he claims, the attempt to violate international law provoked a backlash, and Congress refused to appropriate funds requested by the administration except for basic research that would not violate the treaty. By 1993, President Clinton had declared that the United

States would continue to comply with the ABM treaty. Koh pronounced international law vindicated in an article published in 1996.[60] This conclusion turned out to be premature. In 2001 President Bush announced that he would pursue a space-based missile defense system, and he unilaterally withdrew from (or violated, if you prefer) the ABM treaty.

What happened? The simple story is that in the 1970s it was in the joint interest of the United States and the USSR to refrain from building ABM systems. Détente was at its height, and Americans were optimistic that the United States and the USSR could coexist in peace. Then came the invasion of Afghanistan by Soviet forces in 1979 and the chilling of relations in the 1980s. The Reagan administration took an aggressive stance against the Soviets, and a massive increase in military defense spending was part of this strategy. Wisely or foolishly, so was SDI. However, the Reagan administration was not able to obtain much cooperation from Congress, which funded some research but imposed significant limitations on how the money could be used. For Koh, the reluctance of Congress was due to the legal force of the ABM treaty. But SDI was highly controversial for other reasons. As noted above, many scientists doubted its merits, and many strategic thinkers feared that it would destabilize the cold war equilibrium in a way that greater defense spending would not.[61] Without a consensus among the foreign policy elite, Reagan could not make headway with SDI. He could, however, preserve it as an option by rejecting Gorbachev's proposals to trade concessions on arms control for a strengthened version of the treaty.

Clinton's support for the ABM treaty is, for Koh, evidence of the power of the law; but the world had changed between Reagan and Clinton. The Soviet Union had ceased to exist, and an expensive space-based ABM system was no longer necessary. The reason for Clinton's decision to comply with the ABM treaty was that there was no longer any need to violate it: the United States would not have built an ABM system in the early 1990s even if the treaty had not existed.[62]

But the international scene changed once again. As the 1990s progressed, the new preeminent concern of American foreign policy — with the USSR now gone — was the proliferation of nuclear weapons and ballistic missile technology to rogue states such as North Korea.[63] As it proved increasingly difficult to prevent the spread of weapons of mass destruction and missile technology, an ABM system began to look appealing again.

Indeed, an SDI-style ABM system would likely be more attractive against North Korea than against the USSR — as the USSR could relatively easily develop countermeasures, or overwhelm the system with the sheer quantity of its missiles, and it is not clear that North Korea and other small states and terrorist organizations could do the same.[64]

So the United States withdrew from the ABM treaty in 2001. This act produced little international reaction, and there has been no evidence that it has had repercussions for the United States.[65]

The ABM story lends itself to a simple interpretation. When the United States and Russia had a joint interest in limiting their military competition, they did so. When the United States decided that this type of cooperation with Russia no longer served its interests, it stopped. Domestic pressure to comply with the ABM treaty was due to skepticism about abandoning the doctrine of mutually assured destruction, and about the viability of SDI itself. It was not driven by a desire to comply with international law for its own sake.

Alvarez

In 1990, agents working for the U.S. Drug Enforcement Agency kidnapped a Mexican doctor on Mexican soil and brought him to the United States, where he was indicted for assisting in the torture and murder of a DEA agent.[66] The doctor, whose name was Humberto Alvarez-Machain, argued that the illegal kidnapping — in violation of an extradition treaty with Mexico as well as traditional notions of state sovereignty — deprived U.S. courts of jurisdiction, but this defense was rejected by the U.S. Supreme Court in 1992.[67] Mexico and other nations objected to the Supreme Court's decision. So did various American politicians and international organizations. In response to this pressure, the United States agreed not to engage in any more transborder kidnappings of Mexican nationals, and the extradition treaty between the two nations was modified so as to reflect this understanding. Alvarez-Machain was acquitted of any wrongdoing and subsequently brought a civil suit against his kidnappers under the Alien Tort Statute.[68] For Koh, these consequences show once again the power of transnational legal processes.[69]

But an alternative explanation is available. The U.S. government knew that kidnapping Alvarez-Machain violated international law, but it also felt that Mexican authorities could not be trusted to indict and prosecute him; it was frustrated that Mexican drug criminals could operate with impunity. Mexico's fierce reaction took the United States by surprise,[70] and it backed off. The United States needed Mexico's cooperation in the drug war, as well as in a host of other crossborder issues, and crossborder kidnapping was not so valuable—Alvarez-Machain was acquitted, which suggests that the case against him was never strong—that inflaming the Mexican public was a price worth paying to maintain the policy. But in its dealings with states with weaker governments and law enforcement systems, the United States has maintained its policy of crossborder kidnappings as well as assassinations in some instances, despite their questionable international legality.[71]

Land Mines

Anti-personnel land mines are effective defensive weapons, but they are also highly dangerous to civilians because they remain hidden but still armed long after hostilities cease. For this reason, states have for a long time tried to restrict their use, just as they have tried to restrict other weapons and tactics that are particularly dangerous to civilians.[72] After false starts in the 1970s and 1980s, a series of meetings were held in Ottawa, and in 1997 more than one hundred states signed a treaty that banned land mines. The signatories did not include the main users and producers of land mines—including the United States, Russia, and China—but it is possible that in future some of these states will either sign the treaty or express their agreement with it.

Koh's discussion of these events emphasizes the role of NGOs (such as Human Rights Watch, a "transnational issue network"), American politicians who urged the U.S. government to sign the treaty, governmental units such as the Pentagon and the State Department, and "transnational norm entrepreneurs," such as Jody Williams, who won the Nobel Prize for her efforts, Bobby Muller, Princess Diana, and Pope John Paul II.[73] He argues that "elaborate ad hoc nongovernmental networks, working with smaller governmental powers, can create a treaty norm that pulls through various forms of internalization even the most powerful nations toward compliance."[74] However, this is a non sequitur. Although various extragovernmental people and groups influenced the international lawmaking process and may have encouraged some governments to enter a treaty that they would otherwise have ignored, Koh must—in order to support his thesis about the internalization of international law — provide evidence not about the *formation* of the treaty, but about *compliance* with it.

Here he comes up short. He does not provide evidence that any of the signatories have complied with the treaty in any significant measure. His evidence is limited to the case of the United States — a nonsignatory — and he merely quotes a few government officials who express optimism that the United States will eventually "obey" the treaty as a matter of policy.[75] However, in 2004, the United States announced that it would *not* sign the treaty.[76]

Have signatory states complied with the land mines treaty? And, if so, was it because of "transnational legal processes"? This question is difficult to answer.

The first problem is that the states that depend most heavily on land mines — that is, states that are at war or frequently go to war — refused to ratify the treaty. These states include Armenia, Azerbaijan, China, Cuba, Egypt, India, Iran, Libya, Nepal, North Korea, Pakistan, Russia, Somalia, South Korea, Syria, the United States, and Vietnam.[77] Finland has not ratified the treaty, no doubt because of its long border with Russia. After Russia's invasion of Georgia in 2008, which has also not ratified the treaty, Ukraine ought to wonder whether it made a mistake by entering this treaty. The other states listed above are at war, have recently been at war, or are embroiled in disputes that could at any time lead to war. That these states will not ratify the treaty creates the suspicion that the parties that have been willing to enter the treaty consist only of states that lose nothing by complying with it — because they have no domestic land mine industry that profits by exporting land mines, and because they have no current or expected security needs that can be met only with a stockpile of land mines.

Indeed, Canada and Belgium, which led the campaign against land mines, had decided to abolish their stockpiles of mines before the land mines treaty was signed or ratified. Thus, these countries, and many others like them, could comply with the treaty without changing their behavior.

However, several states with security concerns did sign the treaty and appear to have destroyed some or all of their stockpiles. These states include Afghanistan (acceded to treaty in 2002), which continues to be torn by strife; Albania (ratified in 2000), which is in a dangerous part of the world; Bosnia (1998); Croatia (1998); and Mozambique (1998).[78] Defenders of the land mines treaty point to the activities of these and similar states as evidence for the effectiveness of the treaty.

But there are two problems for this view. First, we need to control for other factors that might cause states to destroy land mines. Many states that ratified the treaty did so at the conclusion of an interstate or civil war. These states — including the Balkan states mentioned above, Angola (2002), and Cambodia (1997) — likely would have destroyed some or all of their unused land mines stockpile, even if they had not entered a treaty. For these states, ratifying the treaty may have been a useful form of public relations but did not otherwise change their behavior. And other states that have ratified the treaty but still have security concerns, such as Eritrea (2001), have not complied with all of its provisions. In sum, the jury's out on whether the land mines treaty has had its intended effect.

Second, there is no evidence that any particular state's decision to comply or not can be traced to the activities of nonstate actors. Putting aside the observation that only individuals can make decisions for state, a useful disaggregated state model must say something about which nonstate actors matter and which do not. Such a model would enable us to explain and predict the compliance of some states rather than others. However, no such model does so, and so we do not know whether Albania has complied while Eritrea has not because of differences in the behavior of nonstate actors or because of differences in their security situations, which would be captured by a traditional unitary state model. Some international NGOs specialize in monitoring compliance with the land mines treaty, but clearly the existence of international NGOs cannot explain interstate variation in compliance with the treaty.[79]

The question is not whether a treaty like the land mines treaty can affect the behavior of states. The question is whether attention to the behavior of NGOs helps one understand the conditions under which states enter treaties and comply with them. Because the NGOs directed their attention at all states, but only some states ratified the treaty, and fewer still have complied with it, the use of NGO behavior as an explanatory variable fails: it cannot explain interstate variation.

The American War against Nicaragua

In the early 1980s, the Reagan administration decided to support a military insurgency in Nicaragua, which at that time was governed by a Commu-

nist regime backed by the Soviet Union. In addition to providing training, financial support, and weapons to the Contras, as the insurgents were
known, the Reagan administration directed the CIA to mine some Nicaraguan harbors, which it did in early 1984.[80] When this operation came to
light, the Nicaraguan government brought suit against the United States
in the ICJ. The United States objected to the jurisdiction of the court, but
the court took the case anyway and held against the United States. The
U.S. government rejected the decision and showed no inclination to obey
it. Here is how Koh describes subsequent events:

> At that point, the Nicaraguans shifted from an international interpretive
> forum — the World Court — to a domestic enforcement forum: The U.S.
> Congress, where resolutions were introduced terminating future aid to
> the Contras for activities that violated the World Court's ruling. In other
> words, Congress internalized the World Court's ruling into U.S. law. Al-
> most immediately thereafter, the Reagan Administration stopped mining
> the harbors. In short, an interaction, interpretation, and internalization of
> an international norm into domestic law helped force the United States
> into obedience.[81]

The U.S. government complied with international law because of internal
and external political processes.

Koh's claim that the law has causal force can be cashed out in two ways
in this context. First, did international law regarding state sovereignty
cause the Reagan administration to refrain from using force against Nicaragua? Obviously not. The U.S. government ordered the mining of the
harbors. To be sure, one could argue that the United States would have
acted more aggressively if there had been no international law barring the
use of force against foreign states. But there is no evidence for this view,
either: the United States had routinely used force against Latin American
states for a century or more, and the modern use of force rules embodied
in the UN charter did not affect this longstanding policy. To add to the
complexity here, the U.S. argument that it was acting consistently with
international law by honoring its defense commitments to El Salvador and
Honduras, which claimed to be victims of insurgencies supported by Nicaragua, was not obviously wrong.

Second, did the ICJ judgment cause the U.S. government to stop using force against Nicaragua? Yes, says Koh: the ICJ judgment mobilized

domestic and world opinion. But there are several problems with this argument.

Initially, the mining occurred and ended before the ICJ's first ruling (in May 1984) and long before its final ruling (in June 1986). Thus, the ending of the mining was not in a direct sense caused by the ICJ's ruling. Although there was not a subsequent hostile action by American forces, American public opinion opposed military intervention. Indeed, Reagan's Central American policy was unpopular in the United States from the beginning. As early as 1981, the public disapproved of the handling of related events in El Salvador by 32 percent to 23 percent (there was not yet any polling on Nicaragua); in 1982 these figures worsened to 64 percent to 23 percent.[82] The earliest polling on Reagan's Nicaragua policy found that 56 percent disagreed with it and 25 percent agreed in April 1983, and 65 percent disagreed with it and 24 percent agreed in August 1983.[83] These figures stayed roughly the same through the 1980s: disapproval stayed in the 40 percent to 64 percent range, and approval stayed in the 20 percent to 30 percent range.[84] Americans did not approve of Communist regimes in Latin America, but they also did not approve of American military intervention.[85] They also opposed Contra aid during the entire period.[86] When its extent became publicly known, the mining operation—whose secrecy was compromised in any event—was no longer sustainable. Public disapproval of Reagan's Nicaragua policy thus preceded the ICJ's judgment. There is no evidence that public opinion was affected by the ICJ's judgment. The low poll numbers did not get any lower in the wake of either of the rulings.

In addition, there is no evidence that the ICJ's judgments affected Reagan's Nicaragua policy through some other mechanism than public opinion. Reagan's policy became even more aggressive after the ICJ's judgments. Although Reagan bowed to American opinion and stopped mining the harbors, the United States did not offer to remove the mines and refused to pay compensation for damage to vessels.[87] Instead, it repudiated the ICJ decision and withdrew from the ICJ's compulsory jurisdiction.[88] Aid to the Contras continued. The Senate approved $100 million in aid to the Contras shortly *after* the ICJ judgment (the House had already approved the aid prior to the judgment). And although aid to the Contras declined the following year, there is little evidence that the decline was caused by the ICJ judgment or any concerns about international law.[89]

Congress reduced aid to the Contras because of concerns about misappropriation of the funds, the Iran-Contra scandal, and new optimism about diplomatic solutions that could be derailed by the insurgency.[90]

To sum up, the evidence does not support Koh's claim that the ICJ's decision — or international law in general — played a causal role in the American decision to stop mining Nicaraguan harbors.

Human Rights

Several scholars have argued that international law governing human rights has caused states to "internalize" human rights norms. Lutz and Sikkink's study of the experiences of six countries in Latin America is one of the most careful efforts to document this process.[91]

In the early 1970s, Uruguay and Paraguay were both governed by authoritarian governments. Uruguay had signed the International Convention for Civil and Political Rights (ICCPR); Paraguay had not. NGOs, domestic opposition groups, and other individuals and institutions complained about both governments, which engaged in widespread torture of political opponents, but the rest of the world did not pay much attention. In 1977, President Carter took office after an election campaign in which he promised to pressure authoritarian governments to improve their human rights practices. Carter kept his promise, and the United States threatened to withdraw aid and military assistance from states that committed human rights abuses. Carter did not distinguish between states that had ratified the ICCPR and states that had not, and both Uruguay and Paraguay bowed to American pressure. Thus, the treaty could not have been a causal factor, at least in any straightforward fashion.

At roughly the same time, Honduras and Argentina were governed by authoritarian governments, which also engaged in systematic human rights abuses, including the practice of making political opponents "disappear." Honduras had signed the American Convention on Human Rights; Argentina had not. NGOs and domestic opposition groups complained about the governments, but again no one else paid much attention. As in the prior case, both governments eventually abandoned the worst of their practices, in large part because of the pressure of the Carter administration. Again, Carter did not distinguish between states that violated international obligations and states that did not.

The final example involves a comparison of world reaction to a coup in Uruguay in 1973 and a coup in Guatemala in 1993. The world reacted with indifference to the first, but foreign countries vigorously protested the coup in 1993. Lutz and Sikkink argue that international legality accounts for the difference in reactions, but in fact Guatemala had no legal obligation to maintain democratic institutions in 1993, no more than Uruguay did in 1973. The difference in world reaction had many explanations—including the wave of democratization in Latin America in the 1980s—but international law was not one of them.

The fact is that there is virtually no evidence that states have internalized international human rights law. Human rights did improve in the 1980s and 1990s, but this was mainly because of rising living standards[92] and the end of the cold war. Empirical studies have found no correlation between ratification of human rights treaties and improvement of human rights practices.[93]

Lutz and Sikkink, and others like them, point to the activity of NGOs, and argue that NGOs and related organizations spread human rights norms from country to country. This may be true—though the evidence is exceedingly thin—but whether or not NGOs mattered in this way, this says nothing about the propensity of states to comply with international law. It is true that letter-writing campaigns and other forms of publicity forced authoritarian governments, in isolated cases, to release political opponents. But the NGOs did not use these strategies only against treaty signatories; it used them against all states that violated human rights. Thus, whatever effect that NGOs have had on the human rights practices of states, it has not been tied to international law.

The Kellogg-Briand Pact

I have so far used examples cited by supporters of the disaggregated state model, but there is no particular reason to limit oneself in this way. As a test of Koh's methodology, let's consider one of the greatest failures of international law and see whether we could tell a story in which transnational legal processes would have predicted the failure.

Of the many international law failures that one could choose from, perhaps the most famous is the Kellogg-Briand Pact of 1928, which outlawed war shortly before the most destructive war in human history and has had no observable impact on the propensity of states to go to war in general.

NGOs played an important role in the creation of that agreement. They included the Bureau International de la Paix, an international organization that won a Nobel Prize for its efforts to coordinate national peace organizations; America's Carnegie Endowment for International Peace, World Peace Foundation, Woodrow Wilson Foundation, and World Alliance for International Friendship through the Churches; Britain's League of Nations Union, which had nearly 500,000 members in 1927; Germany's Friedengesellschaft, which had 28,000 members; and France's Ligue des Droits de l'Homme, which had 120,000 members.[94] Other participating organizations included the War Resisters' International, the Fellowship of Reconciliation, and the Women's International League for Peace.[95] Many trade unions and political parties also supported the Kellogg-Briand Pact. These organizations drew money and membership from people all over the world who were exhausted by war and inspired by Woodrow Wilson's vision of peace.

Countless "transnational norm entrepreneurs" also participated in the process, including Nicholas Murray Butler and James Thomson Shotwell of the Carnegie Endowment for International Peace; Salmon O. Levinson, a wealthy businessman who founded the American Committee for the Outlawry of War; Colonel Raymond Robins, a former coal digger who became an effective orator in support of the Kellogg-Briand Pact; Jane Addams; John Dewey; and Senator William Borah of Idaho.[96] There were also the diplomats—foremost among them the intelligent but ultimately credulous American secretary of state Frank Kellogg and the shrewd French foreign minister Aristide Briand—and politicians and journalists and nongovernmental units such as the U.S. state department. We can certainly call this an "ad hoc nongovernmental network"—why not?—and if Koh was right, this network ought to have pulled "through various forms of internalization even the most powerful nations toward compliance."[97] But it did not.

The truth is that the Kellogg-Briand Pact was the result of diplomatic maneuvering and the exploitation of naive public opinion.[98] After the Americans refused to ratify the charter of the League of Nations, the French desperately sought some way to obtain an American security guarantee. They believed, rightly, as it turned out, that they would not be secure against a resurgent Germany without an American alliance. After French attempts to obtain a bilateral security treaty were rebuffed by an increasingly isolationist American government, the French sought a more modest *negative* treaty—an agreement that the United States and France would not go to war with each other, not a guarantee of mutual assistance—so that at least they could be sure that the United States would not go to war against France if France were drawn into a second world war as a result of its mutual defense pacts with Poland, Belgium, and other countries. At this point, public opinion was aroused in both countries, and the Americans upped the ante by proposing a *multilateral* peace treaty, a cynical maneuver designed to ensure the United States would not be specifically committed to the defense of France. The Kellogg-Briand Pact was the eventual result. It reflected credulous public opinion not diplomatic realities, and indeed the diplomats protected themselves and their governments by submitting interpretive notes that more or less reduced the pact to an empty shell.

Despite the participation of nonstate actors at all levels, and both before its creation and afterwards, the Kellogg-Briand Pact had no discernable influence on the decisions of states to go to war. And there is nothing special about the Kellogg-Briand Pact. Every international treaty or agreement—big or small, successful or unsuccessful—was created through the efforts of nonstate actors. Thus, their presence cannot tell us anything about whether a treaty is likely to be successful.

SOME LESSONS

Methodology versus Substance

Koh and others like him make two distinct arguments that that they repeatedly fail to distinguish. The first argument is one about methodology. Their methodological claim is that states' decisions to make and comply with international law cannot be understood using the unitary state model. The second argument is substantive; it is that nonstate actors cause states to make and comply with international law under conditions under which, according to the unitary state model, with its simple conception of the state interest, international law making and compliance are impossible or unlikely.

These two arguments are analytically distinct: we can easily imagine someone holding variations on Koh's view. One might accept the methodological claim—which is akin to rejecting both realism and its rational choice variants—but argue that, in fact, nonstate actors limit the ability of states to enter and comply with international law. Indeed, despite his reputation as a great realist, Hans Morgenthau made an argument along these lines. He argued that international law was more effective in the eighteenth-century world of the quasi-unitary state—where monarchs, related to other monarchs by blood and sympathy, could treat international relations as an extension of their familial and social relations—than in the twentieth century, when mass movements inspired by nationalistic fervor held power and had no respect for the people of other nations.[99] Because the two claims are distinct, we will evaluate them on their own terms.

The methodological claim is superficially attractive. We all know that states are fictions, and that when a "state" makes a decision, the real decision-making work is being done by individuals who are influenced by local as well as international groups. So it seems plausible that the best understanding of international law must come from disaggregating the state. However, it is a common error to think a more complex and realistic methodology is always better. Too much methodological complexity renders prediction-making impossible.

Initially, to see why accurate premises are not always necessary, I will return to the realist view. The realists argued that the unitary state model is appropriate because all states, regardless of their composition, face the same international environment, which is, in essence, a security competition.[100] The structure of international relations forces states either to adopt a common strategy or cease to exist. The way that states make decisions may be interesting or important, but it is of little help for predicting such things as whether states comply with international law.

The realist view is not necessarily correct, of course, but not necessarily wrong, either. The value of methodologies is always comparative and so we must ask how the methodology of the disaggregated state fares by comparison with the methodology of the unitary state. The problem with comparison, however, is that so few studies relying on a disaggregated state model have been performed. The best and most careful so far are the studies of international trade, but even these are mainly theoretical, and the evidence remains skimpy. As between the disaggregated state model and the unitary state model, then, the jury is out. A hunch is that the disaggregated state model may prove useful for understanding discrete problems of international relations[101] but will never provide a comprehensive theory for why states comply with international law.

I want to turn now to the substantive claim that nonstate actors cause states to comply with (or make, but I shall henceforth assume this) international law in cases where a unitary model would suggest otherwise. It turns out to be difficult to make this argument because the unitary model itself is ambiguous about the conditions under which states obey international law—or, I should say, there are many different unitary models, and each makes different predictions. Koh's modus operandi is to take the most extreme of the unitary models—the kind of severe realism of someone like John Mearsheimer[102]—which seems to predict that states never obey international law except by accident, but this is to load the dice against the unitary model. Then, for Koh, it is simply a matter of showing that states do obey international law sometimes, in cases where they have no clear interest in doing so, thus falsifying the unitary model and proving his own. But many unitary models—including the rational choice view—do predict compliance with international law, so the mere fact of compliance-against-immediate-interest cannot be proof that nonstate actors matter.[103]

To show that nonstate actors matter, one needs to show *how* they matter. One needs a theory, but neither Koh nor anyone else has provided one.[104] The disaggregated state model cannot claim that all nonstate actors matter, equally and indifferently. It must be that certain nonstate actors matter, and others do not, and then we have the beginnings of a theory. Suppose that actors A and B matter, and C and D do not; then we can predict that the state complies with international law when A and B are concerned and not when C and D are concerned. Or, to be more concrete, suppose that the theory is that independent courts matter; then we expect that states with independent courts comply with international law more often that states that lack them. One could make similar arguments about any number of things: the existence of civil society, a free press, separation of powers, a strong legal culture, and so forth. But no one has done this work and so we remain unenlightened about the role of nonstate actors in determining patterns of compliance with international law.

Law Creation versus Law Enforcement

International lawyers frequently neglect the crucial distinction between law creation and law compliance. The neglect is sometimes understandable, but it is methodologically sloppy. States create law when they enter treaties; they comply with the law when they comply with the treaties rather than violating them. Here the distinction is clear. The picture is murkier with customary international law. Customs evolve in a decentralized fashion: states create them by complying with them. Still, the theoretical distinction remains.

As a methodological matter, this distinction matters. When Koh discusses the success of international law and the role of nonstate actors in state "compliance," he frequently lumps together the role of nonstate actors in the creation and their role in compliance. There are two problems with this maneuver. First, creation is never in doubt when we are talking about compliance: if the law did not exist, we would not reach the question why states do (or do not) comply with it. But Koh frequently talks as if the considerable investment of time and resources by nonstate actors in law creation is evidence that states comply with the law. In fact, it is not evidence that nonstate actors cause states to comply with international law; it is evidence only that they cause states to create international law.

Second, the claim that nonstate actors influence the creation of international law is banal. If nonstate actors did not influence the creation of international law, who would? The "state" is a fiction, and can't cause itself to do anything. Much of the busy activity that Koh describes — all the activity of the transnational norm entrepreneurs, politicians, NGOs, corporations, and governmental units — proves nothing, because much of this busy activity occurs during the law making process, not afterwards, when it's time to comply. To be sure, there is also activity during the compliance phase, and this activity is relevant; it's just that Koh's use of the prelaw activity creates an aura of busy-ness that is misleading.

The work in this area would be much improved if scholars focused on the "why comply" question and not the "why make" question. Once we understand whether and when and why states comply with international law or particular international agreements, we will be in a better position to understand why they create international law in the first place. But we are far from that stage of understanding.

Compliance versus Implementation

Much of the disaggregated state scholarship fails to distinguish between compliance with international law and implementation of international law. Compliance means that a state curbs its interests in order to bring its behavior into conformity with the requirements of international law. Implementation refers to the way that the state brings its behavior into conformity with international law. A state that complies with international law may be able to choose many ways of implementing its compliance.

As an illustration, suppose that a state agrees to respect a certain border. In order to comply with this agreement, the state—that is, its government—must enact certain measures, such as laws directed at its own citizens forbidding them to cross the border. These laws could take any number of forms, with different penalties, enforced by different agencies. Suppose, for example, that the government enacts a law that creates a criminal penalty for any citizen who crosses the border without the permission of the other government. The law can be enforced only through the participation of prosecutors, judges, defense attorneys, and other nonstate actors.

Koh's view seems to be that all of this implementation activity—the "transnational legal process"—has something to do with compliance. In a sense, this is true. For the state to comply with its agreement to respect the border, it must rely on officials and other individuals. However, Koh's view is stronger: that these officials may cause the state to comply with the border agreement when the government no longer has an interest in doing so.[105]

It's hard to understand why this could be so. The lawyers and courts implement the border agreement only because it is authorized by legislation; if the legislation is repealed, then they will stop implementing the agreement. The blur of busy nonstate actor activity is certainly evidence that implementation is occurring, but it tells us nothing about whether nonstate actors are forcing the state to comply against its interest.

To be sure, it is conceivable that the officials and courts could try to prevent the state from withdrawing from its border agreement. The prosecutors could threaten to resign; the courts could declare the withdrawal unconstitutional. But there is no reason to expect these people and institutions to do that; and I have not seen evidence of it.

The same points can be made about the literature on networks. Consider Kal Raustiala's case studies, which show that government agencies cooperate with each other across borders when enforcing securities, antitrust, and environmental laws.[106] The agencies do this either because of formal treaties or because they see international cooperation as flowing from their domestic mandates—for example, to catch overseas entrepreneurs who defraud American investors. These case studies show that as more international interactions occur among citizens (driven by the decline in transportation and communication costs and a relatively peaceful security situation) and as states rely more heavily on their bureaucracies to regulate conduct, there will be more international cooperation among these bureaucracies. The case studies do not show that states are more likely to comply with international law if they have bureaucracies than if they do not.

Raustiala's theory is the opposite: he argues that bureaucracies do not simply implement cooperative agreements among states; they make cooperation, and thus compliance with international law, easier and more likely. The theory requires one to engage in difficult counterfactual reasoning of the following sort. Imagine two states, A and B, that have bureaucracies that deal with a relevant international agreement; and two states, C and D, that do not. Raustiala thinks that A and B are more likely to comply with an international agreement than are C and D—or, perhaps, that A and B will enter (and comply with) a more ambitious international agreement than will C and D. The bureaucratic networks disseminate information in a way that fosters compliance; without the bureaucracies, compliance and cooperation are too costly.

At one level, the theory is unobjectionable. States create bureaucracies to implement the law; to the extent that they care about international treaties, they ought to direct their bureaucracies to comply with them. If the bureaucracies do their jobs properly, compliance should be more frequent than it would otherwise be. This is like saying that if two corporations enter a long-term procurement contract, they are both more likely to comply with it if they have bureaucracies than if (say) the CEOs try to implement the contracts themselves (whatever that might mean). But Raustiala's goal seems to be more ambitious: to show that the creation of networks below the level of the government should enhance compliance beyond what might otherwise be in the government's interest.

His three case studies, however, do not provide evidence for this view. They are narrative descriptions of how bureaucracies cooperate. In the area of securities law, the United States' SEC has persuaded other countries to adopt U.S. securities policies, which has made it easier for the SEC to enforce American securities law and policy overseas. Other countries have benefited from the SEC's expertise in creating and enforcing securities rules. In the area of competition policy, a similar phenomenon has occurred, except here the world has divided, with some countries clustering around the American system and other countries following the European system. In the case of environmental law, Raustiala discusses the way that Mexico's environmental regulators benefit from the expertise of the American EPA.[107] These case studies are ambiguous. They might show the networks constraining their governments; but it is just as plausible that the bureaucracies are following the directions of their governments, which have ordered them to cooperate with each other.

International Law versus International Morality and the Diffusion of Norms

Confusion also arises from the neglect of another distinction, this one between international law and international morality. The neglect of this distinction is interesting as well as confusing; it results in part from a real complexity about international law. Many international law scholars claim that international law is not just positive law—that is, the result of states consenting to certain rules—but it is also circumscribed by natural law. There are certain norms—jus cogens norms—that states cannot override.[108] For example, there can be no treaty that authorizes genocide.[109] Such a treaty would not be valid international law.

From this premise, advocates point to the spread of human rights norms and argue that advance of human rights shows that states care about international law. The ratification of treaties—rather than compliance with them—is considered the relevant evidence that the rule of international law has progressed.

To understand this argument, let us offer some definitions. Let IL(P) refer to rules of international law that can be traced exclusively to state consent and have no independent moral or "natural law" component. Let IL(R) refer to IL(P) supplemented with—and limited by—natural law rules to which states have not consented. IL(P) could permit genocide, for example; IL(R) could not. Old-fashioned positivists believe that IL(P) exhausts international law; most modern international lawyers believe that IL(R) defines the contours of international law.[110]

The question, now, is whether states that "comply with international law," to the extent that they do, comply with IL(P) or IL(R). Consider our discussion of human rights. The IL(P) thesis predicts that only states that ratify human rights treaties refrain from human rights abuses when those abuses would otherwise be in the states' interest. The IL(R) thesis suggests that even states that do not ratify human rights treaties will be influenced by those treaties, or perhaps an emerging "norm" reflected in the behavior of the states that do ratify the treaties.[111] Thus, the IL(R) thesis might predict that as more states ratify and comply with human rights treaties, the pressure on the holdouts increases.

Stated this way, the IL(R) thesis converges with a view held by many sociologically oriented political scientists and law professors, which is that states imitate each other regardless of what international law says, although the norms of behavior may eventually make their way into international treaties. In fact, this thesis seems implicitly to be held by Lutz and Sikkink.[112] That may be why they are less interested in whether the states they study formally ratified the human rights treaties than whether their behavior changed over time. Another example comes from Goodman and Jinks, who point to the spread of women's suffrage at an increasing rate after a few states initially adopted it, as though by a contagion effect.[113]

States do imitate each other; in particular, new and unsuccessful states imitate successful states. Japan imitated Western political and military models after its isolation was penetrated in the 1850s. France imitated the German educational system after it lost the Franco-Prussian War. Authoritarian political systems gained popularity after the perceived failure of democracy in Germany, Italy, and France in the 1920s and 1930s. And the free market policies of Western nations were widely imitated after the collapse of the Soviet Union. With these examples before us, the spread of human rights, including the ratification of human rights treaties, seems like more of the same: citizens and governments imitating the successful Western states.

Whatever its merits, the relationship between this line of thinking and traditional debates about international law is obscure. One view might be that treaties play no causal role at all: governments enter treaties in order to show their citizens and the world that they have decided to imitate other states. The treaties are effects, not causes, and if circumstances change—human rights seemed like a great idea yesterday but no more today—the treaties will not prevent states from changing their behavior. Another view, which is more congenial to the literature, is that the treaties and other forms of international law serve as an accelerating force. Once states enter a treaty, events that would otherwise cause them to stop imitating other states no longer have this power. Although this theory might be true, it would be extremely difficult to test it, as one would have to show that a treaty accelerated behavior rather than merely changed it. To my knowledge, no study provides evidence.

GLOBAL LEGALISM AND THE DISAGGREGATED STATE

None of this is to say that disaggregating states is pointless or futile. The biggest problem with the unitary state model is that defining a state "interest" in the abstract, without any reference to the desires of citizens, interest groups, and elected officials, seems fruitless. Some political scientists have assumed that states seek "security" or "relative security" but this assumption cannot be the whole story, as not everything a state does is tied to security. We know that governments pass domestic laws that respond to the concerns of interest groups and citizens, and that these concerns involve issues other than security; why wouldn't foreign policy as well?

In order to define a state's interest for the purpose of analyzing international behavior, then, one must rely on a theory, even if a very rough-and-ready theory, about how the interests of citizens are translated by the political process into government policy. One might assume, for example, that democratic governments roughly express the preferences of the public at large, while authoritarian governments express the preferences of an elite. Whatever the case, it seems sensible to assume that trade law reflects state interests in advancing the prosperity of exporters and import-competers, human rights law reflects people's altruism, the law of the sea reflects merchant and other commercial interests, and so forth. In general, states seek to maximize wealth and security of their people (or elites), and this general policy manifests itself in particular trade, human rights, security, and other foreign policies.[114]

All of this is commonplace. But it is one thing to say, for example, that interest groups influence the kind of treaties that states enter, and to say that a particular interest group may have an interest in ensuring that the government complies with a (favorable) treaty. It is quite another thing to say that interest group theories suggest that compliance with international law ought to be greater than the level that would be predicted by a model based on a unitary state interest. As I noted above, interest groups may encourage governments to violate international law as well as comply with it, and there seems to be no reason to think that interest group pressures add anything to a state's general reputational interest in complying with international law. At least, such a claim would have to rely on a theory about why interest groups tend to promote law compliance rather than law violation, and such a theory has not yet been advanced.

It follows that the disaggregated state model, as currently developed, has no particular implications for the question why states comply with international law or with international norms that have not been legalized. The usual argument — if you look at nonstate factors you will understand why states comply with international law or norms more than realists say — is no more plausible than the opposite view, which is that if you look at nonstate factors, you will conclude that states ought to comply with international law less than international legalists think they do. Although some nonstate factors push in favor of compliance and cooperation, others push in favor of violation and conflict. How these factors balance out remains unresolved.

The upshot is that the main efforts to provide theoretical and empirical support for global legalism have failed. Global legalism is a faith, or set of assumptions, or attitude; it is not a theory grounded in a plausible reading of the evidence.

Globalization, Fragmentation, and the Law

In chapter 1, I observed that commentators have long dreamed of a unified world state or some other type of world governmental organization that would prevent war from occurring and solve the other problems that exist on a global scale. As hope for such a state has faded, global legalism has emerged as a freestanding international creed. The rule of law at the international level, however, is in tension with the state system. In the absence of a world government, powerful states have little reason to comply with the rules that they agree to, except when doing so remains in their interest. Rather than being universal, applying to all equally, as domestic law does, international law consists of the rules that emerge from discrete bargains between different states and is vulnerable to shifts in the balance of power.

Global legalists, however, have taken comfort in what they see as the decline of the nation-state. As powerful states weaken, they will have increasing trouble resisting global institutions that implement the rule of law. And it is true that states have weakened. Two of the most important trends since World War II are the fragmentation of the state and globalization. At the end of World War II, the world was dominated by the United States and three empires—the Soviet Union, Britain, and France. China was a huge country but was wracked by civil war. Japan and Germany, of course, had collapsed and were occupied. The numerous small independent states in Latin America and Europe had marginal influence on world affairs. There were, in all, fewer than seventy states, of which fifty-five were members of the United Nations. And putting aside the lingering elements of wartime cooperation, crossborder flows tended to be limited, and regional or internal to empire.

Today, the picture is entirely different. One hundred ninety-two states exist—more, if one includes states and quasi-states that do not belong to the United Nations. The Soviet, British, and French empires have dissolved, as have the smaller empires of the Netherlands, Belgium, Spain, and Portugal. Decolonization alone accounts for more than one hundred new states; in addition, Yugoslavia split apart, East Timor seceded from Indonesia, Eritrea split off from Ethiopia, and Czechoslovakia divided into the Czech and Slovak republics. The United States is the only globally powerful state, but an increasing number of states must be counted as significant regional powers—including China, Russia, Japan, Indonesia, India, and Brazil. The European countries are consolidating into the EU, a quasi-state with immense economic power that is still a military weakling. International trade is at a historic high; foreign investment is also of great significance. Migration has not reached historic levels but remains important; uncontrolled, illegal migration is a headache for most major states.

These trends have received much attention from economists and political scientists but less from lawyers. International lawyers who have thought about fragmentation and globalization tend to see it as a good thing. The breakup of states and their increasing weakness in the face of global forces shows the declining influence of national sovereignty, which is then interpreted as a sign that governments will be unable to resist the constraints of international law. Meanwhile, the consolidation of Europe is also seen as a vindication of international law: populations are increasingly submitting to legal bodies above the national level. For the global legalist, sovereignty is a dirty word. Smaller, weaker states will need to cooperate with each other, and to do so they must yield sovereignty to international legal bodies.

This chapter takes a more jaundiced look at these trends. Fragmentation is a threat to international law because international law depends on powerful national governments and cannot exist without them. Small states might be more willing to yield to international bodies than large states are, but international bodies are powerful only when large states support them. Globalization itself is not a threat to international law—only to the extent that it has contributed to fragmentation; its long-term effect in this regard is also baleful, or should be considered so by the international lawyer.[1] The fragmentation of states poses a threat to, not an opportunity for, global legalism.

THE STATE

A state is a political entity that joins a territory and a population. People on the territory are in the state and subject to its jurisdiction. The state acts through a government, which may change over time, even as the state itself remains constant. The government typically has a monopoly on the lawful use of force within the territory of the state.

Because the government of a state has a monopoly on force, it can provide public goods to its citizens. It finances the public goods by taxing and regulating citizens, and it prevents foreigners from free riding by controlling its borders. The standard list of public goods includes security, environmental quality, the provision of market institutions, education, and social insurance.

The nature of a public good is such that the cost of supplying it does not increase proportionately with the population. If a state provides adequate border defense, then an increase in its population does not change this: more people benefit from border defense, but border defense is no more difficult. At the same time, the cost of maintaining defense can be spread over the larger number of people, so each individual pays less. All this suggests that larger states can supply public goods more efficiently than smaller states can, so that it is better to live in a large state than in a small state and that over the long run large states should have advantages over small states in the competition for the world's resources. And although some collective goods are not "pure" public goods—that is, they are optimally supplied at less than the maximal scale—the largest states can ensure that those goods are supplied optimally by delegating their provision to regional or local governments.

If the cost of supplying public goods declines with the size of the state, then the optimal size is global. Why, then, is there not a single world state? A world state would be able to spread the fixed costs of public goods over the largest possible population, and thus supply them more cheaply than any smaller state. There is no reason in principle why a world state cannot exist, but history suggests that the problem is one of heterogeneity. As the size of a state increases, the diversity of the population increases as well. Diverse people do not benefit from public goods to the same degree. For example, some people might be willing to pay a lot in taxes for a cleaner environment while others are not. If the government supplies the environmental policy preferred by the citizen with median preferences, those with stronger environmental preferences will be disappointed that the environment is not cleaner and those with weaker environmental preferences will be disappointed that they must pay high taxes for an environment whose cleanliness they consider excessive. The government can try to adjust taxes and use transfers so as to ensure that those with weaker preferences pay less and those with stronger preferences pay more, but this is costly and difficult and can lead to other distortions in people's behavior, further suppressing economic growth.

Heterogeneity does not just interfere with the production of environmental and other run-of-the-mill public goods. When it takes the form of ethnic hatred, it interferes with the most basic functioning of the state and can result in civil war. Successful states are either largely homogenous or have institutions that enable ethnic groups to avoid antagonizing each other or have developed norms of getting along. Unfortunately, most states have significant problems with restive ethnic minorities, and all the major state breakups of recent years, as well as those that are likely to come in the future, have occurred, or will occur, along ethnic lines.

Heterogeneity costs limit the ability of a government to supply public goods. Thus, given a large population, the average individual might be better off if two states exist than if one state exists. A single state could produce public goods more efficiently — in the sense of spreading the cost across the larger population — but it might not be able to produce public goods that one or the other half of the population desires. If the population can be divided into two states that are more homogenous than the single state, then each of the two states can cater to the preferences of its own population. Although they supply public goods at a higher cost, they can also supply public goods of the type that their own population prefers. Thus, the fundamental reason for the existence of multiple states is the heterogeneity of preferences (defined broadly to include interests, values, and so forth).

The theory that the size of states reflects a trade-off between scale economies and heterogeneity costs has been advanced most recently by the economists Alberto Alesina and Enrico Spolaore in their book, *The Size of Nations*.[2] The theory obviously simplifies extremely complex phenomena, and there are many other competing theories, as well,[3] but I will rely on it because of its parsimony and because it adequately serves present purposes.

One more point should be mentioned. Alesina and Spolaore never discuss the possibility that small states can obtain economies of scale by entering treaties with other small (or large) states.[4] We can put the small state's problem this way: supposing that it does not have access to optimal economies of scale, should it attempt to merge with another state or should it enter a treaty with another state? Merger of states is an immensely complex and difficult process and will generally not take place unless the similarities between the populations are considerable. Throughout most of history, the merging of states took place as a result of war — either wars of conquest or wars against external enemies that posed a common threat to the group of merging states. Although treaties can be difficult to negotiate and enforce, these costs are manageable, and so states generally use treaties to produce public goods at a supra-state scale. The larger point is that if treaty making is a substitute for merger, then states might be less likely to merge, and more likely to break apart, as the transaction costs of treaty making decline. If transaction costs decline, then states, recognizing that they can obtain public goods by entering treaties, will break up so that heterogeneous preferences can be better satisfied.

Thus, we have three variables. In addition to scale economies and heterogeneity costs, transaction (or treaty making) costs determine the size and number of states, as well as the "amount" of international law. As transaction costs rise, the size of states could increase (and their number decline), and the amount of international law could decline. As transaction costs decline, the size of states could decline (and their number increase), and the amount of international law could increase.

GLOBALIZATION AND FRAGMENTATION

If the Alesina/Spolaore approach is correct, then states are not fixed entities; governments must constantly handle pressures to expand and contract. If economies of scale increase, then populations or perhaps elites will pressure governments to merge states, conquer territory, or impose their will on foreign territory. If economies of scale decline, then populations that share a territory with other population might try to separate. Similarly, if heterogeneity across states declines, states might merge; if heterogeneity within states increases, states might fragment.

Of course, states do not smoothly expand and contract in response to these pressures. Borders are often rigid because natural characteristics like mountains, oceans, and rivers supply convenient demarcations; because people living on either side of the border develop a vested interest in keeping the border where it is; and because the stories and principles that legitimate national rule have territorial referents. Thus, the Serbs tried to hold onto Kosovo rather than yield it to the control of its majority ethnic Albanian inhabitants because of the role of the Battle of Kosovo in the national mythology—or so we are told (this claim, like so many having to do with the claims of ethnic groups on territory, is controversial). These rigidities contain both centrifugal and centripetal pressures most of the time, but they collapse when conditions change enough.

Alesina and Spolaore argue that the increase in the number of states since World War II was due to the rise of free trade and the benign postwar security environment.[5] As tariff barriers came down, states benefited less from having a large internal market. Producers could export goods rather than find domestic buyers; consumers could buy imported goods rather than find domestic producers. Large populations were also no longer necessary to supply and pay for mass armies. No longer needing to provide large internal market and mass armies, states broke up so that governments could better cater to the smaller and more homogenous population that would form within the new borders.

This argument faces some problems. The number of states did not increase during the last free trade era prior to World War I.[6] In addition, large internal markets are better than free trade as long as borders exist; different governments and regulatory systems substantially increase the cost of trade even when trade barriers are nominally zero. If free trade has made large internal markets unnecessary or of little importance, why have the European countries consolidated into a customs union at the same time that other countries fragmented? As for international security, the environment was hardly benign. Numerous wars were fought between states during the postwar period, involving all the major powers and many minor powers as well.

A more complete theory of fragmentation would explain why free trade has become more popular. A plausible answer lies in technological changes. Since the late nineteenth century, the cost of communication and transportation has declined dramatically. As a result, people could increasingly benefit from access to distant markets. As the benefits of large markets increased, economies of scale increased. In the nineteenth century, this led to the consolidation of smaller states into large states (as occurred in Germany and Italy), imperialism (which involved the conquest of weak states), and reduction in trade barriers.

The two world wars and global economic disruption temporarily halted this process, but it continued after World War II. At this stage, the United States and its allies believed that international trade had security as well as economic benefits, and put in place global trade and financial institutions that would facilitate the expansion of trade.

An important factor continued to be economies of scale; and as communication and transportation costs declined, the benefits of trade would continue to rise, and increased trade was therefore predictable. But instead of the further consolidation of states, as Alesina and Spolaore's model predicts, the opposite happened. This can be attributed to the other two variables.

First, World War II saw the reassertion of nationalism, which emphasized ethnic differences. As people came to stress their ethnic differences, their enthusiasm for multinational states would decline. Nationalism in Africa and Asia helped stimulate decolonization. Nationalism, which is a linguistic and territorial phenomenon, manifests a type of heterogeneity. Increasing heterogeneity costs may well have offset the continued rise of economies of scale, so that states broke apart rather than consolidated.

Second, the decline in communication and transportation costs also contributed to the rise of treaty making. With low communication and transportation costs, states can, with relative ease, negotiate new treaties, modify old treaties in light of changing conditions, and monitor the behavior of treaty partners. Although treaties can be hard to enforce, they are more attractive than consolidation of states. Populations can remain homogenous while obtaining economies of scale along whatever dimensions of international cooperation that will generate joint benefits.

There could also be feedback effects and conflicting causal pathways. As transportation and communication costs decline, values and tastes may spread, resulting in more homogeneity. But people could also react with hostility to foreign influences and recommit themselves to traditional values, resulting in more heterogeneity. Greater homogeneity, by creating larger markets, might stimulate further technological innovation, resulting in accelerating reductions in transportation and communication costs.

So the actual story is surely complex and largely unknown. Still, the hypothesis that technological change has been the main driving force in state size — first leading to state consolidation to capture economies of scale, then to increased reliance on treaty making as a way to preserve those economies of scale while limiting heterogeneity costs — has surface plausibility and is a reasonable working premise.

Technological changes have also spurred globalization. Globalization refers to the increasing interaction among people around the world — in terms of migration, tourism, trade, investment, communication, and, in general, crossborder influence, both good and bad. Globalization is the observable consequence of mainly hidden changes in technology, customs, and habits of mind. People demand diverse products, services, experiences, and interactions; as the costs of communication and transportation decline, they can obtain these goods through cross-border travel and trade. Fragmentation and globalization are different phenomena: globalization could occur through the consolidation of states, such as the development of a world state. The technological changes that have made it easier to negotiate, monitor, and enforce treaties have also made it easier to trade and in other ways interact — that is why increasing economies of scale have resulted in both more interaction and a larger number of states.

COOPERATION AND INTERNATIONAL LAW IN A FRAGMENTING WORLD

Globalization's defenders celebrate increasing trade which they argue, with much evidence, enhances the well-being of most people. They also argue, echoing Norman Angell, that crossborder trade and other forms of cooperation promote peace and the rule of law. Critics of globalization argue that it has done little for many hundreds of millions of people, mostly concentrated in sub-Saharan Africa, and possibly has made them worse off. Greater openness has created new resentments, as people see their traditional cultures overcome by external forces that they do not understand and cannot control, and it has created new opportunities for greedy corporations, terrorists, and viruses.

Both sides accept a premise: that globalization has resulted from or has been greatly accelerated by international law. Alesina and Spolaore think that international trade law had made possible international trade, which is the central component of globalization. If they are right, then the fragmentation of states was only mediately caused by trade; the ultimate cause was international law. Alesina and Spolaore's argument implies that populations, in effect, choose state size and the level of international cooperation in a manner that maximizes national well-being, resulting in both the creation of larger international structures and the fragmentation of states into smaller entities that can better funnel the benefits back to the population.

This premise is questionable, however. Populations depend on governments to maintain these larger international structures. Treaties do not enforce themselves; governments must manage them — negotiate them, monitor compliance, and threaten retaliation or a diminution in cooperation if treaty partners breach their obligations. So in the process of creating international structures and reducing the size of their states, populations also weaken the only entities that can maintain those structures.

Globalization and fragmentation march forward hand in hand. But fragmentation potentially undermines the benefits of globalization by weakening the international legal structures that produce these benefits.

The process is not hard to understand. Suppose that two countries, X and Y, enter a treaty that provides for the creation of a public good such as clean air. X and Y enforce the treaty by implicitly threatening to back out of it if the other side does not discharge its obligations. So if X pollutes, then Y will retaliate by polluting, and vice versa.

Now suppose that separatist movements win independence from X and Y and form two new states, X' and Y'. Suppose further that the clean air public good encompasses the territory of all four states, so that, optimally, all four will participate in the creation of that public good. The difference, of course, is that now cooperation must take place between four states rather than two. It is conventional wisdom that cooperation becomes more difficult to sustain as the number of participants increase; that is why governments are needed to enforce cooperation above the level of family or clan. States X, Y, X', and Y' will cooperate less well than states X and Y alone, and if the four states divide further, cooperation may become difficult or impossible.

This problem can be put more concretely. All states have foreign ministries charged with the task of maintaining good relations with other states. Suppose that a hundred states exist, and most of them have various treaties with each other. The foreign ministry of each state has the task of negotiating additional treaties as new problems arise (for example, Internet security), updating old treaties in light of new technology and changing relations, monitoring the activities of other states for treaty violations, protesting violations, entering negotiations in order to resolve disputes over treaty interpretations, and on and on. These are highly labor intensive activities and few states can afford to undertake them with the care that they would seem to deserve. A new state, the hundred and first, comes into existence. As a result, the hundred existing states must decide whether to enter treaties with this new state. Potentially, one hundred pairs of negotiations must be started, and if treaties are ratified, then dozens or hundreds of new treaty relationships must be monitored, enforced, and so forth.

Now, this is not in fact what happens. Most new states cannot enter such complex relationships, and so instead limit their treaty relationships, confining themselves to relationships with neighbors and one or two major states such as the United States or the former imperial power if there is one.[7] But the patron-client relationship is troubling to the global legalist, who believes that each state should stand on equal footing under international law. Patrons demand concessions in return for their patronage. Witness, for example, the United States' insistence that many states, especially the poorest and weakest, commit not to hand over Americans to the International Criminal Court.[8] This strategy has outraged legalists, who see it as an attempt to undermine the ICC's universalistic role.

Another approach, which became popular in the twentieth century in the midst of the fragmentation of states, is the multilateral treaty. A new state, the hundred and first in our example, need not negotiate hundreds of bilateral treaties, because it can instead accede to existing multilateral treaties that lay out the rules for the most common type of interstate relationships—diplomatic and consular rules, principles of treaty interpretation, the treatment of refugees, and so forth. But the multilateral treaty is, at best, a limited solution. The new state must accept a package of rights and obligations that do not necessarily fit its particular needs and, if negotiation costs are avoided, the cost of monitoring and enforcing remains high. Multilateral treaties are not self-enforcing, and so the new state must monitor the activities of other states and be prepared to protest if other states violate its treaty rights and to retaliate if the violations continue. It also must be prepared to monitor its own people, be able to stop them from violating the treaty rights of other states, and also be able to defend them and itself when other states claim treaty violations that did not actually occur or are ambiguous. Again, most states, and certainly most new states, cannot afford these costs.

It is hard to prove that international legal institutions weaken as the number of participating states increase, but there is some suggestive evidence. Most states are small and poor; these states rarely use international legal institutions in a meaningful way. They might send delegates to participate in negotiations to create them, but they rarely rely on them. As we will see, the WTO dispute resolution mechanism is rarely used by developing countries; the ICJ is faltering. The legally binding activities of the UN are controlled by a small number of rich countries. Underneath the universalistic rhetoric, policy is determined by a small club. However, proof of my thesis will have to await more systematic evidence that showed (for example) that, for a given international legal regime, compliance declines as membership increases. Europe would be the obvious place to test this thesis, as various European institutions (including the European Union and the European Court of Human Rights) have added members over the years.

Global legalists do not believe that the fragmentation of states weakens international institutions; they do not discuss this issue at all. But if asked, the answer would surely be that populations transfer their loyalty, or some of it, from national governments to international institutions. Putting aside Europe (which I will discuss shortly), there is little evidence for this view. Few people around the world, or even in the most advanced democracies, know anything about international institutions (true international institutions, as opposed to European institutions, NATO, and so forth). The United Nations is well known, but that is about it. Consider how much people know and think about their national governments by contrast.

Even in the case of the United Nations, it would be odd to think that people have transferred, or are willing to transfer, any amount of loyalty to it. The UN is controlled by national governments. Thus, it can enforce international law only as long as the national governments make it do so. But if people are not very loyal to their national governments, why would they trust them to make the UN operate correctly? And if they are loyal to their national governments, then they could not be loyal to the United Nations. To be sure, certain international actions have greater legitimacy when endorsed by the UN, but that is most likely because it acts only when most states (and usually all the major states) consent to its action, which means, of course, that people will not hear their own governments objecting to that action.

The central tenet of the global legalist view is faith that if international law advances, then eventually true international law-enforcing (and eventually law-making) institutions will follow in its wake, and *then* people will transfer their loyalty, or some of it, to those institutions. For all this to work, these institutions cannot be controlled by the states; they must be, at least in some part, independent. For them to be independent of governments, populations will have to oppose their own governments when those governments refuse to follow the dictates of international institutions. There is no international institution for which this can be said to be true.

Despite its negative implications for the international rule of law, it is not necessarily a bad thing when states break apart, and to evaluate fragmentation one needs to know why the divisions occurred in the first place. There are a number of possibilities.

First, X and Y might have divided because the populations within X and within Y became more heterogeneous. Suppose, for example, that a new religion spreads among a minority in X, and that people with this religion become hostile to people who have not converted. Or suppose that migration into Y over many years results in a large enclave of ethnically homogenous people who reject the interests and values of the original population of Y. If the original populations control the levers of government and refuse to make concessions to the converted or new populations, or if the groups just share too few interests to be able to maintain a viable government, then the division of the states is predictable, and may not be a matter of regret. But even if the new states can better cater to the interests of the populations, the populations will not be able to cooperate with each other as well across borders, and thus the treaty regime with which we began might fall apart.

Second, X and Y might have divided because scale economies in some aggregate sense declined. Suppose, for example, that external security risks have declined or that free trade has increased. X and Y no longer need to maintain large armies or internal markets. If it is less important for the states to be large, pressure will form for them to divide. Yet this does not mean that there are some areas of international cooperation, such as environmental cooperation, that might be of great importance to the respective populations. When X and Y divide into four states, it may become more difficult for the four states to obtain the environmental amenities that X and Y could obtain in their bilateral treaty relationship.

Whether particular populations or people in general benefit when states break up depends on context,[9] but that is not the relevant question here. The point is rather that as states break up, international cooperation will become more difficult, and international law will become weaker.

So there is an apparent paradox of international law. When few states (or few major states) exist, international cooperation is relatively easy, and so formal international legal institutions become less important. The states can cooperate in an informal sense rather than try to issue and enforce formal rules that apply generally. At the same time, because the large states can create most collective goods internally, the demand for international cooperation is relatively low. When many states (or many major states) exist, international cooperation is both more desirable and more difficult. Because it is more difficult, formal international legal institutions become more attractive; however, because cooperation is necessary to sustain those institutions, the latter are likely to be weak. One might speculate that the relationship between number of states and international law follows an inverse U-shaped curve. When states are few or many, international law is weak; it is most robust at an intermediate point.

EUROPE

European states are bucking the global trend—sort of. On the one hand, the decades-long project of unification has generated an enormous, economically powerful quasi-state, the European Union. Although its member states retain a great deal of sovereignty, the EU increasingly acts as a single agent. Of great importance, national institutions such as courts accept the authority of EU law. A plausible reading of events is that the governments of EU states usually (but not always!) refrain from defying the EU government, because they believe that the long-term benefits of cooperation exceed any short-term costs.

On the other hand, many of the EU's member states are experiencing strains. Spain has had to grant significant autonomy to Catalonia and the Basque region. In Italy, the Northern League, which seeks to create a new northern Italian state, has substantial political power, though a breakup does not appear likely anytime soon. The British government has had to devolve power to Scotland and Wales. In Belgium, the Flemish have been making noises about separation. In all cases, the source of the separatist pressure is the inability of the national government to develop policies that satisfy the heterogeneous groups that make up the state. Note that the rejection of the national government should not be confused with rejection of the EU. It may be that separation from the national government is attractive because the group in question expects to retain the benefits of EU membership. If there is a common European market, the nation no longer supplies an otherwise vital public good—the large internal market.

The development of Europe is a good thing for international law and cooperation, at least to the extent that the twenty-seven member states can act as one. This has indeed been the case with respect to international trade. Until recently, one could say with little exaggeration that the trade system was the outcome of three-way cooperation between Japan, the United States, and the EU. The EU members would determine a common trade policy before negotiating with Japan and the United States. The success of the trade regime can be attributed, at least in part, to the relative straightforwardness of three-way cooperation. If the EU did not exist, then the United States and Japan would have to negotiate with twenty-seven European states, although no doubt the smaller states would have played little role, and so the relevant actors would be the UK, Germany, France, and perhaps Italy and Spain. Cooperation among eight states is more difficult than cooperation among three; international trade law would likely have been less robust and effective. This magic works because Europeans have placed some of their political loyalty in the hands of the European government.

If all this is true, however, the fragmentation of the globe outside Europe is a matter of concern. Indeed, one rarely hears the global legalist who celebrates the EU's contribution to international law acknowledge this corollary that fragmentation outside the EU spells trouble for international law. Fifty or sixty states can more easily cooperate in controlling greenhouse gas emissions, ocean fishing, and nuclear proliferation, than can two hundred.

Instead, the global legalist argues that if European states, with their long history of conflict, can merge into a single state, then why can't all states submit to international legal institutions? But note the non sequitur. As noted in chapter 1, no one today thinks that a global EU is possible—that states can or will merge into a single world state or quasi-state. For that to happen, Indonesians, Paraguayans, Swedes, and Sudanese would have to transfer their loyalty to international institutions in the same way that Europeans have transferred some loyalty to European institutions. Today and for the foreseeable future, such a profound psychological change is implausible. And if no such transfer of loyalty to international institutions occurs, then it will be up to governments to uphold international law. This brings us back to our claim: as states fragment and governments weaken, enforcing international law will become harder, not easier, and international law will become weaker over time.

GLOBALIZATION, FRAGMENTATION, AND LEGALISM

Fragmentation ought to warn us of the possibility that international law will become weaker rather than stronger. But conventional wisdom is the opposite. And there is much to be said for the conventional wisdom. There are thousands of international treaties. States negotiate and enter more of them every day. New international institutions like the International Criminal Court are being created, and older institutions like the trade regime are being strengthened. Governments nearly always profess that their behavior is consistent with international law even when it is not, and they criticize other governments for failing to comply with their international legal obligations. It is possible that the world is moving up the inverse U-shaped curve rather than down the other side—that is, that the most effective level of international law occurs when the number of state exceeds the current amount.

There is no way to prove that this conventional wisdom is wrong because there is no way to measure the "strength" of international law at any given time. But there are reasons for being skeptical about the conventional wisdom.

The denominator problem. There are more treaties today in part because there are more states today. In the early 1990s, Yugoslavia broke up into four states: Slovenia, Serbia, Croatia, and Bosnia and Herzegovina. Suppose that after the breakup, each state enters a single treaty with another state, a treaty that established a minimal level of cooperation such as that necessary to establish embassies and other aspects of diplomatic relations. Each state, then, would enter three treaties—one with each of the other three states—so that in total there would be six new treaties where before there were zero, since there was a single state. Does the fact that the total number of treaties throughout the world has increased by six mean that international law is "stronger" than before? Surely not. Perhaps in some sense international law is more important, given that the domestic law of a single state can no longer regulate the entire population of the territory that had been under the sovereignty of Yugoslavia. But that does not mean that international law is stronger or more reliable, or entitled to more respect, than before. Yet the greater-than-threefold increase in states since World War II surely accounts for much of the international legal activity—the treaty making, the institution building—that we continue to observe today.

The relevant question is whether the people who live in the former Yugoslavian territories benefit more—in the sense of obtaining more valuable public goods—when the territory is controlled by a single state than when it is controlled by six or more states that may (or may not) have treaty relationships. A single state can, in principle, supply public goods at a larger scale than six or more states, given the difficulty of managing treaty relationships. But as events have proved, a state with a highly heterogeneous population may not be able to function. The fragmentation of Yugoslavia followed by the development of new international legal relations among the successors, is perfectly ambiguous from a normative perspective: there is more law, but people may be better or worse off.

This point can be put in quantitative terms. When only 50 states existed, the number of possible state pairs was 1,225. With 190 states, the number of state pairs is 17,955. If we think of each state pair as a possible avenue of cooperation, one that is ideally governed by one or more treaties, then the vast increase in the number of treaties since 1945 (on the order of about 50,000, very roughly) does not seem so great. To be sure, most states do not have any bilateral treaties at all with most other states, and indeed most of the treaty activity has involved the 10 or 20 biggest states. But this is just to say that the growth of international law has had more to do with the activities of a small number of states. Indeed, these states are akin to nodes in a network, connected with each other by thick treaty relationships and then with different groups of small states (dominated by former colonies, except in the case of the United States). The small states, which compose the overwhelming majority, have very weak relationships with each other or none at all. Again, we cannot call this development progress without knowing whether the international legal changes have produced better lives for the people affected.

Big states versus small states. In the nineteenth century, international law was thought to apply mainly to the Great Powers—Britain, France, Russia, Prussia (then Germany), the Austro-Hungarian Empire, and (maybe) Italy. Japan and the United States later joined this list. The many other countries of the world, especially those in regions where there were no formal states in the Western sense, were given either second-class status or no status at all. International law regulated the conduct of soldiers in wars between Britain and France, but not in wars between France and the political entities that occupied North Africa. The reason was that weak states and quasi-states could not cooperate on the same terms as the Great Powers. Many of them, for example, were too weak to control their populations, at least enough to ensure that police would protect foreign property and subjects. Great Powers that sought to penetrate the markets of weak states thus would send military forces to protect their subjects, violating the sovereignty of the state in question to a degree that would be an act of war between great powers. In the extreme, of course, foreign states would conquer, colonize, or exert territorial control over the weak state. This would all happen even while the leaders of the Great Powers insisted that international law was universal.

Today, we must also consider whether the rhetoric of international law has much to do with the way it is actually used. No one doubts that the largest states have the most influence over the development of international law, and that they can more easily break it than small states can. Currently, international law might have its great appearance of stability because the United States is the sole superpower and its chief sponsor. The United States therefore has a strong interest in maintaining and advancing international law—appearances, sometimes, to the contrary. This is anomalous, as a matter of history. As American supremacy wanes and new Great Powers claim their rightful position, we could very well have a system of international law that resembles that of the nineteenth century, with the United States, China, Japan, the EU (maybe), Russia, and possibly India as the Great Powers. Small states will choose their patrons, and the universalistic aspirations of global legalism will continue to erode.

Form versus substance. Do formal treaty relationships translate into real cooperation? In many cases, certainly, yes. Many bilateral treaties, such as arms control treaties, have resulted in measurable cooperation, and so have some multilateral treaties, such as the Montreal Protocol, which restricted the emission of chemicals that deplete atmospheric ozone. Unfortunately, there has been very little effort to collect evidence of compliance in a systematic way. In the best studied area, human rights, the level of compliance seems low. The Western liberal states enter these treaties but add reservations where the treaties would require a change in the states' human rights practices; other states do the same (for example, the treaty will be interpreted so as to be consistent with Islamic law); and still other states enter the treaties and then ignore them. The problem is that it is hard to design a rigorous empirical study that tests the hypothesis that states comply with international treaties and that addresses in a satisfactory the troublesome possibility that a particular state would have acted in the same way even in the absence of a treaty. For example, a state making the transition from an authoritarian system to a liberal system may well improve its human rights practices while joining human rights treaties, but that does not mean that the treaties cause the improvement.

It is worth emphasizing at the risk of redundancy that the view I am advancing is not that international law does not matter and that states never pay attention to it. My view is, rather, that we do not know how much states comply with international law, and until we do, it is hazardous to draw strong conclusions about the prospects of global legalization in a world of fragmenting states.

The burst of international lawmaking activity that has occurred since 1945 explains, in part, the appeal of global legalism. What else could explain this activity but an increasing international consensus that the solutions to the world's problems lie with international law? Global legalists believe that the lawmaking and institution-building activities of the last sixty years show that ordinary people and elites have thrown their lot with international law—international law has entered their value systems, and this is all to the good.

Missing from this picture is the fragmentation of the globe. When imperial powers lose their colonies, they try to maintain some sort of economic and military relationship, and this relationship is embodied in often elaborate treaty systems. Thus, as an empire crumbles, international law soars, but not because everyone sees the error of old ways and seeks to replace power relationships with relationships of legal equality. The empire-replacing treaties represent joint efforts by former imperial power and former colony to maintain some good cooperation even as they jettison the bad. The relationship is likely to remain one of substantive inequality even if of formal (sovereign) equality. And as states multiply, other states scramble to keep up. Since they can no longer cooperate with the former colony by dealing with the government of the foreign imperial power, they must try to establish a new relationship with the former colony. This will usually be a slow, painful process, and the flurry of treaty making is better seen as a rear guard action to minimize the loss of cooperation as large states fail, than as a vindication of the international rule of law.

We might thus speculatively advance a counter-story to the widely accepted Whig version of the history of international law, which ignores the fluctuation of state size and treats international law as a kind of independent entity that progressively develops, acquiring a stronger and stronger grip on states that they accept passively. In the counter-story, the great empires are like large firms that have spun off divisions which, as newly independent entities, establish legal relationships with the empire's various other successors including the mother country herself. The system of newly independent states may well be more appealing than the empire that they replaced but the aggregate level of cooperation among the populations that live in the territory once controlled by the empire is likely to be lower than it once was, holding constant technological change. International law becomes more necessary and important as states crumble into smaller and smaller bits, but only because states can accomplish less for their populations when they are small than when they are large.

GLOBAL LEGALISM VERSUS
INTERNATIONAL COOPERATION

The focus of this chapter, however, is the claim that the fragmentation of states does not imply that international law is becoming, or will become, stronger, as global legalists assume. It does imply that the demand for international law will increase, but it does not imply that states will be able to supply it. Demand will increase because as states shrink, they can no longer supply public goods above a certain scale without cooperating with other states. Treaties become more important, and so does customary international law, and so do all the international institutions that are necessary to support international law. But supply will fall because international law depends on states for those same structures of institutional support. As states fragment, they will find it more difficult to cooperate and thus to provide financial and diplomatic support for global institutions.

Global Legalism and Domestic Law

In recent years, a new battleground between global legalists and their adversaries has appeared. The battle involves the extent to which international law is to be given direct legal effect in the United States—that is, without first receiving the endorsement of the political branches. Consider the following examples.

Hague Invasion Act. The International Criminal Court has jurisdiction not only over the citizens of the states who have ratified the Rome Statute; it also has jurisdiction over citizens of other states when those citizens have committed international crimes on the territory of ICC members. Suppose, then, that American soldiers commit international crimes while on the territory of an ICC member like Sierra Leone. In principle, that state (or other ICC members) should capture the soldiers and turn them over to the ICC. When this possibility came to the attention of Congress, it passed a statute that authorized the president to use "all means necessary and appropriate to bring about the release of any [American soldiers or officials, as well as certain others] being detained or imprisoned by, on behalf of, or at the request of the International Criminal Court."[1] This statute was dubbed the "Hague Invasion Act" because of the menacing tone of the language, which echoes the language Congress uses to give the president authority to use military force.

A bill to prevent reliance on foreign law. In recent years, the Supreme Court decided several prominent cases involving the interpretation of the U.S. Constitution on the basis, in part, of foreign law and international law. In *Roper v. Simmons*, for example, the Supreme Court struck down a statute that applied the death penalty to people who committed capital crimes while juveniles.[2] While the court based its judgment on the eighth amendment's prohibition of cruel and unusual punishment, in doing so it noted that "cruel and unusual" is a function of international norms as well as domestic norms, and international norms are reflected in foreign law and international treaties, both of which disfavor the juvenile death penalty. In response to this case and others like it, two congressmen sponsored a bill that prohibited the Supreme Court from relying on foreign law when deciding cases interpreting American law or the American Constitution.[3] It has also become customary for Senators to question Supreme Court nominees about their attitudes toward foreign law and for nominees to deny that they would permit foreign law to influence their interpretations of the U.S. Constitution.

Avena. The United States is party to the Vienna Convention on Consular Relations, which, among other things, obligates states to give certain protections to foreign nationals who are arrested because of suspected criminal activity. When police arrest a foreign national, they must give him notice that he has a right to the advice of his foreign consulate. In the United States, several cases arose where the police failed to give notice; defendants were subsequently convicted of capital crimes and sentenced to death; and defendants lost their chance to challenge the conviction on the basis of the treaty violation, because their lawyers neglected to raise this challenge during the initial trial, and state procedural default rules prohibited them from raising the challenge in collateral (habeas) proceedings. After the International Court of Justice held that the state procedural default rules violated the treaty, Congress enacted a statute that provided that state procedural default rules take priority over the ICJ judgment.[4] After a further adverse judgment, the United States withdrew from ICJ jurisdiction over this type of treaty dispute. And then in 2008, the United States violated yet another adverse ICJ judgment when Texas executed one of the Mexican nationals involved.

These examples all involve negative domestic political reactions to efforts by both domestic and foreign actors to extend the influence of international law over activities traditionally regulated by domestic U.S. law and without the consent of the political branches of the U.S. government. Traditional American constitutional understandings provide that the political branches — Congress (sometimes just the Senate) and the president — determine when international law becomes a part of domestic law. In the case of treaties, the president largely determines, with the consent of the Senate or the majority of both houses, whether the treaty will become part of domestic law. Sometimes, the treaty provides for domestic application itself; in other cases, a subsequent statute incorporates the treaty or some elements of it into domestic law. In the case of customary international law, Congress has the constitutional power to incorporate customary international law into domestic law. In limited circumstances, federal courts have incorporated customary international law norms by themselves, but pursuant only to certain narrow federal common law powers, themselves typically derived from statutes or the U.S. Constitution.

In the three cases described above, pressure is put on these traditional understandings. In the first case, foreign nations shrink America's freedom of action on the battlefield without obtaining American consent. In the second case, American courts incorporate foreign and international law so as to constrain the political branches (and states). In the third case, Congress prevents an international institution of which the United States was already a member from interpreting international law contrary to Congress's own goals. The latter case is related to the general problem of "international delegation."[5] International delegation occurs when states by treaty create an international organization that has the power to create rules or issue judgments that bind states — even in cases where the states do not explicitly consent to those rules or judgments. Congress made clear to the domestic courts that they were not to defer to the International Court of Justice's judgment, reflecting traditional American reluctance to bind the United States to rules and judgments issued by international organizations.

What seems to be particularly troublesome to critics of these trends is not that international law constrains the United States — that is hardly new — but that the constraints of international law are to be interpreted and implemented by foreign institutions — the International Court of Justice, the International Criminal Court, or a vague collectivity of foreign states.[6] Further, the U.S. government would not have the option to reject these interpretations as incorrect; it would be bound by its own courts, which would give deference to the interpretations and demand that the U.S. government comply with them. The government cannot ignore the orders of American courts as easily as it can the orders of international courts. The U.S. government almost never disobeys the orders of American courts, for if it were to do so, a constitutional crisis could ensue.

Advocates of global legalism approve of these forms of penetration of domestic law by international and foreign law, or what I will usually call "incorporation" of international law into domestic law. The distinctive point here is that, for the advocates, it may be desirable for foreign actors—at least, international organizations and possibly collectivities of foreign states—to be able to directly affect the rights and obligations of Americans in America (or elsewhere not traditionally subject to foreign jurisdiction) without going through the political branches.

THE GLOBAL LEGALIST CASE FOR INCORPORATION

The case for incorporation of international law rests on a simple premise: that the United States would be more likely to comply with international law if international law was "part of our law," in the famous words of the Supreme Court.[7] If international law was automatically incorporated into domestic law, then it would be subject to the jurisdiction of the courts. The key point here is that all international law—including non–self-executing treaties, customary international law norms not already incorporated in statutes, the decisions of international tribunals, general principles, and so forth—would be enforceable by domestic courts. International law would not be watered down by Congress or the Senate with reservations, declarations, and understandings; it would not be subject to the interpretations of presidents; perhaps it would be even difficult or impossible for the political branches to prevent international law from becoming a part of domestic law. Some scholars have argued that treaties, once entered, should prevail over domestic law;[8] this is a possible, though extreme, kind of incorporation. But even if not, the automatic incorporation of international law into domestic law would make it more difficult for the political branches to control how international law had domestic effect. And this would be all for the good, the argument continues. Individuals subject to American judicial jurisdiction would be more tightly and routinely constrained by international law, which means that the United States itself would be more consistently in compliance with international law. And the U.S. government would be prevented from violating international law for opportunistic reasons, which happens from time to time under the current system.

International law is nothing if not spongy and complicated, and so one might worry about whether American domestic judges, in interpreting international law, might be less competent, than the executive branch. Advocates of incorporation discount this concern, or at least believe that the danger of judicial error is less than the danger of opportunism by the government. Elected officials are too easily swayed by short-term political interests and systematically discount the long-term value of international law. They are thus unwilling to incorporate international law into domestic law to as great a degree as is optimal from some undefined normative standpoint. On this view, elected officials should be discouraged from thinking about international law in narrow cost-benefit terms — "we should violate this rule of international law if the gains exceed the costs." The fear is that if officials take this approach, the authority of international law will be eroded, and many of its benefits will be lost. By the same token, judges, who are generally more far-sighted and public spirited than elected officials are, should be encouraged to incorporate or defer to or in other ways respect and even extend international law. If judges did this more often, international law would be strengthened; citizens and elected officials alike would be forced to take account of international law, for otherwise they would end up disobeying domestic judges and provoking a constitutional crisis.[9] The model for this type of judicial behavior can be found in the countries of the European Union, where domestic courts, without the express permission of elected officials, applied EU law in a manner that ended up constraining the national governments. National governments could more easily defy the European Court of Justice than their own domestic courts; thus the actions of the domestic courts strengthened the ECJ and European law generally.

Another, narrower version of this view can be found in a recent book by Robert Scott and Paul Stephan.[10] They call incorporation of international law "formal enforcement" and contrast it with "informal enforcement," which is the traditional method of government-to-government retaliation in case of breach. Informal enforcement works best when parties on both sides can easily observe each other's actions — or, at least, those actions necessary to generate the bargained-for cooperative outcome — and thus are in the position to retaliate if the other side fails to act properly. Against the baseline of informal enforcement, formal enforcement has benefits and costs. The main benefit is that the independent tribunal can discover facts that the states might otherwise conceal from each other. Scott and Stephan claim that formal enforcers, unlike victim states using informal enforcement, can extract otherwise hidden information from the parties by threatening to rule against them if they do not disclose it. This information, which is not available for informal enforcers, enables the tribunal to determine whether the states' activities in fact breached their obligations. The richer informational environment permits forms of international cooperation that are not possible with informal enforcement.

The main cost of formal enforcement, aside from the administrative cost of operating an independent tribunal, is that the tribunal has limited capacity relative to the states themselves to evaluate information that is not concealed from the states. Borrowing from contract theory, Scott and Stephan draw a distinction between information that is verifiable by third parties, such as tribunals, and information that is not verifiable but known only to the parties themselves. The tribunal is assumed to be able to observe verifiable information only, so it can be effective only to the extent that the parties' optimal obligations turn on verifiable information. Thus, formal enforcement is most likely to be optimal when the nature of the cooperative relationship between the parties is such that the production of maximal joint value depends on complex, hard-to-observe but verifiable actions on each side. Otherwise, it contributes nothing, in which case, reliance on formal enforcement simply creates costs—the cost of administering the tribunal, plus any risk resulting from judicial error, plus some possible "crowding out" of informal cooperation.

Although they do not draw this conclusion in so many words, Scott and Stephan's argument implies that incorporation of international law into domestic law is to be welcomed whenever domestic courts can contribute to enforcement. They emphasize the domestic court's ability to obtain information about the states' conduct under a treaty; one could also point to the tradition of impartiality among American courts. Foreign states might be more willing to accept an interpretation of international law that is produced by an American judge than one from the U.S. State Department—though there are complicating factors here. The judge might be more impartial, on the one hand, but the State Department's interpretation might reflect its greater expertise and judgment about the impact of particular outcomes on the relationship between the United States and the foreign state in question. Finally, there is the simple point that if international law is to be given domestic effect, American courts will almost always be involved. The U.S. government can comply with extradition treaties only if judges are willing to release detainees into the custody of foreign governments; judges will do that only if authorized by law. In principle, these considerations carry over to international tribunals as well.

RABKIN'S CRITIQUE: SOVEREIGNTY AND DEMOCRATIC THEORY

Jeremy Rabkin argues that domestic incorporation of European law in European states is not a good model for the treatment of international law in the United States, and indeed, that it has not served the Europeans well, either.[11] He argues that incorporation of international law into domestic law and other forms of deference to the judgments of international institutions — what he collectively calls "global governance" — violate America's constitutional traditions and the attractive mixture of freedom and security that these traditions support. Global governance is bureaucratic, insensitive to democratic pressures, and indifferent to local variation in values and interests. Further, liberty requires the rule of law, and the rule of law can prevail only in a sovereign state. Global governance undermines sovereignty and thus undermines the rule of law and freedom as well.

Rabkin has no objection to international law per se. As long as international law is created by the governments of sovereign states, which retain the option to violate or withdraw from treaties, it can do much good. What he objects to is the transfer of loyalty of the general public and important domestic institutions, such as courts, from the constitutional government of the state to international institutions or vague international norms or standards that are advanced by busybody NGOs. Rabkin fears that Americans will be tempted to succumb to rule by the mainly foreign employees of international institutions because it promises security, prosperity, and promotion of human rights; will become accustomed to such rule; and then will not realize until too late that they have lost the capacity to engage in self-government. And given that international institutions coddle tyrants, appease aggressors, and impose elite values on the common people, Americans will realize too late that they have lost more than they have gained.

The viability of the European Union, according to Rabkin, is due to the dirigiste, bureaucratic, and aristocratic traditions of the continent. Rabkin believes that the Europeans want to foist their idealistic commitment to global governance on the Americans as well, whatever damage it might do to American democratic and constitutional values. Europeans might like the EU, but that is because they discount the values of self-governance and freedom. For Americans, the European Union shows what happens when state sovereignty gives way to supranational institutions.

Ironically, Rabkin's argument echoes the worries of the early critics of the U.S. Constitution. These critics feared that the sovereignty of the former colonies would be lost to a distant, imperial national government, and with the loss of sovereignty would come the loss of prized traditions of self-governance. These critics lost the battle in the 1780s and were forever silenced by the Civil War. American constitutional traditions celebrate freedom, but they also embrace empire. Power, prosperity, and prestige were the benefits gained in return for yielding elements of local self-government to a remote national elite. To be sure, the federalist system preserves local autonomy to some extent, but the final product is very much a compromise and certainly permits further expansion if warranted by the gains. Advocates of global governance as well as critics like Rabkin can find ammunition for their views in American constitutional traditions.

Rabkin's argument thus depends less on American constitutional ideals than on a theory about the limits of lawmaking. Rabkin thinks that only sovereign states can make and enforce laws that serve the interests of the people, and he appears to think that the size of sovereign states has a natural limit. When states become too large — at the extreme, a world state — they lose the power to enforce the law, and, to the extent that they can, they become imperial, bureaucratic, remote, and soulless. But nobody today equates "global governance" and a world state. Rabkin argues rather that the intermediate institutions advocated by supporters of global governance fall short of a world state but nonetheless are harmful in similar ways.

But why should this be the case? There is no good theory about the optimal size of a state. If one were to take as a normative baseline the median state, which has a population in the neighborhood of only ten million citizens, the United States itself would seem vastly too big and highly unlikely to have a responsive democratic government at the national level. If the United States is not too large, then on what grounds can one assume that the optimal state size is not even larger? Rabkin also has trouble distinguishing the type of international institution that is malignant and the type that is benign. If the WTO and NATO are acceptable, then why not the ICC and the Kyoto Protocol?

For similar reasons, the exhaustive debates about whether supranational institutions are insufficiently democratic are largely beside the point. All democracies delegate significant authority to domestic agencies, and although people worry about whether these agencies are sufficiently democratic or not, these worries are theoretical rather than practical, while the benefits of delegation are clear, both as a matter of theory and practice. In the United States, concerns about delegation have made little headway since the 1930s. It is sufficient to note that the decision to delegate is made by a democratically elected legislature, and no legislative body can, as a practical matter, make all decisions itself.[12] The same points can be made about international bodies. And if these bodies always include foreigners with no particular loyalty to the United States, the only relevant question is whether the bodies make decisions in their member states' interests or not.[13]

AN ALTERNATIVE PERSPECTIVE

If Americans transfer loyalty, or some of their loyalty, from the U.S. national government to international institutions, this would not necessarily be a bad thing. In effect, the scale of government would increase for some types of policy. Americans would have less influence on the projects chosen by the international body than they have on projects chosen by the national government, but with costs spread across a larger population, the benefits for Americans might be large enough that the loss of influence would be tolerable. Much would depend on how the international institution operated and how the interests of people from different states were aggregated. But as long as American interests received sufficient weight, the institution would be acceptable. It does not even matter much whether other members of the institution are democratic states or not. If not, then maybe their citizens will benefit less from the institution than elites or other groups within those states, but that should not necessarily be a concern for Americans who otherwise benefit from the institution.

Indeed, as noted above, a similar decision was made at the end of the eighteenth century. The American states were sovereign, but the populations of those states decided to yield some of their sovereignty to a national government. The national government would have certain powers, such as national defense, while the states would retain certain powers, such as local policing. The ability to engage in local self-government was thus reduced, but the gains—in terms of defense and economic growth—were thought to be considerable. There is no reason to think that the national government more than two hundred years later is the optimal level of government for some or all regulatory powers; perhaps some of those powers should be located at a higher—regional or international—level. In a very limited way, the NAFTA review tribunals reflect such a judgment. They have the authority to award compensation without the consent of the involved governments.[14]

But it is one thing to say that supranational organizations whose judgments have binding legal effect may be desirable in certain instances, or to say that it is theoretically possible though highly unlikely that Americans would be better off if the United States merged with another state. It is quite another thing to say that international law should be generally considered to have domestic effect. There are several problems with this view.

International law is ambiguous, often by design—but in any event, like all law, it is necessarily so. States might negotiate a treaty that creates obligations without being concerned about how those obligations are translated into domestic practice. Suppose the United States and Canada agree to limit crossborder pollution. The United States might discharge this obligation by strengthening tort laws, while Canada issues an administrative order requiring factories to relocate farther from the border. As long as the United States and Canada are concerned only about the pollution, they should be indifferent to how pollution is reduced, in which case there is no reason for the treaty to provide rules governing how pollution is to be controlled.

In a regime in which international law is incorporated into domestic law, we can imagine domestic courts responding to the crossborder pollution treaty in a number of ways. Suppose that a citizen of Canada (or the United States) sues the United States for failing to adequately implement the treaty through the strengthening of the tort system. A court would no longer have the option of holding, as it would probably today, that the treaty is non–self-executing, and therefore, the claim fails. Instead, it might order the government to revise the tort system or undertake the revision itself. If, for example, the defect in the tort system is that the damages remedy is too low, the court could order the government to change the remedy or else, through ordinary litigation, change the remedy by holding that the treaty obligation supersedes the tort system. Similar arguments would allow American courts to enforce international human rights treaties and customary international law. In the weaker version of incorporation, such enforcement would occur only when Congress has not subsequently superseded international law with explicitly inconsistent statutes; in the stronger version, such enforcement would supersede even explicitly inconsistent statutes that are enacted subsequent to the international rule in question.

As noted above, the obvious appeal of such a system is that it would make it more difficult for governments to enter international obligations and then violate them. But the costs of such a system are significant as well. We can divide these costs into two categories, ex post and ex ante.

Ex post costs. As noted above, courts would either need to order the government to pass implementing legislation for treaties that today would be considered non–self-executing or develop the implementing rules themselves. We might imagine that the pollution victims in Canada would bring a lawsuit in the United States, and a court of the United States would issue an injunction ordering the government of the United States to strengthen pollution controls or award damages to the Canadian citizen on account of the United States' failure to do so. The court could also permit the victim to sue the offending firms directly under the treaty. Whatever the case, the court would need to make policy judgments about what type of program is required by the treaty. Otherwise, it cannot evaluate whether the government eventually brings the legal system into compliance with the treaty, which would presumably end the injunction or eliminate claims for damages. But courts do not have the expertise for developing the policy instruments for implementing the treaty, and so they are likely to do a poor job of either evaluating the policy instruments adopted by the state or developing their own—a phenomenon familiar from litigation over schools, prisons, and other institutions that violate constitutional standards and are redesigned by judicial order. These are the ex post costs of a system in which courts implement treaties by developing policy—they are just the costs of error that result when courts rather than governments make policy. They are likely to be even higher when courts try to implement customary international law than when they implement treaties, because customary international law is so vague.

Ex ante costs. In a regime of domestic incorporation, governments would anticipate the judicial response to treaties and customary international law. We know already that the U.S. government frequently prefers that treaties be non–self-executing because the government often takes that position in litigation and writes non–self-execution provisions into treaties or reservations. In the strong regime of domestic incorporation, where courts would ignore non–self-execution clauses, the government would be put to the choice of entering a treaty that has domestic effect, entering no treaty at all, or (what is most likely) entering treaties with weaker substantive obligations than it would prefer. Given that the treaty has less effect, the cost of judicial error in implementation is correspondingly smaller. This is hardly an improvement, as it simply eliminates an important policy instrument that governments use to comply with treaties—administrative implementation rather than judicial enforcement. The U.S. government will be particularly wary about entering treaties, because other states do not provide for automatic judicial enforcement of their treaties, and many states do not have independent judiciaries anyway. As a result, the United States would be bound by its courts while the parties on the other side of the treaties would not. This disadvantage would further reduce the attractiveness of treaties and weaken the incentive of the government to enter them. The same is true for customary international law. The government would be more cautious about endorsing developments in customary international law and supporting international tribunals with the authority to develop customary international law if it knew that these rules would be enforced by domestic courts.

Against these points, supporters of domestic incorporation typically stress the virtues of courts and the vices of governments, including both executive officials and legislatures. A common claim is that judges are more impartial and farsighted than election-sensitive governments are, and therefore they are more likely to enforce international law impartially.[15] This ought to increase the attractiveness of international law as a mechanism for international relations. If the U.S. government can tell potential treaty partners that judges will enforce the treaty, the treaty partners would have more confidence that the U.S. government would not turn around and violate the treaty while asserting a thin rationalization.

The claim that elected officials act for the short term and judges act for the long term is superficially appealing but dissolves under inspection. Political parties, bureaucracies, bond markets, and other institutions constrain elected officials to take account of the long-term impact of their choices. When elected officials have farsighted constituents, elected officials must be farsighted as well. As for judges, they are human beings, too, and they are usually elderly and not subject to party discipline; so it is far from clear whether their time horizons are broader than those of policymakers.

Time horizons are only one relevant factor, of course. Even if judges are more farseeing, they are less sensitive to the interests and values of the public than elected officials are, because judges do not depend on the goodwill of the public in order to enter and retain office. This is of significance, because whether and how to incorporate international law into domestic law is a matter of policy as well as legal analysis. There are typically multiple ways in which a treaty obligation or norm of customary international law can be complied with; thus, the international legal obligation itself does not determine the optimal form of domestic compliance. The choice among options, then, is a policy rather than legal choice.

Judges are bad at policy, not just because they have little sensitivity to public opinion, but also because they are nonexperts. Executive branch officials are in a better position to evaluate international law and determine the extent to which complying with it serves America's interests. Here, it is important to emphasize that the question is rarely one of overt violation versus compliance; the question is usually one of shades of meaning. International law, especially customary international law, is frequently vague, and it is very much a part of international relations for states to advance their particular interpretations of international law in the hope of persuading other states to agree to them. The preferred interpretation of a particular state will serve its interests more effectively than alternative interpretations. Often, an interpretation of international law or a general willingness to comply with a particular norm depends on what other states are doing — whether they recognize the norm, whether they comply with it, and whether they do so enthusiastically or minimally — so that knowledge about the attitudes and activities of dozens of foreign states is a key element in deciding how to comply with international law. Elected officials, assisted by bureaucratic experts, are in a better position to engage in these inquiries than are judges.

A final point is that the notion that judges are farsighted while elected officials are shortsighted would, even if true, have at best ambiguous implications for the question of incorporation. When judges invoke international law, they nearly always invoke international law that the political branches endorsed or created at some earlier point. Thus, judicial enforcement of international law in the teeth of political branch opposition means enforcement of the judgments of earlier shortsighted officials rather than the judgments of later shortsighted officials. There is no particular reason to think that doing this serves the interests of the public. And when elected officials recognize that foreign states are more likely to join a treaty if judicial enforcement is stipulated, then they have the incentive to include a self-execution clause.

In *Mingtai v. United Parcel Service*, the resolution of a dispute involved the interpretation of a treaty that listed China as a signatory but not Taiwan.[16] As a matter of American law and policy, Taiwan is officially not a state but a province of China; at the same time, American law recognizes Taiwan as a de facto independent entity, and the United States has made clear that it opposes any effort by China to use force to exert control over Taiwan. Friendly relations between the United States and China depend heavily on maintaining the fiction that Taiwan is a part of China. The court was faced with the choice of interpreting the treaty consistently with the legal fiction or with fact. To bind Taiwan to a treaty that it did not sign would violate the U.S. commitment to Taiwanese independence until such a time as Taiwan and China voluntarily merged; to refuse to bind Taiwan to the treaty would risk offending China and damaging American-Chinese relations. Wisely, the court deferred to the United States' position in an amicus brief to the effect that Taiwan was not bound to the treaty. The argument that the court should have decided on its own because it is farsighted while the U.S. government is nearsighted is particularly dubious in light of cases like Mingtai.

The argument so far rests on the straightforward claim that the political branches are in a better position than courts to determine when and how international law should be incorporated into domestic law. A further factor concerns the extent to which other nation-states allow for judicial incorporation of international law into *their* law. Most states do not permit their courts to incorporate international law to the extent that global legalists advocate, though the facts are extremely murky. Some states have constitutions that provide for the enforceability of customary international law,[17] but no state I am aware of provides that treaties are automatically a part of domestic law even when the government that enters them does not so intend.[18] Further, most states do not have highly independent judiciaries like the United States'; in fact, most states have weak and corrupt judiciaries that can be manipulated by governments. Thus, judicial incorporation of international law in the United States would be a unilateral—or at least highly unusual—act, one that other states are unlikely to reciprocate, and one that in many instances the United States would not want other states to reciprocate because it has less confidence in the foreign judiciary than in the foreign government.

Against these claims, supporters of incorporation advance the example of Europe. In 1951, six Western European states agreed to create a coal and steel "community," essentially a common market in these products governed by a common legal regime. In 1957, the states extended the common market to cover nearly their entire economies. Over the years, this union broadened and deepened; today twenty-seven states belong to the European Union, and the EU government has quite extensive functions. A key step along the way was the decision of national courts to apply European law, so that it would supersede inconsistent domestic law. In addition, national courts deferred to the European Court of Justice's interpretation of European law. National governments apparently never intended for their domestic courts to defer to the ECJ, but they have acquiesced, and this has strengthened the rule of European law and diminished national legal differences.

If Europe, why not the world? Suppose that U.S. courts incorporated international law, including the judgments of international tribunals like the ICJ. It is possible that other national courts would as well, and that therefore international law would gain strength at the expense of inconsistent national laws. But although it is theoretically possible that this could happen, it seems unlikely that it would.

There are several reasons for this. First, and of utmost importance, national judiciaries in most countries—nearly all developing countries and even in some advanced countries—are extremely weak, as just noted. Many foreign judges, unlike American judges, have low status and little power. In a country like India or Bangladesh, one might need to wait a decade or more between submitting a complaint and obtaining a judgment. In many countries, features of the judicial process that Westerners take for granted—an available record of written opinions, a compilation of relevant laws, a usable courthouse—do not exist. In many countries, judges are easily bribed, or they take orders from political superiors, or they render judgments that no one pays attention to. So it is hard to see how such judges can be given the task of upholding international law.

Second, judges in most countries are not internationalists; often they are the most conservative and locally minded of all government officials. In many Muslim countries, for example, they are likely to interpret the International Covenant for Civil and Political Rights in the light of Sharia law or other religious traditions, or local customs. To be sure, some judges in Turkey and Pakistan have distinguished themselves as relatively liberal, but this is not the norm.

Europe is special—not a good model for the world as a whole. European countries are Western; they share Western values and interests. There, elites and, to some extent, the public are committed to supranational (albeit only at the regional level) governance. These commitments are closely tied to Europe's recent historical experiences with war and genocide.[19] The European experience provides no more evidence that incorporation could work for international law than the fact that American states were willing to defer to national (federal) courts, starting in the late eighteenth century. In that instance, too, what was special was the commitment of elites as well as substantial portions of the public to national (but initially, "regional" or "supranational") institutions. One should also remember that, even in Europe, the road to union has not been smooth, and in recent years a backlash has developed.[20] A proposed European constitution was rejected in referenda held in France and the Netherlands in 2005, and an effort to obtain the same substantive ends through treaty making was blocked by Ireland in 2008. At the time of this writing, one can still be optimistic about continued European integration. But if Europe integrates, we may at some point start calling Europe a nation or a quasi-nation, but the lesson for global legalism would be obscure. Consider the possibility that as Europe becomes a powerful nation, its commitment to international law will weaken.

One need to look no farther than international trade law, where Europe, acting as a bloc, has emerged as no more likely to comply with international law than the United States. The European Union, like the United States, breaks the rules or drags its feet when the rules conflict with public sentiment or commercial interests. Its massive economic power, the result of integration, gives EU countries the ability to break international law, where, acting individually, they might have refrained for fear of retaliation. European trade barriers on genetically modified organisms, beef hormones, and bananas are the most famous examples. In another area of international law — human rights — a similar phenomenon has begun to emerge. The European Court of Justice has held that the human rights commitments of European countries take precedence over Security Council resolutions that would otherwise prevail as a matter of international law.[21] The European Union has begun to tread down the trail blazed by the United States, which for decades has maintained that the United States cannot consent to, or be made to comply with, international law norms that are inconsistent with the U.S. Constitution. The ECJ's attitude toward international law is converging with that of the U.S. Supreme Court.

In sum, it is in the interest of the United States to incorporate international law only if — at a minimum — other states do as well. But other states do not do this, or rarely do so. The European countries do not incorporate international law into domestic law; they incorporate *European* law into domestic law, and when European law and international law conflict, European law takes precedence.

The significance of these considerations is highlighted in an article by Laurence Helfer, which describes a similar backlash in several Caribbean countries.[22] Jamaica, Trinidad and Tobago, and Guyana had seen their death penalty laws rendered useless as a result of several decisions by the Privy Council that relied heavily on international human rights treaties and decisions that disapproved of long waits on death row. Stuck with slow domestic judiciaries and the delays introduced by rights of appeal to international human rights bodies, the three states cut their ties with the Privy Council and withdrew or modified their consent to the First Protocol of the International Covenant on Civil and Political Rights. As Helfer points out, the states had entered the human rights regime with the understanding that they would be able to retain their death penalty statutes. The Privy Council interpreted the states' obligations in a manner heavily influenced by legal developments elsewhere such as Europe but without any sensitivity to the underlying bargain and hence the political needs of the states in question.[23]

AN INTERNATIONAL JUDICIAL ALLIANCE?

Courts in different nations have always cooperated with each other, albeit in a very narrow way. They enforce each other's judgments when the defendant has crossed national borders. They interpret treaties, and in doing so they pay attention to how foreign courts have interpreted those treaties and make an effort to ensure that treaty interpretations are consistent. When disputes cross national borders, courts try to ensure that the dispute proceeds in the more suitable country — for example, where most of the relevant events occurred and the parties are located — and they will even enforce foreign law in certain conditions. These practices go back many years, and they have never been troubling or thought to require special justification. The reason is that the courts are just taking instructions from their own government — that is what a treaty does — or are engaging in practices that their own government would almost certainly approve of, and deferring when the government says otherwise.[24]

Today, something new seems to be afoot. The innovation is that courts are increasingly restraining their governments by drawing on international law and foreign legal sources. Courts can do this in several ways. They can interpret hard-to-change constitutional provisions in light of international and foreign law and give them a gloss that restricts the government. They can draw on foreign interpretations of treaty language and reject their own government's interpretation. They can aggressively interpret statutes in light of international and foreign legal sources. Even when governments have the formal power to rewrite statutes, reject judicial decisions, and in other ways resist the pressure from their courts, these judicial activities at least raise the cost of acting in the way that the government wishes to act.

What are we to make of this phenomenon? Initially, the evidence that has so far been adduced for it is less than overwhelming. In the United States, there is a great deal of skepticism about whether the Supreme

Court's sporadic references to international and foreign sources actually mean that those sources play a role in its decision making. And even if it does, there is quite a difference between looking at foreign sources for epistemic purposes—which is hardly new[25]—and trying to coordinate legal outcomes across borders. It is much harder to interpret the behavior of foreign courts, but merely noting that judges from foreign countries talk to each other will not do.[26] Nor does it do much good to count up references to foreign sources. The traditional business-as-usual involves resolving crossborder disputes, which almost always involves discussion of foreign law; one cannot resolve a treaty dispute without citing the treaty.

Eyal Benvenisti discusses three examples in a recent article.[27] He makes a plausible case that courts in a handful of developed countries have been keeping an eye on each other's counterterrorism-related decisions and argues that by citing foreign cases, these courts are able to provide something like a united front in the face of possible resistance by their governments. Similarly, courts in South Asia have drawn on international and foreign law in order to strengthen environmental standards. And the courts in many (but not all) "destination" nations (that is, mainly Western nations) have tried to come to a common interpretation of the 1951 Convention Relating to the Status of Refugees. However, it is most doubtful that the decisions of the South Asian courts have had real impact: the court systems in those countries just do not have much power. And, as I noted earlier, courts have always referred to foreign decisions when interpreting treaties. And this point can be made about the first example, which is Benvenisti's strongest. Most of these cases involve interpretations of human rights treaties. It will be a long time before we know for sure whether an international judicial alliance really exists.

Benvenisti argues that judges have banded together to provide a common front against their own governments. He argues that by tying the hands of their governments, judges actually increase the government's bargaining power in their dealings with other governments. He seems to have in mind the following sort of case. Suppose that Weak Country is negotiating a bilateral investment treaty with Strong Country. Strong Country demands that certain environmental or human rights laws be waived so that they cannot be used as a pretext for expropriating or regulating investments. The government of Weak Country is prepared to cave in to this demand, but it turns out that it cannot, because its courts will not allow it to. Strong Country therefore drops this demand. That is certainly a possible outcome. But another possible outcome is that the bilateral investment treaty no longer has value to Strong Country. Rather than making concessions, it just refuses to enter the treaty. Unless courts are prepared to evaluate these sorts of diplomatic risks and determine the benefits and costs of the treaty for their citizens, they cannot improve outcomes for their government by tying its hands.

There is a second step in Benvenisti's argument. He thinks that judges cannot engage in such behavior unless they can rely on shared international norms reflected in foreign law and international law. Perhaps the idea is that judges would lack legitimacy if they simply asserted that the treaty concession is a bad idea, but would have legitimacy if they could point to these other sources of law. Or perhaps the idea is that judges fear that if they unilaterally constrain their governments, while other judges do not do the same with respect to *their* governments, then a domestic judge will just put his country at a disadvantage internationally. So the court of Weak Country restricts its own government only if the courts of other countries do the same; then Strong Country cannot take its business elsewhere and might as well make the concession to Weak Country.

All this is possible, but Benvenisti does not explain why the governments would not do the same, and much more effectively than their courts. If (say) developing countries want to increase their bargaining power vis-à-vis wealthy countries, they can do so by agreeing among themselves to form cartels, such as OPEC. Governments have every incentive to enter these agreements; they don't need their courts to force them to. Courts acting on their own that instead rely on an international judicial alliance are constrained by whatever foreign or international materials happen to exist, but there is no reason to think that those materials maximize national welfare. An environmental declaration or human rights treaty, if interpreted consistently, will provide the same level of environmental quality and human rights activity for every single country, regardless of their very different circumstances. If very restrictive, developed world–level environmental laws are put in place in very poor countries, they will reduce rather than increase national welfare. And if courts do not interpret these treaties consistently, then the international judicial alliance serves no purpose.

Finally, advocates of an international judicial alliance do not rest their case on the benefits that it would supposedly bring to weak countries. There is a more ambitious idea that the judges can force governments of strong as well as weak countries to adhere to a set of international values or constitutional norms that otherwise would not receive universal consent. This idea is the same as that of world or global constitutionalism, and it gets around the problem (mentioned in the preface) that sovereign states outside Europe have so far shown no interest in such an idea. If governments do not consent to certain norms, then their courts can consent for them, and as long as governments obey their courts, government consent is de facto.

Why would (say) American judges hold their government to "international" (that is, mainly European) norms? Judges who have advocated the use of foreign and international sources to interpret the United States Constitution have not answered this question with any clarity, and a perfectly harmless answer is that these judges are simply using foreign and international law as a source of factual and possibly moral information where Constitutional interpretation calls for it—a bit like consulting an academic study.[28] But there are two more ambitious possible answers.

First, the U.S. courts use foreign and international law as evidence of universal international values, that is, what used to be called natural law, and they are trying to impose these values on the American constitutional system. Suppose, for example, that natural law frowns on the death penalty. The absence of the death penalty in many countries provides evidence that this natural law indeed exists. American courts, therefore, perhaps relying on inherent judicial powers, or on an interpretation of the U.S. Constitution that allows for incorporation of natural law principles, strike down the death penalty—or, as has happened so far, strike down particular applications of it to mentally retarded persons and to people who committed crimes as juveniles.

Natural law has been philosophically disreputable for quite some time, but even if natural law principles exist, their content is certainly very controversial. It requires a further argument to explain why courts, rather than democratically legitimate governments, should determine what these principles are and incorporate them into domestic law. As I have tried to argue, the populations in different states are highly diverse and the heterogeneity of values is one reason why the world is divided into states in the first place. It hardly seems proper for judges to fight against this process by defying the judgments of the government on the basis of the judges' own fallible speculations about what natural law requires. To be sure, when laws in other states are uniform, judges can ground their speculations in evidence, but this evidence is just as available to governments as it is to judges.

Second, U.S. courts might rely on foreign and international law to "make a good impression," as former Justice Sandra Day O'Connor has said.

> Doing so [citing foreign sources] may not only enrich our own country's decisions; it will create that all important good impression. When U. S. courts are seen to be cognizant of other judicial systems, our ability to act as a rule-of-law model for other nations will be enhanced.[29]

The statement, taken literally, suggests a vision of U.S. courts interpreting the American constitution in a manner that, at least at the margin, defers to foreign sensibilities, in return for which foreign courts follow American jurisprudence — again, at least at the margin. On the American side, the Court would cut back on constitutional norms that many Americans approve of — say, freedom of speech or the permissibility of the death penalty. On the foreign side, American constitutional norms would increasingly influence their national law — say, stronger abortion rights or a right to bear arms.

American judges confer benefits on Americans — perhaps strengthening their rights in foreign countries or perhaps advancing their presumed political/constitutional interests in those lands — in return for which American judges accept constraints on American constitutional norms at home. In a stronger form, perhaps it is not even necessary for American norms to travel abroad. In the weaker form, reciprocity occurs, albeit of an odd sort. From our perspective (not theirs), foreigners benefit from the extension of American constitutional norms to their states, while from their perspective (not ours) we benefit from the extension of their norms to our state. We want them to accept our norms; they want us to accept theirs.

This idea is certainly odd and has no known adherents. Are Americans to give up the death penalty in exchange for Europeans adopting American norms of free speech or religious freedom? Why should either side make such an exchange? And even if they should, it is not clear why judges rather than governments should have the decision-making role. We would need to suppose that American judges restrain the American government, because otherwise the American government would shun opportunities to advance the rights and interests of Americans by making deals with foreign governments. Because of democratic failure, the U.S. government neglects to protect Americans abroad by offering fair process to detainees in counterterror operations; and because of democratic failure, the U.S. government (or state governments) neglects to influence European constitutional norms by rejecting the juvenile death penalty. Neither of these propositions has any plausibility. Because these benefits — protection of Americans abroad, influence on Europe — would go to Americans generally, rather than to a particular minority, these failures are not democratic failures.[30]

And even if we were to accept the idea that courts should make constitutional deals directly with foreign constitutional courts, with our courts restraining our government for the sake of foreign interests so that foreign courts restrain their government for the sake of American interests, there is no evidence that Americans are getting anything out of these bargains; indeed, most foreign courts do not have the power to deliver their governments. This leaves the suspicion that there are no exchanges, that the influence is really going only one way.

AN INTERNAL DISAGREEMENT AMONG GLOBAL LEGALISTS

Global legalism is not monolithic; internal disagreements exist. One of the most interesting divisions among global legalists pits those who believe that international tribunals alone should adjudicate breaches of international law of general concern, and those who are willing to tolerate domestic adjudication.

To understand the difference between these views, consider an international criminal such as Slobodan Milošević. Milošević almost certainly violated international criminal law prohibiting various crimes against humanity, though he expired before his ICTY trial did. For the purist, it was essential that Milošević be tried by an international court. The problem with domestic adjudication was not just that a Serbian or Bosnian court would probably be unable to conduct a fair trial or (in the Serbian case) any trial at all. The problem with domestic adjudication was that Milošević committed crimes against the world, and thus, a world court is the appropriate forum for adjudication. For this reason, the purist would object to a domestic trial in some other county that had granted its courts jurisdiction over international criminals, even those with no connection to that country, regardless of the quality of that country's judiciary.[31]

The purist's view is easy to understand. All national governments have biases, even those that are not directly involved with the defendant, either as victim or abettor. Ideally, then, an international tribunal would exercise jurisdiction. The problem, as we will see in chapter 8, is that international tribunals have their own set of biases. And even when international judges are unbiased, they realize that they are not perceived that way, bend over backward to grant process, and end up taking too much time and too much money, thereby severely limiting their usefulness.

For this reason, more pragmatically inclined global legalists have watched the emergence of domestic adjudication of international crimes with mounting excitement. Spain's effort to extradite Pinochet from Britain for trial in Spain for his crimes while dictator of Chile, was the most spectacular manifestation of this trend, although Spain was ultimately unsuccessful. The workhorse has been the Alien Tort Statute, which we will see again in chapter 9. The ATS is a civil, not criminal, statute; victims can obtain monetary damages only, and these are rarely paid. Nonetheless, ATS suits have determined over and over that various foreign officials have committed international crimes and in recent years have tried deep pocketed corporations suspected of complicity.

The pragmatists see these ATS cases as an opportunity for pressuring corporations to avoid doing business with regimes that violate human rights. But it is not clear how they reconcile these cases with their commitment to global legalism. The courts that enforce the ATS are American courts, and American courts have American biases. Indeed, the courts have made clear that they will give special weight to the views of the executive branch of the U.S. government.[32] This means that, in practice, the ATS will put pressure on corporate activities that are inconsistent with the aims of the U.S. government. Thus, the ATS is an instrument of the U.S. government—albeit an unwieldy one—a fire hose that is always on, squirting in all directions, except when the executive branch turns it off. It is in this way a clumsy method of imposing sanctions on countries that displease the United States — although in some cases it might be politically risky for the government to intervene.

A third alternative has emerged, one that splits the difference between the fully international tribunal and the domestic tribunal: this is the hybrid tribunal. As we have seen, the international tribunal avoids the problems of domestic politics: it is either impartial or, even if not, less vulnerable to the claim that it represents the interests of a particular national government than a national tribunal is. But in the process of insisting on its impartiality, the international tribunal renders itself expensive and ineffectual. The national tribunal, by contrast, is less likely to be impartial but more likely to be effective, at least if enforcement of international law serves the national government's interest. Hybrid tribunals include both national and international (that is, foreign) judges; the latter tend to be more professional and to have a proven devotion to international law.

Hybrid tribunals have been set up in East Timor, Kosovo, Bosnia and Herzegovina, Sierra Leone, and Cambodia. The experiences so far can best be described as mixed.[33] But the main significance of these tribunals, for our purposes, is that the establishment of these tribunals by the UN is inconsistent with the legalistic ambitions embodied in the International Criminal Court.[34]

These debates might be said to pit domestic legalists against global legalists, with the former seeking to bring all kinds of international wrongdoing within the ambit of domestic courts, and the latter seeking to strengthen the capacity of international courts to handle it. The domestic legalists can argue that legalism has served America well, and if Americans ask domestic courts to make policy as well as decide cases, then courts should make foreign policy as well as domestic policy. For the global legalist, if the domestic legalist's faith in courts is appealing, his or her faith in domestic courts is not. Better to confine the jurisdiction of domestic courts, even if they can theoretically do some good, lest efforts to internationalize adjudication be crowded out.

Legalist thinking does not contain the conceptual resources that are needed to resolve this debate. Law does not have any intrinsic moral valence, nor does adjudication. The relevant question is — or ought to be — whether people around the world do better when international law is incorporated as a part of domestic law, and thus put into the hands of domestic judges, international law remains mainly in the hands of governments, or international law falls to a greater degree to the discretionary authority of international agencies such as international courts. If, as I have argued, international agencies are too weak (and must be too weak as long as the state system prevails), and if domestic judges are disqualified by their lack of expertise and decentralization, then governments will remain the institutions that have the primary responsibility for making, interpreting, and breaking international law.

Adjudication in Anarchy

Global legalism is a way of thinking that has many intuitively appealing features—it promises a way to solve global collective action problems in a world that cannot be governed in any conventional way, that is, *with a government*—but it lacks a plausible theoretical defense. Law cannot solve problems without institutional support. Normally, such institutional support is called government. If a world government is unavailable, then the type of law that we can expect to prevail on the international stage will have to be weak, limited, malleable, and vulnerable. It is the conceit of global legalism that people—ordinary people, government officials, bureaucrats—will obey law even though they would not obey or consent to the international versions of government institutions that we all agree are necessary to make law workable at the domestic level.

In the twentieth century, a concerted effort was made to create world institutions that could manage international law. There have been a few successes at the regional level—such as Europe—and with respect to certain issues like trade, but effective international institutions with legislative and executive authority remain virtually nonexistent. What has emerged is an international judiciary of sorts—but not the type of judiciary that exists in a sovereign state. National judiciaries are hierarchical systems controlled by a high court to which citizens are subject, whether they like it or not. Courts can call on the coercive machinery of the executive to enforce judgments, and they can rely on funds from the legislature to keep them going. The international judiciary is a fragmented and decentralized collection of tribunals with no hierarchical superior and undefined relationships with one another. Few of them enjoy mandatory jurisdiction—in the sense that states must bring their disputes to them—and even those that nominally have mandatory jurisdiction have no practical means for forcing states to appear or to comply with their judgments. Yet some (not all) tribunals have a fair amount of work and enjoy a degree of compliance with their judgments.

How do we account for adjudication within the anarchy of the international system? In the second part of this book, I contrast two views of adjudication. One sees international tribunals as practical devices for helping states to resolve limited disputes when the states are otherwise inclined to settle them. The courts help resolve bargaining failures between states by providing (within limits) information in (within limits) an impartial fashion. On this view, courts are agents of states, and they are subject to the control of states. It follows that states will submit to the jurisdiction of tribunals where doing so serves their interest, and will insist on limits and conditions as necessary, and will withdraw or reduce cooperation if and when tribunals disappoint their expectations. The second view is that of the global legalist: international courts advance international justice. They are impartial and independent, and they do justice in the face of the efforts of states to exercise power for gain; and they are indispensible for necessary forms of international cooperation.[1] I will explain how this tension has helped shape international courts and thinking about those courts, and argue that only the first view makes sense of recent history.

International Adjudication:
Its Promise and Problems

CHAPTER SIX

International adjudication is the most distinctive and lasting contribution of global legalism, as well as a phenomenon to which global legalists point with pride. Understanding international adjudication is thus an important part of this study. Any discussion of international adjudication must start with the International Court of Justice, often called the World Court, which was established in 1945, at the same time as the United Nations as an organ of that institution. The founders of the UN hoped that an international court would be able to resolve disputes between states, thus heading off war by applying law.

Why did the founders believe that an international court was needed? International law, like domestic law, is often ambiguous; and governments, like ordinary people, can exploit legal ambiguities in order to attain their ends. Indeed, government officials rarely admit that state policy violates international law; instead, they argue that state policy is consistent with international law, rightly interpreted. When the United States invaded Iraq in 2003, critics charged that the invasion violated the UN charter, because it was not in self-defense and was not authorized by the Security Council. The U.S. government replied that earlier Security Council resolutions that had ended the first Gulf War implicitly gave the United States the authority to resume hostilities if Iraq refused to cooperate with UN weapons monitors. These resolutions suspended hostilities but also obligated Iraq to cooperate in the disposal of its weapons of mass destruction, which Iraq did not do. (Iraq did eventually dispose of its weapons, but not openly, so that inspectors could not confirm that it had done so.) Both arguments have surface plausibility, and what might have resolved the conflict between the United States and its critics was an authoritative interpretation of those resolutions by an impartial court. For reasons that we will shortly discuss, that could not happen, but in principle, such a court could have resolved a conflict that damaged numerous diplomatic relationships.

Many other long-running conflicts would also benefit from impartial adjudication. The dispute between Britain and Argentina over the Falklands/Malvinas Islands, which exploded into war in 1982, seems impervious to diplomatic resolution. China-India border disputes led to war in 1962, and many still have not been resolved. China and Japan have a serious disagreement about their maritime boundaries, and thus, rights to underwater resources. India and Pakistan dispute the status of Kashmir. Turkey and Greece have fought over Cyprus, Britain and Spain cannot agree about the status of Gibraltar. Russia, Denmark, and Canada have overlapping claims to mineral resources in the Arctic seabed. Israel and several of its Arab neighbors have disputed Israel's right to exist for decades. Countless other such conflicts exist. Many are minor, and many others have been resolved. But some are serious and disrupt the lives of people who live in the affected area, and occasionally lead to war.

That adjudication of some sort can resolve disputes between states, at least in some cases, is not open to serious question. In the nineteenth century, the United States and Britain used arbitration panels to resolve numerous disputes, including disputes over the location of the U.S.-Canada border and over Britain's assistance to the Confederacy during the Civil War. The U.S.-Britain example influenced other states, and by the end of the nineteenth century, ad hoc international arbitration had become a thriving institution. But arbitration was only as good as the intentions of the states with a dispute; if they did not trust each other, they would not set up an arbitration panel or comply with its judgment. Many people therefore argued that what was needed was a permanent international court with compulsory jurisdiction. Only such a court could compel states to bring their disputes to it, and in this way ensure that wars did not break out between states otherwise unwilling to resolve their disputes with voluntary arbitration.

For the global legalist, the move from arbitration to adjudication was natural, perhaps inevitable. No domestic legal system lacks a judiciary; therefore, the international legal system needs a judiciary as well. Indeed, legalists have long envisioned an international court system that would have a hierarchical structure similar to that of domestic court systems:

judges would be independent; jurisdiction would be compulsory and general. And judges would not only interpret treaties; they would develop customary international law.

Yet the history of international adjudication during the twentieth century has not gone according to plan. The Permanent Court of International Justice, set up after World War I, performed poorly, and the ICJ, which replaced it after World War II, has also failed to live up to the ambitions of its founders. Adjudication today remains marginal to world affairs. Splintered into many specialized systems with no clear relationship to one another, international adjudication has worked well only in narrow conditions. This chapter will argue that the move from episodic arbitration to a full-fledged international court could seem natural only to global legalists. The failure of the ICJ has much to say about the pitfalls of global legalism.

HISTORY

States in conflict can choose from a range of methods to resolve disputes short of the use of force or coercive sanctions, including diplomacy, mediation or conciliation, arbitration, and adjudication.[1] While the distinctions between these categories are not sharp, international legal scholars traditionally distinguish arbitration and adjudication from negotiation or mediation because in the former a formally binding decision is reached according to a legal rule.[2] Before any permanent courts were established, states often relied on ad hoc arbitration. In the typical arbitration case, two states involved in a dispute would each appoint a single arbitrator, the two arbitrators would then jointly appoint a third, and the three arbitrators would together hear arguments and deliver a judgment. International lawyers date the modern era of arbitration to the Jay Treaty of 1795.[3] Since then, hundreds of arbitrations have occurred, and they continue to the present day. For example, the currently operating Iran-U.S. claims tribunal, which was created to hear and adjust claims arising from the Iranian Revolution in 1979, falls within this tradition.[4] Interstate arbitrations have concerned a wide range of disputes, including controversies over borders, damage to property during wars and civil disturbances, and collisions between ships at sea.

While different in many respects, international arbitration shares a key characteristic with international judicial processes: reliance on third parties to resolve a dispute between two states. Third party dispute resolution has many attractions: it introduces (in theory) a neutral body to a dispute — one whose views are not colored by interest or passion.[5] Arbitration involves the third party in the most limited way possible: an arbitral panel is set up to resolve only one dispute or class of disputes, and it follows an ad hoc set of procedural and substantive rules that remain within the control of the parties. Arbitration's main weakness is that the disputing states, whose interests and passions *are* engaged, need not consent to a panel's jurisdiction, nor need they comply with its judgment, though they frequently do. A fully fledged international court has different features, including: (1) compulsory jurisdiction — the court would have automatic jurisdiction over a certain class of disputes; (2) a permanent judiciary whose members do not depend on the disputing states for their appointment or salary; and (3) regular procedures that would not be renegotiated from dispute to dispute.[6]

The first steps toward this ideal were taken at the turn of the nineteenth century. The delegates to the Hague conferences of 1899 and 1907 agreed to establish a permanent arbitral body, the Permanent Court of Arbitration (PCA).[7] The PCA had the modest goal of encouraging states to use arbitration; it did this by providing a set of procedures for choosing arbitrators from a group of people identified in advance as potential candidates. However, parties did not use the PCA as much as its advocates hoped, and it went into desuetude for a very long period, though it has recently enjoyed a rebirth.[8]

The next step was the establishment of the Permanent Court of International Justice (PCIJ), which, along with the League of Nations, was supposed to maintain international order after World War I.[9] The PCIJ's innovation was an authentic panel of judges who served for fixed terms and so in theory would be at least partly independent of the influence of states. In addition, states could submit to compulsory jurisdiction by making unilateral declarations, and many did. In other ways, however, the PCIJ lacked independence, and could be and was ignored. Its failure set the stage for the International Court of Justice, the judicial organ of the United Nations, which continued in 1946 from where the PCIJ left off.[10] The compulsory jurisdiction of the ICJ has been more significant than the compulsory jurisdiction of the PCIJ. As I will discuss, compliance with ICJ judgments has been more than occasional, although not routine.

At roughly the same time that the ICJ began its operations, drafters were putting the finishing touches on GATT, a legal framework for international trade that eventually resulted in a relatively systematic form of arbitration. After several decades of operation, during which 298 cases were decided, the GATT arbitration system gave way to the more court-like dispute settlement mechanism (DSM) of the WTO in 1995. Unlike standard arbitration systems like GATT's, the DSM had compulsory jurisdiction, and states would (as a practical matter) be unable to refuse consent to the creation of tribunals and their adjudication of a dispute. There have since been several hundred WTO cases.

Starting in the 1950s, several regional courts were created. The European Court of Justice (1952) adjudicates disputes arising under European law.[11] The European Court of Human Rights (1959) adjudicates disputes involving the 1950 European Convention for the Protection of Human Rights and Fundamental Freedoms.[12] The Inter-American Court of Human Rights (1979) hears cases involving the 1969 American Convention on Human Rights.[13] These are only the best-known regional courts; others deal with human rights and commercial relationships in other parts of the world.

Another important development was the creation of the International Tribunal for the Law of the Sea (ITLOS) in 1996, which has jurisdiction over a range of maritime disputes governed by the UN Convention on the Law of the Sea (UNCLOS).[14] It has compulsory jurisdiction and an independent, permanent group of judges. Another area of growth in international adjudication has been in the area of war crimes. The Nuremberg and Tokyo tribunals after World War II were followed, after a long hiatus, by the International Criminal Tribunal for the Former Yugoslavia (1993) and the International Criminal Tribunal for Rwanda (1994).[15] All four of these tribunals were established by states or the UN after the disputed behavior occurred. The drafters of the Rome Statute of 1998 aspired to turn these episodic judicial interventions into a permanent court, the ICC, which would be open to proceedings brought by a regular prosecutor.[16] This system would be the most independent to date; it would have compulsory jurisdiction, independent judges, and a prosecutor with the authority (with certain exceptions) to bring cases against defendants. The prosecutor has begun to investigate cases and bring charges but no trials have yet occurred.

In this mass of detail we can identify two trends. First, international tribunals have become more formally powerful over time. Compulsory jurisdiction has become more common, and the judiciaries have become more independent of the states that establish them. Second, international tribunals have become more diverse and specialized. Contrary to some expectations, the world has not moved toward a single judicial system comparable to a domestic hierarchical judiciary; instead, jurisdiction is parceled out to coequal institutions, with no higher appellate authority to resolve jurisdictional conflicts.[17] This second trend is an important clue, and I will return to it.

THE INTERNATIONAL COURT OF JUSTICE

The ICJ is the judicial organ of the United Nations and the only international court with general subject matter jurisdiction over international legal disputes. As such, it has important symbolic value and embodies the hopes of global legalists who seek to advance the rule of law in interstate relations. Its actual record, however, is mixed. States frequently refuse to submit to its jurisdiction or comply with its judgments. It has not resolved any major international controversy between great powers. And although several controversies have ended with an ICJ judgment with which the loser complied, one cannot always isolate the ICJ's contribution to the resolution from that of regular diplomatic processes.

At one time, scholars could blame the ICJ's problems on the cold war; indeed, the ICJ's docket increased in the 1980s and 1990s. But this short-term increase only masked the long-term trend. Adjusted for the increase in the number of states over its sixty-year history, usage of the ICJ has unmistakably declined.

Background

The ICJ derives its authority from the statute of the International Court of Justice, which is independent of, but referenced by, the United Nations charter. All members of the United Nations charter are parties to the statute, so virtually every state has potentially been a party to litigation from the ICJ's founding.

The ICJ obtains jurisdiction in three main ways: by special agreement, by treaty, and by unilateral declaration under the optional clause. For some cases, jurisdiction is based on more than one source.

Jurisdiction by special agreement arises when the disputing states agree to submit their dispute to the ICJ. The ICJ, in special agreement cases, serves as an elaborate arbitration device. To be sure, unlike traditional arbitration, the state parties that use the ICJ do not select most of the judges, so that the ICJ, unlike traditional arbitration panels, may be willing to decide cases in a way that reflects the interests of states other than the two parties. In some cases, however, the parties to the special agreement have persuaded the court to appoint a limited number of judges to hear the case.[18]

Next, we have treaty-based jurisdiction. Many treaties provide that if a dispute arises under the treaty, the ICJ will have jurisdiction. The Vienna Convention on Consular Relations is one such treaty; one of its optional protocols, because signed by the U.S. and Mexico, authorized ICJ jurisdiction in the recent *Avena* case, in which Mexico accused the United States of failing to provide proper notice of their consular rights to Mexican nationals who had been arrested by local police.[19]

Finally, many states have filed a declaration of compulsory jurisdiction by which they confer jurisdiction to the ICJ in advance of any dispute. The obligation is strictly reciprocal: a state can be pulled before the ICJ only by another state that has itself filed the declaration. In addition, many states have, through reservations, consented to compulsory jurisdiction only for a narrow range of cases.

In theory, any dispute involving international law can come before the ICJ; in practice, a few types of dispute have dominated its docket: aerial incidents (mainly from the cold war), border disputes, use of force, and conflicts over property.

Fifteen judges sit on the ICJ. Each judge has a nine-year renewable term. Their terms are staggered so that the composition of the court shifts by one-third every three years. No two judges may share a nationality. Judges must have the standard qualifications, and typically they have significant experience as lawyers, academics, diplomats, or domestic judges. Judges are nominated by states[20] and then voted on by the Security Council and the general assembly. If a state appears before the court as a party, and a national from that state is not currently a judge, the state may appoint an ad hoc judge who serves only for that case but otherwise has the same powers as the permanent judges.

If there are fifteen slots but nearly two hundred states, how are the states that receive representation determined? The slots are distributed by region, currently as follows: Africa—3; Latin America—2; Asia—3; Western Europe and "other" states (including Canada, the United States, Australia, and New Zealand)—5; Eastern Europe (including Russia)—2. This distribution is the same as that of the Security Council, and the permanent members of the security council have, by custom, one slot each. Thus, the United States, Russia, Britain, China, and France have always had a judge on the court;[21] other states rotate. Among the rotating states, larger states—such as Japan and Germany—have had more representation on the court over time than smaller states, many of which have not had any representation at all.

Decline

The decline of the ICJ is best seen from its usage data. Figure 1 shows the history of filings of contentious cases.[22] The bars show the number of filings in a given year; they range from 0 (in various years) to 17 (in 1999); the line shows the five-year moving average. One can perhaps discern a gradual trend upward, driven almost entirely by the spike in 1999. What does seem true is that ICJ usage enjoyed a recovery in the 1980s and 1990s from a trough in the 1960s and 1970s. Eyeballing the graph, it's not clear whether the recovery brings us back to the earlier level or to a higher level.

But the raw data in figure 1 are misleading for several reasons.

1. They do not take account of the large increase in the number of states that can in principle benefit from ICJ dispute resolution. In 1946, there were only 55 UN members; today there are over 190. Adjusting for the increase in the number of states, the "U" shape of the curve remains, but the decline is more precipitous, the recovery more gradual, and the initial usage level is never matched.

2. We have counted many cases that never progressed beyond the filing stage and required the ICJ to make a nonministerial decision. These cases only add noise because the ICJ does not actually perform any function.

3. The final decade of the ICJ's existence contained one anomalous case. In 1999, Serbia and Montenegro filed proceedings against all the NATO countries for violating international law during the intervention in Kosovo. Thus, we count 10 cases for what is essentially a single case with multiple respondents.

FIGURE 1. Filings

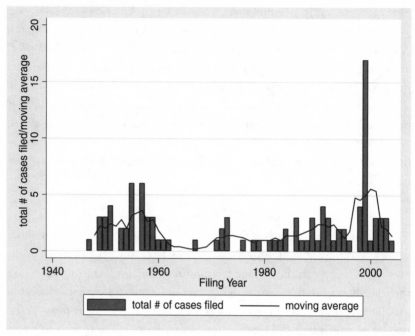

When the figures are adjusted, a new pattern emerges. We see a decline in usage of the ICJ with, at best, a very gradual recovery during the 1990s, but not to the levels seen in the 1950s.[23]

The conclusion that the popularity of the ICJ has declined is bolstered by several factors.

First, the ICJ is being abandoned by the major powers. Consider the countries that currently have the ten largest economies: the United States, China, Japan, India, Germany, Great Britain, France, Italy, Brazil, and Russia. Four of these states — China, Japan, Brazil, and Russia — have never brought a proceeding and never been a respondent beyond the filing stage. Table 1 lists cases involving the other major powers, excepting special agreement cases.

In the first twenty-year period, a major power was an applicant in 60 percent of the cases and a respondent in 60 percent of the cases. In the second period, a major power was an applicant a little under 50 percent of the time, and a respondent a little under 50 percent of the time (depending on how one counts India). In the last period, a major power was an

TABLE I. Cases involving major powers.

Applicant	Respondent	Filing year
1946–1965		
United Kingdom	Albania	1947
United Kingdom	Norway	1949
France	United States	1950
United Kingdom	Iran	1951
Greece	United Kingdom	1951
Italy	France	1953
France	Norway	1955
Portugal	India	1955
Switzerland	United States	1957
Cameroon	United Kingdom	1961
1966–1985		
India	Pakistan	1971
Germany	Iceland	1972
United Kingdom	Iceland	1972
Australia	France	1973
New Zealand	France	1973
United States	Iran	1979
Nicaragua	United States	1984
1986–2005		
United States	Italy	1987
Libya	United States	1992
Libya	United Kingdom	1992
Iran	United States	1992
New Zealand	France	1995
Paraguay	United States	1998
Yugoslavia	France	1999
Yugoslavia	Germany	1999
Yugoslavia	Italy	1999
Yugoslavia	United States	1999
Yugoslavia	United Kingdom	1999
Pakistan	India	1999
Germany	United States	1999
Republic of the Congo	France	2003
Mexico	United States	2003
Romania	Ukraine	2004
Costa Rica	Nicaragua	2005

applicant in only 12 percent of the cases; a major power was a respondent in *88 percent* of the cases.[24]

This trend is suggestive. Increasingly, major powers are not applicants that drag other states into court; they are respondents being dragged by other, usually weaker, states into court. It thus would not be surprising if major powers have begun to sour on the court.

The decline of major power interest in ICJ adjudication is reflected not only in these usage statistics; also recall that with the United States' withdrawal from compulsory jurisdiction in 1985, France's in 1974, and China's in 1972, only the UK among permanent Security Council members is subject to this form of jurisdiction. Among the top thirty states (measured by current GDP), only Japan, Great Britain, India, Canada, Mexico, Spain, Australia, the Netherlands, Poland, the Philippines, Pakistan, Belgium, and Egypt have submitted to compulsory jurisdiction; among these states, Japan, Poland, the Philippines, and Egypt have never appeared before the ICJ—as respondent *or* applicant—under any head of jurisdiction. The ICJ has historically been dominated by the United States, Great Britain, and France. In the last twenty years, these states, in the aggregate, brought a case only once.

Second, although the number of states that have submitted to mandatory jurisdiction (the ironically named "optional clause") has roughly doubled since 1946, the fraction of states that have filed has declined, and so has the practical value in providing the ICJ with jurisdiction. In 1950, 60 percent of the states were subject to compulsory jurisdiction; today, this fraction has declined to 34 percent. And of these states, few have been involved in ICJ litigation. Focusing on cases where the applicant successfully invoked compulsory jurisdiction and then prevailed on the merits,[25] we count four instances from 1946 to 1965, eleven instances from 1966 to 1985, and three instances from 1986 to 2004. Thus, the doubling of states subject to compulsory jurisdiction has had no impact on its usage.[26] This may be due in part to states' use of reservations to limit their consent to ICJ jurisdiction even when they submit to compulsory jurisdiction.

Third, states have shown less and less enthusiasm for treaty-based jurisdiction.[27] From 1946 to 1965, states entered (on an annual basis) 9.7 multilateral or bilateral treaties that contained clauses that granted jurisdiction to the ICJ. This number dropped to 2.8 per year for the period from 1966 to 1985, and to 1.3 per year from 1986 to 2004.[28] These numbers are abso-

FIGURE 2. ICJ Treaty-Based Jurisdiction

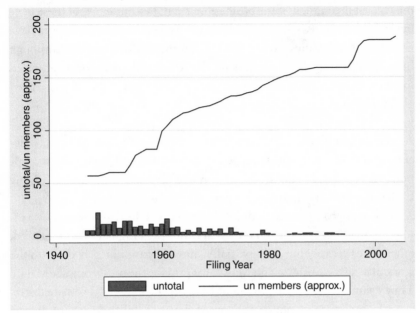

lute; recall again the number of states tripled during this period. Figure 2 provides the trend; the line shows the number of states. The United States, which was an enthusiastic user of ICJ treaty clauses in the 1950s and 1960s, apparently has not used this type of clause a single time since the early 1970s.[29]

Fourth, the only positive trend for the ICJ has involved special agreement cases. The ICJ had only four such cases during the first half of its existence; it has had ten during its second half. But in special agreement cases, the ICJ is just a glorified arbitration panel; indeed, states now routinely exclude most of the ICJ judges from the panel that hears the case. While the ICJ may serve a useful function as an arbitration panel, this was not its purpose.

Fifth, during the period of the ICJ's existence, global interaction has expanded dramatically. There are far more opportunities for (say) aerial incidents today than in the past because there is far more crossborder air traffic, even holding the number of states constant. Thus, in determining relative usage, using the number of states as the denominator probably exaggerates the ICJ's importance.[30] Cutting the other direction, there are many more international courts than in the past—the ECJ, for example, may have taken much of the business of the ICJ—but many of these have business that the ICJ has never had (the WTO), and many others have not had much business so far (the Law of the Sea tribunal). So although it is probably impossible to measure the ICJ workload correctly adjusted for the expansion of global interaction, it seems likely that it has lagged globalization.

A note on compliance. One might ask whether usage of the ICJ has declined because states have failed to comply with its judgments. This question just begs the further question why states would not comply with the ICJ's judgments, but the data may be interesting nonetheless.

Measuring compliance with ICJ judgments is difficult for various reasons: many states comply but only years after the judgment was rendered; other states comply but only partially; and so forth. I largely defer to the work of others. Ginsburg and McAdams provide the most complete data.[31] They examined the post-judgment behavior of states and classified it as either compliance or noncompliance. I depart from their coding in one respect: I drop contentious cases in which the respondent prevailed. The reason is that if the respondent prevails, it is not clear whether the applicant "complies": it might pursue its claim diplomatically, for example. Indeed, an applicant could do this consistently with international law, for an adverse judgment based on jurisdiction or prudential grounds does not negate a claim under international law. By contrast, it seems reasonably clear that a respondent who loses a case either complies with it by giving the applicant what it sought or violates it by refusing to change its behavior.[32] (I include all special agreement cases, which do not technically have an applicant and respondent.)

I divide the cases into twenty-year periods and compute the mean compliance rate. I provide separate figures for all cases and for compulsory jurisdiction and treaty-based cases, as special agreement cases are more like arbitration than like judicial cases. The results are in table 2.

The table shows that the compliance rate—whether including or excluding special agreement cases—was much higher in the ICJ's first twenty years than in its last twenty. This is consistent with the conjecture that states have lost confidence in the ICJ after an initial honeymoon pe-

TABLE 2. Compliance trends.

Period	All cases		Excluding special agreement cases	
	N	%	N	%
1946–1965	6	83	5	80
1966–1985	5	20	4	0
1986–2004	7	29	6	17
Total	18	44	15	33

Note: Compliance trends are limited to cases for which we have compliance data and either the applicant prevailed or jurisdiction was based on special agreement.

riod. There has been a slight recovery in the last few years, however. In any event, there are too few observations to have much confidence in the statistics.

The usage data (and also the compliance data) are vulnerable to the objection that they result from selection effects. It is theoretically possible that usage of the ICJ has declined because with every judgment international law has become clearer, and thus more and more states are able to settle their disputes without resort to adjudication. Similarly, one might argue that compliance rates have declined because states have brought harder and harder cases to the ICJ in response to its earlier successes. Both of these claims are implausible. Hundreds of treaties are ratified every year, and every new treaty creates new legal issues. We need only compare the ICJ with the European Court of Justice, which has enjoyed steadily increasing usage, to see how implausible they are, for on this account, the ECJ's increasing usage statistics would suggest that it has been a failure.

In sum, substantial evidence shows that the ICJ has been declining over its history, though it enjoyed a small shot of adrenaline when the cold war ended. Some scholars disagree,[33] and no doubt there is room for disagreement, but I want to turn now to the question of why. I will suggest below two possible explanations. The first is a theory of institutional failure; the second is a theory of geopolitical conflict.

AN INSTITUTIONAL THEORY OF DECLINE

A first hypothesis for the decline of the ICJ is that its judges have decided cases in an impartial manner. The logic of this argument is simple. Suppose that two states enter a treaty, and, anticipating that ambiguities may arise in the future, also agree that the ICJ will resolve those ambiguities. Suppose further that it turns out that the ICJ is biased in favor of a certain type of state—rich or poor, northern or southern, eastern or western. The ICJ's biases initially may be hidden, but as they become clear, whichever states are disfavored by the bias will be reluctant to agree to grant the ICJ jurisdiction by treaty. Similarly, disfavored states will withdraw from compulsory jurisdiction, or narrow it with reservations, or not submit to compulsory jurisdiction in the first place. Or states will submit cases by special agreement only when they can eliminate certain judges from the panel that hears the case. We have seen that all these things have been happening. But is there evidence of judicial bias—where bias means failure to apply international law in an impartial manner?

Consider the voting patterns of ICJ judges. Table 3 provides the raw data.

About 90 percent of the time, judges vote in favor of the state that appointed them (in the case of ad hoc judges) or the state of which they are nationals (in the case of permanent judges).

What about the judges whose home states are not parties of the dispute? One might think that they would vote impartially. Miguel de Figueiredo and I tested the hypothesis that these judges would vote in favor of the state with closer political or economic links to their home states. We looked at

TABLE 3. Votes of party and nonparty judges in proceedings.

Judge	Vote in favor of applicant		Vote in favor of respondent	
	Ratio	%	Ratio	%
National party	15/18	83.3	34/38	89.5
Ad hoc party	57/63	90.5	37/41	90.2
Total	72/81	88.9	71/79	89.9
Nonparty	656/1356	48.4	638/1358	47.0

Source: Eric A. Posner and Miguel de Figueiredo, *Is the International Court of Justice Biased?*, 34 J. Legal Stud. 599 (2005).

a variety of measures—including membership in OECD or NATO, regional blocs, and so forth. Our best predictors of judicial votes were the following. First, judges voted in favor of the state party whose economy was closer in size to the economy of the judge's home state. Judges from wealthy states voted in favor of wealthy states; judges from poor states voted in favor of poor states. Second, judges voted in favor of the state whose political system was closer to that of the judge's home state—measured by the extent of democracy. Judges from democratic states voted in favor of democratic states; judges from authoritarian states voted in favor of authoritarian states. We also found weaker evidence that judges tended to vote for states whose religion and language were the same as those of the judges' home states.[34]

There are various possible interpretations of these results. The first is that judges vote the interests of home states, and home states tend to share interests with other states that are like them, economically and politically. Thus, we have long seen divisions between wealthier countries (the OECD) and poorer countries, for example, in international trade. In addition, during the cold war, the states divided into democratic and authoritarian blocs, though of course there were important exceptions. A second possibility is that judges just happen to feel more sympathy to states that are like their own. The power of the linguistic and religious variables is consistent with this claim, although they could also reflect postcolonial political and economic ties. There is also evidence of a fair amount of politicking and vote trading in the selection of ICJ judges,[35] suggesting that states may try to ensure that judges serve their interests. But whatever the truth, it is hard to believe that governments would be pleased to learn that economic, political, or linguistic affinities affect judicial interpretation and enforcement of the treaties that they negotiate and the customary international law to which they submit.[36]

A GEOPOLITICAL THEORY OF DECLINE

Another possible explanation for the decline of the ICJ is that it was a victim of geopolitics. The ICJ could flourish only if a sufficient number of states were willing to use it and comply with its judgments. To attract this sufficient number, whatever it was, the ICJ had to decide cases in a way that persuaded these states that using the ICJ served their interests. But the

ICJ failed to persuade this critical mass of states that it could and would act consistently with all their interests. It failed because the states' interests diverged so greatly that there was no moral and legal consensus on which the ICJ could base its decisions.

To understand this problem, one can usefully begin with a comparison of the Security Council and the ICJ. The United Nations was never intended to be a parliament of nations. The five countries that were believed to be the major powers at the time that the UN was founded—the United States, the USSR, China, France, and the United Kingdom—were given permanent seats in the Security Council and the veto right. This meant that the United Nations could not act in any significant way without the consent of a major power.

The International Court of Justice was not so explicitly under the thumb of the major powers. The ICJ operates by majority rule, and this means that a major power can always be outvoted—unlike in the Security Council.

The immediate consequence of this was that the Soviet Union refused to submit to the jurisdiction of the ICJ, and never appeared before it in any capacity. Nor did any of the Soviet satellites. The reason is clear. The states represented on the first court were Belgium, Brazil, Canada, Chile, China, Egypt, El Salvador, France, Mexico, Norway, Poland, Russia, the United Kingdom, the United States, and Yugoslavia. Of these states, a clear majority (1) belonged to the bloc of major Western powers (Belgium, Canada, France, Norway, the United Kingdom, and the United States); or (2) were dominated by them either because of their regional or postcolonial status (Brazil, Egypt, El Salvador, and Mexico). At the time, the United States and the United Kingdom could have believed that China, their wartime ally, would generally take their side in disputes. With a large majority arrayed against it, the Soviet Union could expect to be outvoted in any case in which its interests were pitted against those of the west.

With the Eastern bloc absent, the advanced Western states dominated the docket until the 1960s, with occasional participation by developing countries. In the beginning of that decade the participation of developing countries increased somewhat. However, in 1966, the ICJ held in the South West Africa case that it did not have jurisdiction to hear a dispute over a UN Trust territory controlled by South Africa. The ruling outraged the emerging bloc of postcolonial states, which loathed the racist South

African regime and blamed the outcome on Western domination of the ICJ's bench. The developing nations stopped bringing cases to the ICJ. Apparently in response to the outcry, the court reversed itself in its Namibia advisory opinion of 1971, but—with the exception of some disputes between India and Pakistan—developing nations refrained from using the ICJ until the late 1970s and early 1980s.[37]

The South West Africa brouhaha hastened reform. It had long been realized that representation on the Security Council and the ICJ no longer reflected geopolitical realities. In 1965 the Security Council was expanded from eleven to fifteen members, and greater representation was given to the postcolonial states. Meanwhile, the general assembly had almost doubled since World War II, and the new states were all developing countries. These changes mattered for the composition of the ICJ, because election of ICJ judges required majorities in both the security council and the general assembly. And indeed, the 1966 election of ICJ judges resulted in greater representation for new states from Africa and Asia.[38]

This change in representation alone suggests that the ICJ would subsequently tilt in favor of developing nations. It might also have been the case that even Western judges realized that the ICJ needed both legitimacy and users, and that as long as it decided cases in a manner that pleased Western powers but outraged developing nations, it would have little global legitimacy—it would be seen as a puppet of powerful states. And although the handful of Western powers might continue to use it, it would lose the business of the dozens of nations that came into existence in the period of decolonization after World War II. In short, the ICJ had to develop a jurisprudence friendlier to the weaker states. It accomplished this task by softening its commitment to positivism—which meant enforcing treaty structures largely developed by the Western powers—and developing a "progressive" jurisprudence, one based more on the judges' notions of global fairness.[39]

The turning point came in the *Nicaragua v. U.S.* case (1984). This was the first major case in which a developing country challenged a major power. The United States had been secretly providing military support to an insurgency in Nicaragua in the hope of bringing down the government, which had allied itself with the Soviet Union. After it was revealed that the CIA had directed operations to mine Nicaraguan harbors, Nicaragua brought a case before the ICJ. Nicaragua argued that the United

States had violated international law by mining its harbors; the United States responded that the ICJ did not have jurisdiction over the case, and in any event that the United States was acting legally by participating in the collective security of Honduras and El Salvador in response to Nicaragua-supported insurgencies in both countries. The American defense was reasonably strong,[40] but the ICJ found in favor of Nicaragua.

Shabtai Rosenne, an expert on the ICJ, suggests that this case may have encouraged nonaligned, developing states to bring proceedings before the ICJ;[41] what he does not mention is that it appears to have seriously dampened the enthusiasm of Western states for the ICJ. As I noted above, these states have all but stopped using the ICJ.

We can think of the United States and the other Western states as being in a position analogous to that of the Soviet Union and its satellites in the late 1940s and 1950s. The Western states can no longer expect that a majority will favor them on the court. And, in some respects, the Western states are in a worse position today than the Soviet Union was, because there are many cleavages among them, as well. Like the Soviet Union, the Western states are withdrawing from the court, although gradually. As the developing states came to dominate the membership of the court, they used it more often, but their many conflicting interests are likely to put a limit on usage.

As of 2008, the states represented on the court are China, France, Germany, Japan, Jordan, Madagascar, Mexico, Morocco, New Zealand, Russia, Sierra Leone, Slovakia, the United Kingdom, the United States, and Venezuela. The court reflects complex cleavages: north versus south, east versus west, wealthy versus poor, and so forth. It is more likely today than in the 1950s that the major Western nations that used to be the court's most frequent users — the United States, France, and the United Kingdom — will find an unfriendly audience in the judges. But it is also not clear whether developing nations can expect a sympathetic hearing. The problem for the ICJ is just that there are too many cleavages, and so states cannot expect the ICJ judges to take account of their interests. By contrast, the early court was a club dominated by a handful of Western powers that shared powerful strategic and economic commitments. It might be that a court of general jurisdiction like the ICJ cannot exist in the current international environment where interests are fragmented. On this view, the best hope for international adjudication lies with regional courts (like

INTERNATIONAL ADJUDICATION ‡ 149

the European Court of Justice) and courts that have a narrow jurisdiction over an area of international law in which interests substantially converge (like the WTO dispute settlement mechanism).

In sum, the ICJ was the victim of conflicts among states. A realist might argue that the ICJ was doomed from the start, but it is hard to know how one could prove this claim. The better view is that with the cold war, decolonization, and the rise of new powers like India and Brazil, the ICJ could not find an international legal or moral consensus on which it could make judgments that states would respect. This may have reflected the nature of geopolitics, or it may just have been the result of a failure by the ICJ judges to act with sufficient political sensitivity.

THE ICJ AND GLOBAL LEGALISM

Legalists established the ICJ hoping that it would provide a forum in which states could peacefully resolve their disputes. There is no doubt that some states have resolved some disputes there, but the ICJ has worked best in cases where disputes were small in scale and the states involved already inclined to cooperate with each other, which suggests that it has done little more than offer a modest alternative to interstate arbitration. With no world government to enforce its judgments and no world legislature to change laws that had gone out of date, the ICJ had to depend on the goodwill of states, and that goodwill was often absent.

Disappointment with the ICJ has not caused states to abandon international adjudication. Instead, they have worked around it, creating courts that are more specialized and have more limited jurisdictions. The next chapter examines these courts.

The Fragmentation of International Justice

CHAPTER SEVEN

The international adjudicatory environment is a bewildering jungle of judicial, quasi-judicial, and advisory bodies, some global and some regional or bilateral, with overlapping jurisdiction and no hierarchical structure to ensure uniformity in the law. Aside from the ICJ, there is an International Tribunal for the Law of the Sea, which was established in 1996, and the World Trade Organization Dispute Settlement Mechanism, which was established in 1995. An International Criminal Tribunal for the Former Yugoslavia hears criminal cases arising from the civil wars and interstate wars that took place during the disintegration of Yugoslavia, and an International Criminal Tribunal for Rwanda hears criminal cases arising from the Rwandan genocide. Today, the International Criminal Court has general jurisdiction over international crimes committed by nationals of member states or on those states' territories. The European Court of Justice hears cases involving European treaty law. There are also a Common Court of Justice and Arbitration of the Organization for the Harmonization of Corporate Law in Africa, a Court of Justice of the Common Market for Eastern and Southern Africa, a Court of Justice of the African Union, a Court of Justice of the Western African Economic and Monetary Union, a Court of Auditors of the West African Economic and Monetary Union, and an East African Court of Justice. The European Court of Human Rights adjudicates disputes among members of the European Charter for Human Rights; the Inter-American Court of Human Rights adjudicates disputes among members of the American Convention on Human Rights. There are many more such institutions, including various claims and arbitration tribunals.[1]

The proliferation of international tribunals raises a number of questions.[2] Why are there so many? Why isn't there a hierarchical system of the type that exists in nation-states? After surveying the international judicial landscape, I will argue that the fragmentary tribunals are the result of a collision between the ambitions of global legalism and the realities of politics.

THE INTER-AMERICAN COURT

In 1969, several American states adopted the American Convention of Human Rights, which established the Inter-American Court on Human Rights (IACHR).[3] The convention, which entered into force in 1978, protects primarily political and civil rights, such as the rights to life, liberty, personal integrity, due process, privacy, property, equal protection, and freedom of conscience and expressions. The IACHR started operating in 1979; it is a permanent court.[4]

Before the adoption of the convention, human rights in the Americas had been the subject of the American Declaration on the Rights and Duties of Man, a nonbinding declaration that was adopted at the same time as the creation of the Organization of American States (OAS).[5] The IACHR monitored compliance with the declaration, primarily by conducting visits of nations and issuing country reports about their human rights performance. It continues to exist; one of its functions is to screen petitions and forward those that make out a plausible cause to the IACHR.

Not all members of the OAS are parties to the American Convention. The United States and Canada, for example, are parties to the OAS but have not ratified the convention and therefore are not subject to the jurisdiction of the IACHR. The American Convention has been ratified by twenty-five of the thirty-five American states; of these states, twenty-one have accepted compulsory jurisdiction.[6] The IACHR may hear petitions alleging a violation brought by either the Inter-American Commission on Human Rights or by a state party to the convention, but not by an individual. Under the American Convention, the decisions of the IACHR are legally binding and not subject to appeal.[7]

The IACHR is composed of seven judges nominated by state parties to the convention and elected by majority vote of the state parties.[8] The judges serve for six-year terms and may be re-elected once. Ad hoc judges ensure representation on the court for parties before it.

Contentious cases between state parties may arise in one of three ways. A state may accept the jurisdiction of the IACHR through a general acceptance of compulsory jurisdiction; a limited acceptance of reciprocal jurisdiction in suits brought by countries that take on the same obligation; or ad hoc acceptance of jurisdiction in an individual case.[9] Individuals and NGOs have no authority to bring a suit before the court directly, but by bringing a matter to the attention of the commission, they might prod the commission — after investigating, issuing a report, and seeking a settlement — to submit the case to the court on their behalf. The court may hear only cases involving a claimed violation of the American Convention. It has the authority to order remedial actions or compensation for violations.

The court has heard relatively few contentious cases. According to one count, as of 2000, it had heard only thirty-two contentious cases and issued only fifteen judgments.[10] This is a usage rate of 0.07 cases per state per year. This count may miss cases; the Web site reports seventy cases as of 2000, and one hundred eighty cases as of July 2008. In any event, the number of cases is extremely low. As we will see, this usage rate is much lower than usage of the European Court of Human Rights. As one scholar of the IACHR has written, "whereas the European system has during its forty-year history generally regulated democracies with independent judiciaries and governments that observe the rule of law, the history of much of the Americas since 1960 has been radically different, with military dictatorships, the violent repression of political opposition and of terrorism and intimidated judiciaries for a while being the order of the day in a number of countries."[11] As a result of the recent political history, "human rights issues in the Americas have often concerned gross, as opposed to ordinary, violations of human rights. They have been much more to do with the forced disappearance, killing, torture and arbitrary detention of political opponents and terrorists than with particular issues concerning, for example, the right to a fair trial or freedom of expression that are the stock in trade" of the ECHR.[12] There are many cases, it is fair to say, that have arisen in Latin America in the last twenty-five years over which there is no dispute that grievous violations of the American Convention have occurred.[13]

Compliance with IACHR decisions is mixed. The IACHR often orders two types of remedies in a case: the trial and punishment of offenders within a state party and changes in domestic law, and monetary compensation for the complainant. It appears that states routinely ignore the requirement that they try and punish offenders or change their domestic laws, but that they will often pay financial compensation. Before 2000, there was only one case in which a nation fully complied with an IACHR decision. Even in that decision, the *Honduran Disappeared Persons* case, the defendant state, Honduras, did not pay the award until eight years after the court had rendered its final judgment. In all the other cases, it appears that nations had not fully complied and the court continues to "supervise" compliance.[14] This amounts to an approximately 5 percent compliance rate. In the 2007 IACHR report, twelve instances are identified where the relevant nation is classified as in "total compliance" with the recommendations of the IACHR, for less than a 10 percent compliance rate.[15] In general, states have been more likely to comply with orders to pay compensation than with orders to change their laws and practices.

There are the usual problems with selection effects. But given the low usage and compliance rates, we can be reasonably confident in concluding that the IACHR has not been a very effective tribunal. In recent years, however, its record has improved, perhaps because more Latin American countries have become consolidated democracies.

GATT/WTO

GATT was created in 1947. It was initially intended as a temporary framework for international trade negotiations, but was indefinitely extended when the treaty creating the International Trade Organization was not ratified by the United States. GATT's charter did not provide for formal adjudication of trade disputes; instead, states submitted their disputes to arbitration under the GATT secretariat's auspices.

The informal panel system handled hundreds of disputes over nearly forty years. However, the system did not always work well. States could block or delay the establishment of panels and the adoption of judgments, and although outright blocking was relatively rare, delay occurred frequently. Frustration with these practices led to evasion of the system. States employed unilateral retaliation and during many years did not use the GATT dispute mechanism at all. Dissatisfaction with the arbitration system, as well as with other aspects of GATT, prompted member states to establish the WTO in 1995. The Dispute Resolution Understanding of that year created a more formal, court-like adjudication system.[16]

GATT. The GATT system was essentially a formalized arbitration system. If consultations fail, a party may request the creation of a panel. Because GATT acts by consensus, either party can block the creation of a panel; therefore, as in an ordinary arbitration, a panel will be appointed only if both parties consent. The two parties must agree to the members of the panel, and much delay can occur before agreement is reached. After the panel hears the case and renders a judgment, the GATT members decide by consensus whether the panel's judgment will be adopted. Again, because both parties' consent is needed, the losing party can block adoption of the panel's judgment.

If a panel's judgment is adopted by GATT members, but the losing party does not comply with it, the winner can again seek GATT authorization for the implementation of sanctions. The loser again has the opportunity to block such authorization. This has happened in every case but one.[17] Thus, although losing states did not usually block adoption of a panel's judgment against them, they almost always blocked authorization of sanctions against them. The winning party would then have to decide whether or not to implement unilateral sanctions, which would be a technical violation of GATT. The United States frequently threatened unilateral retaliation, though rarely implemented it.

In 1989, the GATT system was revised; the most important innovation was the elimination of the right to veto a panel. However, because the right to veto adoption of the panel report was retained, the GATT system remained at the mercy of its users.

WTO. The 1995 Dispute Settlement Understanding (DSU) created a system much closer to a court.[18] After consultations fail, the complaining party has a right to request the Dispute Settlement Body (DSB) to appoint a panel. If such a request is made, the DSB, which consists of all members of the WTO, must create a panel unless all DSB members agree *not* to. Since the complaining state would not ordinarily agree to the dismissal of its own complaint, this consensus rule effectively makes appointment of the panel automatic. And although the parties can recommend individuals for the panel, the WTO director-general may appoint a panel if the parties cannot agree. Because of this, strategic delay of the formation of the panel is difficult. The panel consists of three people who are *not* nationals of the disputing parties, unless the parties agree otherwise. After the panel hears the case and renders a judgment, the judgment is adopted by the DSB unless there is a consensus *against* doing so. Again, because the winner is a member of the DSB, and thus can block any effort to refuse to adopt the judgment, the adoption of the judgment is effectively automatic.

The DSU created an appellate procedure. A standing appellate body consists of seven members drawn from the WTO membership. They serve four-year terms. Appellate panels usually consist of three of the members of the appellate body drawn at random. As a result, a national of one of the state parties will not necessarily hear the case. The appellate body's decision is adopted by the DSU unless all members agree otherwise.

If the losing party does not comply with a judgment that has been adopted by the DSU, the DSU may authorize sanctions. Here again, the consensus rule applies against the losing party. It can avoid sanctions only if all members of the DSB, including the winner, agree. Thus, obtaining multilateral authorization for sanctions is effectively automatic.

In earlier work, I argued that the WTO system was no more effective than the GATT system.[19] Although the WTO system has handled about four times more cases per year than the GATT system did, the raw numbers don't account for other factors. Because the number of states with the legal right to use the dispute resolution system has increased rapidly, the volume of international trade has increased exponentially, and new types of disputes (related to services and intellectual property) were added to the system at the same time that the WTO was established, we would have expected the number of disputes to rise even if the WTO was no improvement over the GATT system. In addition, the rate of compliance with WTO decisions has been no higher than the rate of compliance with GATT decisions — though this is predictable, given that states with no intention to comply could block GATT decisions, while states cannot do the same with WTO decisions.[20] In any event, the relevant variable for purposes of evaluating the systems ought to be trade flows, not dispute resolution figures. Chad Bown conducted a test using this proxy on a set of disputes involving allegations of excessive import protection from 1973 to 1998.[21] The dependent variable is the log growth rate of the defendant's imports from the complainant in the disputed sector from one year before to three years after the dispute. He finds no evidence that the WTO adjudication procedures were more effective than the GATT procedures. His main finding is that an adjudication is more likely to be successful (in the sense of increasing trade flows) when the complainant has a large share of the defendant's exports. The retaliatory capacity of the injured state, rather than the details of the adjudication regime, drives compliance with international trade law.

Whether or not this judgment is correct, what is clear is that the GATT/WTO system has been generally successful. States seem satisfied with the WTO dispute resolution system and there is no pressure to change it. This raises the question: Why has the WTO dispute system been more successful than the ICJ? One of the most significant difference between the two systems is that ICJ takes seriously the sovereign equality of states, while the WTO system acknowledges the importance of state power. This difference is manifested in a subtle but significant way. As we have seen, the ICJ issues remedies, including monetary reparations, that are binding to the same extent for weak countries and powerful countries, and the increasing willingness of the weak countries to use the ICJ against powerful countries may have soured the latter on this institution. GATT and WTO do not make this mistake. While formally a weak country can bring a case against a powerful country, the remedy available is limited to authorization to use self-help. But small countries cannot harm big countries by closing their markets to them; they can only hurt themselves by doing this. The remedy thus has value only for powerful countries, both with respect to their relations with each other and with small countries. And, indeed, studies confirm that weaker and poorer countries generally do not use the WTO dispute mechanism.[22] This rather grim constraint may explain why trade adjudication has flourished while ICJ adjudication has not: the former is less legalistic, yielding to practicalities.

ECHR

The ECHR, created by the European Convention of Human Rights in 1953, which was created by the member states of the Council of Europe,[23] was established to monitor compliance by the member states with the convention's substantive terms. The convention protects individual rights, such as the right to life, the prohibition of torture, and freedom of expression and thought. Initially, the convention established a two-stage process in which cases were filtered by the European Commission of Human Rights, which decided whether to attempt mediation of the dispute or refer the case to the Committee of Foreign Ministers of the Council of Europe. If a referral was made, the complaining state or person could seek binding adjudication before the court. In 1998, the commission was eliminated and the court was established as the only institution that hears complaints under the convention.[24]

The ECHR is composed of judges equal in number to the member states of the convention, which currently numbers forty-four. The judges serve for renewable six-year terms. Each state party may nominate three candidates, who may or may not be nationals; they are elected by the Parliamentary Assembly of the Council of Europe.[25] There is no guarantee that every member state will have a national on the court and no restriction on the number of judges of each nationality. Nonetheless, it appears that each member state has one representative, whether its national or not (an ad hoc judge), on the court.[26]

The jurisdiction of the court is broad. Any state party, individual, group, or NGO may bring a suit claiming a human rights violation against one of the member states, as long as domestic remedies have been exhausted. Originally, a member state could choose not to allow jurisdiction over itself in cases brought by non-states, but in 1998 — at the same time as the elimination of the commission — the court's jurisdiction was made compulsory as to all state parties as to all complaints. In sum, the judges are relatively independent, similar to the judges of the ECJ.

Usage of the ECHR has increased steadily since its inception, in response to the expansions in jurisdiction by amendment to the convention. By the time of the 1998 expansion in compulsory jurisdiction of the commission, the annual number of applications had increased from 404 in 1980 to 4,750. The number of cases referred to the court itself had risen from 7 in 1981 to 119. In 2002, the court received 28,255 applications and delivered 844 judgments.[27] In 2007, the court reviewed 41,700 applications and delivered 1,735 judgments.[28] Almost all of this activity involved cases brought by individuals against their own state rather than state-to-state disputes.

The convention does not require that member states follow any specific process for bringing their laws or actions into compliance with ECHR decisions.[29] The ECHR has no method of enforcement in cases where a state party to a case refuses to comply.[30] States have responded in several different ways, including administrative rule making, implementation by national judiciaries, enactment of conforming legislation, and even changes to domestic constitutions. The great majority of state responses, close to 80 percent, involve legislative enactments, and both legislative and administrative responses amount to 91 percent of the cases where a change is sought.[31]

Although some commentators suggest that levels of compliance with ECHR rulings are high,[32] there is in fact no good compliance data that I have found.[33] By mid-1999, the court had addressed more than 1,000 petitions, nearly all of them initiated by private parties. More than 670 were adjudicated on the merits with more than 460 resulting in a finding of a violation of the convention. The court claims that member states have consistently paid damages when ordered to, but it also reports only 294 cases in which states have altered their domestic laws in compliance with an ECHR decision. This would mean, if each merits decision required a change in domestic law, a compliance rate of roughly 64 percent. This figure is highly imprecise, as it is unclear what percentage of human rights violations, if any, might be the result of actions of government officials that are ultra vires of existing law.

Another means of judging compliance is through the Article 41 action, which permits plaintiffs who do not receive full compensation from the losing member state after an ECHR decision to seek additional compensation. According to one study covering the years 1960–1995, Article 41 claims occurred in 48 out of 292 cases in which the ECHR found a violation of the convention (16.4 percent). The percentage of cases that generated Article 41 claims was initially quite high: in 1970, more than 50 percent of all cases that found a violation of the convention were followed by Article 41 claims, and that number hovered around 50 percent until the early 1980s. That number dropped below 24 percent by 1995, but during that period a procedural change occurred that combined Article 41 claims into the actual merits decision, so it is difficult to determine what the actual level of noncompliance is now.

Finally, we should point to the problem of Russia. Russia ratified the European Convention in 1998, yet over the last decade, it has become increasingly authoritarian and less willing to respect human rights.[34] It has lost a number of cases in the ECHR, and although Russia has paid damages to victims, it has not been willing to change its laws or practices.

To sum up, we do not know whether compliance with ECHR judgments has been high or low. We also cannot say whether usage has been high or low compared to that of international tribunals. Although the ECHR caseload of hundreds compares favorably to, say, the IACHR's caseload of dozens, millions of people may file cases with the ECHR, whereas only a handful of states may file claims with the IACHR.

ECJ

The European Court of Justice (ECJ) was established in 1952 as the judicial body for the European Coal and Steel Community.[35] It has remained the principal judicial organ for members of the European Community (EC) even as they have evolved from a loose collection of several communities into the European Union under the 1992 Treaty of European Union and the 1997 Amsterdam Treaty. Its purpose is to settle disputes between the different actors of the European Union, which includes member states, EU institutions (such as the Commission, Council, and Parliament), and sometimes private parties. It also attempts to ensure the uniform interpretation of European law, and national courts may refer questions of European law to it. The substantive law derives from the treaties that have formed the European Communities and the European Union, the regulations and directives issued by European Community institutions in exercising the powers conferred to them by the treaties, and treaties to which the community is a party. It is a permanent court that hears disputes concerning the interpretation and application of the European Community treaties and secondary laws created under their authority.[36]

The ECJ is composed of twenty-seven judges,[37] the same as the number of member states. They are appointed for renewable six-year terms by the unanimous consent of the member states. By tradition, each member state has one representative on the bench. Parties cannot raise objections based on nationality to the membership of a chamber that hears the case.[38]

The jurisdiction of the ECJ covers mainly three types of cases. First are claims brought against member states by the community for violations of EC law; second are claims brought against community institutions; and third are referrals from member states' domestic courts concerning questions of EC law. Cases against member states for violations of EC law can be brought by other member states, but this occurs rarely; cases are ordinarily brought by the European Commission.[39] Cases under the second fount of jurisdiction can be brought by member states, other EC institutions, or individuals that have a direct and particular interest in the outcome. The third type of jurisdiction occurs when a question of EC law arises in the domestic proceedings of a member state's national court. Although it is the decision of the national court whether to seek the referral, the individual parties to the case may participate in the ECJ proceedings. If a question of EC law arises in the national court of last resort, it has an obligation to refer the issue to the ECJ.[40] The member states have an obligation to ensure that ECJ judgments are enforced within their domestic legal systems. Each member state must designate a national authority whose function it is to enforcement ECJ judgments. These characteristics—compulsory jurisdiction, judges with fixed terms, a continuing body, and so forth—are those of an independent tribunal.

The ECJ hears approximately 500 new cases each year and disposes of roughly that amount, with 907 cases still pending as of 2002. From 1998 through 2002, the most recent figures available, the largest number of cases were referrals for preliminary rulings on EC law by national judiciaries, of which there were 241 in 2002; with the next largest class was direct actions, of which there were 215 in 2002. While the number of preliminary ruling cases has varied little, the number of direct actions has steadily risen from 136 in 1998.[41]

Compliance by EU member states with ECJ decisions appears to be significant. One study finds that noncompliance with ECJ decisions by national judiciaries from 1961 to 1995 occurred in only 0.6 percent of cases, and efforts at evasion of compliance occurred in 2.9 percent of cases (through referring the question again, or by reinterpreting the ECJ decision). In 40.9 percent of the cases, the litigants voluntarily agreed to forgo further proceedings leading to a national court decision and immediately implemented the ECJ decision.[42]

However, there is some reason for doubting these figures.[43] Apparently, it is common in some countries to conceal evasion with ECJ decisions or to plead problems with implementation.[44] At the end of the first decade of common market integration under the treaty establishing the European Economic Community (EEC),[45] the ECJ heard a series of cases challenging existing trade quotas on agricultural products among member states, which, after a transition period ending in 1969, were to be abolished and replaced with EU-wide marketing organizations.[46] In one of these cases, France appears to have defied an ECJ decision requiring elimination of an import quota on bananas; in another, France even announced before the ECJ had rendered its decision (which it lost) that it would refuse to comply with a decision requiring it to eliminate a quota on mutton.[47] States that have refused to comply also have sought other means of resistance other than outright defiance, such as supporting other governments that defy ECJ rulings or seeking collective efforts to constrain the ECJ either through secondary EC legislation or even proposals to change the basic EC treaties.[48] One scholar argues that noncompliance with ECJ decisions has increased in response to efforts by the European Commission and the ECJ to strengthen enforcement mechanisms during the period of the deepening of the European internal market in the 1990s.[49]

According to figures supplied by the European Commission,[50] states had ignored judgments of the ECJ in infringement cases—cases where the commission claims a member state has failed to implement an EU directive—thirty times by the early 1980s, and more than eighty times by the late 1980s. The commission reported in 1989, in regard to member state implementation of the EU's internal market measures, that "a fundamental problem is compliance with ECJ judgments; that the increase in infringement proceedings is reflected not only in a less satisfactory implementation of Community law, but also and more particularly in a growing number of non-enforced judgments, gives real cause for concern . . . . The burden of non-implementation of the ECJ decisions is particularly felt in the internal market domain."[51] It does not appear at present that a comprehensive empirical examination of compliance with ECJ decisions has been done.[52]

Nonetheless, it is reasonable to conclude that the ECJ has been an effective tribunal—in some periods, a vital institution that spurred integration when the efforts of national governments flagged. Indeed, the success of the ECJ has fueled global legalism by showing that an international tribunal can work. But the reason for its success is that the ECJ is not truly an "international court" for purposes of comparison with the ICJ, arbitral tribunals, and other courts.

The special character of the ECJ, compared to other courts, can be seen in its daily workings. Virtually none of the ECJ's direct action cases involve suits between member states, much as there are very few inter-state lawsuits in the U.S. system. Rather, most of the direct lawsuits are brought by the institutions of the European Union itself, particularly the European Commission, against member states for failure to comply with their treaty obligations.[53] Further, the close integration of the ECJ with the member states' national judiciaries—in which EU questions are referred by the domestic courts to the ECJ and ECJ decisions are often directly implemented by domestic courts[54]—more closely resembles the relationship between local and national courts in a federal system, than international dispute resolution.[55] The "great bulk of the court's case load is generated by preliminary references from national judges responding to claims made by private actors."[56]

The distinctive character of the ECJ has led several observers to characterize the ECJ as a "constitutional court" for the European Communities, with the supreme law being the various EC treaties.[57] These scholars view the ECJ's primary function, through the preliminary reference system, as promoting a consistent interpretation and application of EC law throughout Europe. This has arisen, however, not through direct actions between member states, but through the mechanism of preliminary references, which have created an indirect method for private actors to bring lawsuits challenging member state or EC decisions.[58] Although the French or German governments were willing to ignore ECJ judgments against them, they were not willing to ignore their own domestic courts, which would order the government to comply with the ECJ judgment. The governments did not provoke a domestic constitutional crisis by rejecting the judgments of their own courts, because they shared with their courts and many domestic interest groups the goal of European integration.[59] If the ECJ embraced integration, it was with the acquiescence of the European governments.[60]

Thus, although the ECJ provides the best case for the viability of international courts, this view does not take account of the special circumstances of Europe. There are two special circumstances that need to be singled out. First, Europe has a richer institutional environment than the world as a whole. The ECJ is just one of a number of European institutions—including the European Parliament, the Council of the European Union, and the Commission—and it works with these institutions to ensure that

European law develops properly and flexibly in response to changing circumstances and the needs and interests of the populations of the member states. International courts, by contrast, lack this institutional structure.

Second, Europeans, especially the elites, have a shared commitment to integration, based on the lessons of World War II, fears about German nationalism, and very successful but also incremental progress in European cooperation across a range of issues over sixty years. No doubt this commitment played a role in the decision of the judges of national courts to give substantial deference to ECJ decisions. This system cannot be a model for international courts, where relationships between states are thin and fraught with conflict.

The Law of the Sea Tribunal

In 1994, the United Nations Convention on the Law of the Sea went into force. Most nations have ratified this treaty — 155 as of July 2008. The United States has signed but not ratified the treaty. The treaty was painstakingly negotiated over many years and governs a host of sea-related legal issues mainly having to do with how nations divide control over the surface of the sea and hence navigation and passage and resources underneath the sea. The treaty also established a dispute resolution system.

The dispute resolution provisions of the Law of the Sea convention are complex. States are permitted to choose among the newly established International Tribunal for the Law of the Sea, the International Court of Justice, and two types of arbitration; they are also permitted to opt out of mandatory dispute resolution for a set of disputes. The ICJ has not had a law of the sea case; ITLOS has had a trivial number of cases — only fifteen over more than ten years, nearly all of them dealing with a very narrow topic — whether bonds set by states that had captured vessels in their coastal seas were reasonable or not.[61]

EXPLANATION: COURTS UNBOUND

The European Court of Justice resembles a national court that enjoys the obedience of those subject to its jurisdiction. The European Court of Human Rights represents an ambiguous case: certainly, many of its judgments are obeyed, but systematic work on compliance has not been done. The Inter-American Court of Human Rights and the International Court of Justice are marginal cases. The GATT/WTO system seems to have been successful, so far. How might we explain this pattern? With so few data points, one can only make conjectures, but a safe conjecture is that courts do best when they exist in a political community that is thickly institutionalized (the ECJ) or when they have limited jurisdiction and remedial power (GATT/WTO). The ICJ, with general jurisdiction over the world and powerful remedial authority, was simply too ambitious.

A central institution in all legal systems is the court. The court's main role is to interpret laws. Strictly speaking, courts do not enforce laws; instead, they issue orders to various executive individuals such as sheriffs, bailiffs, police, and regulatory agencies, who carry out the courts' orders, using force if necessary. The law interpretation function is of great importance, because no law is self-explanatory; there are always ambiguities. If there were no courts, and executive officials were permitted to interpret the laws, there would be a danger that the executive officials would interpret the law in self-serving ways. In the American system, executive officials who interpreted laws in self-serving ways could greatly reduce or eliminate the role of the legislature, which could object to the interpretations and enact new laws correcting the interpretations but would still be helpless, because the executive officials alone carry out enforcement. Many people think that the legislature reflects the will of the people to a greater degree than the executive does, and so if the executive could disenfranchise the legislature by issuing self-serving interpretations, democracy itself would be threatened. An independent concern is that executive interpretations would follow the political winds at any given moment, and thus a practice of executive interpretation would undermine rule of law virtues — the predictability that comes with stable laws with stable meanings.

Courts can play their role only if two conditions are satisfied.[62] First, the judges must have expertise. Interpreting legal documents and resolving legal disputes is difficult craftwork; it takes hard-to-define but real skills, and can be done well or poorly. Outsiders have trouble evaluating the quality of legal work but they can evaluate outcomes; business people, for example, know whether a particular society has a favorable legal climate in which contracts and property rights are respected or not, although any particular judge in any particular case might make a decision for inscrutable reasons. Countries with good judges have good lawyers as well, and a good legal culture with strong professional norms and powerful legal institutions, such as bar associations. Legal expertise consists of familiarity and facility with the norms of legal argument and the sources of law.

Second, judges must be impartial. Impartiality means deciding cases according to the legal merits alone, and not according to legally irrelevant considerations about which the judge might feel strongly for moral, political, or pecuniary reasons. A judge should not favor a party with a weaker legal case because that party belongs to the judge's family, tribe, ethnic group, or political party. Impartiality is a quality of decision-making and not an institutional characteristic. In the United States, federal judges and some state judges are given independence — they cannot be fired — and it is often thought that this guarantees impartiality because judges need not fear that they will be fired for making a decision that is unpopular with the ruling party or the public. But by the same token, the judge is free to decide cases on the basis of political preferences because there is no risk of punishment. Judges in other countries usually have less protection than American judges, but many of them are just as impartial. But judicial independence in a larger sense is necessary for impartiality: judges have to be understood as deciding cases neutrally and not according to the wishes of the government. In that sense, they are politically independent.

Not all domestic judges are impartial or expert; even excellent legal systems have mediocre judges. But numerous institutional safety valves ensure that bad judges have limited influence on people's behavior. When judges misinterpret laws, legislatures can amend the laws so as to eliminate the misleading ambiguities; executive officials can also intervene in court to argue against bad interpretations and soften their impact by modifying enforcement priorities. Multiple layers of review by appellate courts, the possibility of collateral challenges, redundant civil/criminal claims, presidential and gubernatorial pardons, paneling, and so forth, ensure that incompetent or biased judges have limited impact. The ultimate check on judicial abuse is the political system. The government can investigate and impeach judges; it can strip the judiciary of jurisdiction; it can defund the judiciary and harass it in other ways. In most American states, state judges are disciplined by electoral pressures or the threat of nonrenewal by the governor or legislature. In the United States, the balance of power between the judiciary and the other branches has worked over two hundred years. In other countries, where the judiciary has less formal independence, it has functioned well because of elite or popular support.

In the international arena, these safety valves do not exist. If the ICJ misinterprets an international law, states cannot modify the law in the same way that a legislature can modify a misinterpreted domestic law. A legislature operates by majority rule; this eases lawmaking and works adequately when the values and interests are sufficiently homogenous and the political culture is effective. No analogous world legislature can modify the law in question; instead, states must convene an international convention which must operate by consensus. This ensures that small minorities can hold up needed legal change—a problem exacerbated by the enormous variance in the size of states. Nor can states, as a body, modify the design of the court by changing its jurisdiction or its structure—that, too, is frozen in stone. Reappointment of bad judges can, in theory, be blocked; in practice, states' decisions regarding appointments and retentions are driven by national and regional interests.

And this is all assuming that states act in good faith. But out of nearly two hundred states, only a few dozen have judges who satisfy these conditions to a substantial extent.[63] Most states have bad legal systems. The states with good legal systems are, for the most part, the modern, wealthy, liberal democracies. When international courts are established, all states that might have a case before them insist on having a role in the appointment of judges, prosecutors, and other officials. States insist on having such a role because they want to have an influence on the court; they want to have an influence on the court because they believe, correctly as we have seen, that other officials on the court will be loyal to their own nations' interests or perspectives and thus not impartial. And because these states have corrupt or ineffective domestic judiciaries, because they lack a decent legal culture, the states end up appointing people who, even if not corrupt, are not disinterested, and are often not even expert.

So if all states would be better off if they could agree to establish an impartial international court and could agree to obey the court's judgments, they nonetheless cannot create such a court. Free riding occurs at every stage: in the design of the court, in the appointment of officials, in the decision whether to comply with the court's judgments. The extent to which the judges on these courts actually act impartially is, of course, unknown, but the evidence suggests that, at least on the margin, they do not, and that some governments do not trust them to behave impartially.

These factors explain the proliferation of international courts.[64] In 1946, there was one functioning court. Today, there are twenty-one existing international judicial bodies, and another nine that are either getting started or being discussed.[65] There are dozens more quasi-judicial bodies. International lawyers are ambivalent about this trend. More courts imply more international justice, but also conflicting law, jurisprudential overlap, and forum shopping. Some scholars think that these concerns can be remedied; it is merely a question of judges showing respect for their brethren in other courts.[66] However, this response assumes away the most plausible reason for the proliferation of courts: states become unhappy with an existing international court, and they work around it by depriving it of jurisdiction and establishing additional courts or adjudication mechanisms as needed. If a group of states avoids a particular court because they do not like the way it rules, they will not accomplish anything by establishing a new court or arbitration mechanism that follows the first court's lead.

Global legalists believe that the domestic judicial institutions that have proven their worth over the centuries can be recreated at the international level. But courts, like plants, flourish only in the right environment. The political and cultural bases of the adequate domestic judiciaries that exist in the more successful states do not exist at the international level, where interests diverge to a greater degree than within a state, and institutions that correct and support courts are thin or nonexistent. This does not mean that international adjudicatory institutions cannot succeed. But it may be that the type of adjudication that works internationally will look different from, and be more limited than, domestic counterparts. Fragmented jurisdiction, tribunals with narrow scope — this may be the best that one can hope for.[67]

THE RETURN OF ARBITRATION

In international legal circles, there has been a great deal of comment about the recent explosion of arbitration. Unfortunately, many arbitrations are secret, and no one keeps track of all the public arbitrations. Nonetheless, the evidence suggests that indeed arbitration, which never went away even while international courts were being established, is enjoying a rebirth.

TABLE 4. Arbitrations by twenty-year periods.

Period	All states	Involving 2 Great Powers or the United States.
1794–1819	23	ND
1820–1839	9	2
1840–1859	29	3
1860–1879	48	6
1880–1899	116	17
1900–1919	101	16
1920–1939	80	5
1940–1959	18	0
1960–1979	16	4

Source: Compiled from A.M. Stuyt, Survey of International Arbitrations 1794–1989 (3d ed. 1990).
Note: In 1900–1914, there were 86 arbitrations; in 1915–1919, there were 5. ND, no Great Power data.

Consider first some background. Data on arbitrations from 1794 to 1989 are collected in a book by A.M. Stuyt, who provides information on every arbitration during that period.[68] Limiting oneself to those cases where Stuyt provides comprehensive information, there were 467 arbitrations during the period, though many were closely related or stemming from a single dispute. The frequency of arbitration rose gradually and peaked in the decade before World War I. Table 4 provides the number of arbitrations by twenty year period (excluding the last ten years of the data set and arbitrations for which no starting year was given). It shows that the absolute number of arbitrations increased until World War I and then never fully recovered. If we confine ourselves to arbitrations involving two Great Powers or one Great Power and the United States,[69] we can see that even within this limited pool of states the rate of arbitration increased; thus, the increase was not driven solely by growth in the number of independent states during the nineteenth century. The failure of the arbitration rate to recover even after the end of World War II may have been due to the rise of other dispute resolution mechanisms.

Most arbitrations involved two states. The most common topics were, in order, borders (90), personal claims (68), maritime seizures (36), arbitrary acts (29), treaty interpretations (26), war damages (15), indemnities

(12), mutual claims (12), civil insurrections (11), and military actions (8). These are Stuyt's classifications; though not transparent, they give one a sense of the landscape. Of the arbitrations for which this information was given, 306 (about two-thirds) involved a commission of three people or more, and 145 involved a single arbitrator or mediator, typically a head of state. Commissions were popular for civil insurrections, war damages, and personal claims; heads of state were popular for arbitrary acts and maritime seizures.

It is well known that Britain and the United States were early champions of arbitration, and the numbers bear out the conventional wisdom. But there are also some surprises. Table 5 lists the main users of arbitration.

The pattern that emerges is that large countries—not necessarily Great Powers—used arbitration frequently, as one would expect; and that Latin American countries had a special preference for arbitration. But there are problems of selection bias. Large countries should use arbitration more often because they have more interactions than small countries do. The Latin American countries are older than similar smaller countries in Africa and Asia; they came into existence prior to the heyday of arbitration in the early- to mid-nineteenth century. Still, it does appear that the Latin American nations have relied on arbitration more than other states have, and the historical evidence suggests that American influence played a role.[70] There is little evidence that democracy plays a role in the choice to

TABLE 5. Arbitration by state.

United Kingdom	116	Portugal	18
United States	106	Brazil	16
France	81	Netherlands	15
Germany	50	Ecuador	13
Chile	33	Austria	11
Italy	32	Argentina	11
Peru	29	Russia	9
Venezuela	24	Bolivia	8
Mexico	20	Canada	8
Spain	20	China	5
Colombia	19	Japan	4

Source: Compiled from A.M. Stuyt, Survey of International Arbitrations 1794–1989 (3d ed. 1990).

arbitrate; many of the prominent users of arbitration — Germany, Chile, Italy — were not democracies during the relevant periods.[71]

In the abstract, we cannot say that the usage of arbitration is high or low. But it is telling that the popularity of arbitration increased steadily through the nineteenth century, suggesting that states were pleased with the results.

Stuyt provides data on compliance for some of the cases, but the data are difficult to interpret. Of the 220 cases for which Stuyt provides compliance data, he says that compliance occurred in 206 cases, for a very high 94 percent compliance rate. However, Stuyt does not explain how he defined and measured compliance. Further, it is possible that the cases with compliance information are a biased sample. If it is harder to collect information about noncompliance than information about compliance, then it could be that all or most of the 247 cases for which there is no information should be treated as noncompliance cases. If the no-information cases in his data set are cases of noncompliance, the compliance rate is 44 percent.

Stuyt's data end in 1989, and there is no similar collection of data for arbitration since then. However, arbitration remains popular. The Permanent Court of Arbitration maintains a Web site that lists its cases.[72] Its last case before the 1990s was the Island of Palmas case of 1928. After a seventy-year hiatus, an arbitration between Eritrea and Yemen took place. Including that arbitration, there have been ten completed arbitrations since 1998, and there are an additional five pending arbitrations. These are all state-to-state arbitrations; in addition, there are fifteen arbitrations involving a state and a private entity. Other institutions have also been conducting arbitrations — of particular importance, arbitrations between states and private companies under Bilateral Investment Treaties.

What accounts for the increasing popularity of arbitration? With arbitration, unlike adjudication, states retain maximal power over the proceedings. Two states with a dispute choose the arbitrators, give them instructions, and retain the right not to comply with the judgment if they believe that the arbitrators violated their instructions.

Arbitration has taken many forms, and for expository simplicity we will consider a stylized example that captures most of arbitration's standard features. Imagine that two neighboring states have a dispute about the location of their border. Each state asserts a border that enhances the size of its territory at the expense of the other state; between the two asserted borders lies a no-man's-land where neither state can exert full control because of the competing claim of the other state. As long as the border dispute exists, the no-man's-land cannot be put to productive use. The people who live there have uncertain citizenship, cannot be taxed, cannot appeal to a common government to resolve disputes, and so forth. This lost value can be thought of as a "pie" that the two states have an interest in preserving and dividing. As long as they fail to come to agreement, the value of the pie is lost.

If the states choose to arbitrate, they will first enter an agreement that provides for the structure of the arbitration, including instructions for the arbitrators. The instructions lay out the issues that the arbitrators must resolve; they are not permitted to resolve other issues, or consider law or evidence excluded from the instructions. Each state then appoints a single party arbitrator (sometimes, they might appoint more than one party arbitrator, but the states always appoint the same number of arbitrators). The two party arbitrators then meet and jointly choose an umpire (if there are more than two arbitrators, they will usually choose more than one umpire). The two party arbitrators and the umpire form a panel. The states make their case before the panel. The panel then decides the case and issues a judgment, which might or might not be public and might or might not include much reasoning. The losing state then decides whether to comply with the judgment. If it does not, the dispute remains unresolved.

Working backwards, we observe that the losing state will not comply with the panel's decision unless the reputational harm exceeds the cost of compliance. The reputational harm might be severe—a state that rarely or never complies with arbitration judgments will not be able to use arbitration in future and thus will not be able to do better than rely on diplomacy—but compliance can be costly as well. The arbitrators know this, of course, and they may want to take this into account and not impose an excessively strict sanction. If states routinely ignore arbitration judgments, then arbitration will not be used, and the arbitrators will not have future business. On the other hand, winning states may prefer to avoid arbitration if they expect awards to be limited. However arbitrators take these conflicting factors into account, they have an interest in acting consistently with the joint interests of the states.

Indeed, the states will try to select party arbitrators who are loyal, so the party arbitrators will be inclined to support their own state's interest. In addition, they might expect to be used again by their government, as noted above, or be used in other capacities by their government, if they are able to defend the government's interest, though a government can only have partial information (for example, through random audits) about whether it lost because it had a bad case or because its agent did not perform adequately or was disloyal. The main way that the party arbitrator serves his state is to ensure that the umpire is impartial—not biased in the other side's favor—and by persuading the umpire to take his state's side of the dispute. As for the umpire, he has a strong incentive to act impartially so that he will be selected as an umpire in future arbitrations. Because no party arbitrator would consent to the appointment of an umpire known to be biased toward the other side, and the appointment requires the consent of both party arbitrators, a biased umpire should never be appointed, barring ordinary error.

So arbitration makes sense in broad terms. States can use arbitration to convey information about facts, interest, and power, and in this way avoid delay, impasses, and violent conflict. If states can find agents who care about their reputations and develop expertise about various areas of international law and relations, then arbitration can produce more favorable outcomes than diplomacy alone can. The popularity of arbitration over the last two centuries lends empirical support for this conjecture.

But arbitration also has limitations. One limitation follows from the structure of the agency relationship. If agents have interests that are not perfectly aligned with that of their principles, then they will not always take actions that advance the principles' objectives. Arbitrators might not adequately serve the interest of states for a host of reasons: personal ideological or political views at variance of those of their government, a desire for money or prestige, even laziness.

Another limitation of arbitration arises from its episodic nature. States establish arbitration panels on an ad hoc basis in order to address conflicts as they arise. The fixed costs of start-up must be incurred over and over. These costs are not just the result of spending time and money to vet and hire arbitrators, draft instructions, and establish rules. They are also the result of lost expertise from one arbitration to the next. Much better would be a permanent arbitration system or, even better, a court that would be able to develop expertise over time, or, in more familiar terms, a jurisprudence.

To be sure, arbitrators use international law and often take into account opinions of prior arbitration panels, as well as government statements and the like. But arbitrators do not have a strong reason to do this and often have good reasons for not doing this. Governments might demand secrecy, and they often provide narrow instructions that foreclose reliance on international law. Individual arbitration panels do not gain anything by publishing well-reasoned opinions, because they are not likely to rely on them in the future. Arbitration also lacks many features of courts that are designed to maximize consistency and accuracy—including appellate bodies, specialized judicial officers, and compulsory jurisdiction (without which states can simply refuse to resolve their disputes peacefully).

So it is understandable that pragmatic politicians as well as global legalists of the late nineteenth and early twentieth centuries would try to establish international judicial systems. But those things that make courts attractive—mandatory jurisdiction, a permanent body of judges, a consistent jurisprudence that respects sovereign equality—also made them unappealing to powerful states.

ARBITRATION, ADJUDICATION, AND GLOBAL LEGALISM

The history of adjudication, defined broadly to encompass arbitration and judicial action, is long and complex and cannot be easily summarized. But a few points can be made. First, the global legalist Whig style of history that asserts increasing legalization and judicialization of international politics cannot handle the limited success of international courts. Arbitration never left and has been making a comeback. International courts succeed best when they are subject to strict limitations—voluntary jurisdiction, limited jurisdiction, weak remedies, and so forth. True, domestic arbitration flourishes and no one takes the existence of domestic arbitration as a rebuke to domestic courts (except in some countries where the judicial system is weak). But—a crucial difference—domestic arbitration *depends* on courts to enforce arbitral awards, to call on the coercive machinery of the state when the loser refuses to pay. International arbitration panels have no such resource (except in some limited circumstances), and so they are used in more limited fashion.

Second, as noted above, the proliferation of international courts is a sign of the weakness of the international system, not its strength. Scholars have made a similar point about other international institutions.[73] States set up courts and then find they cannot control them. Rather than submitting to their jurisdiction, they set up even more courts or more arbitration panels—ones that they think they *can* control. In the meantime, existing courts see their workload shrink, and the longstanding goal to replace arbitration with courts in order to ensure that international law will develop in a unified rather than fragmented way is defeated.

Third, international judges have failed to win the prestige and trust that domestic judges enjoy in legalistic nations like the United States, and hence also lack domestic judges' ability to expand their authority and withstand pressure from other institutions. Several possible reasons can be cited. American judges emerge from a legalistic culture that incorporates widespread values; so when these judges make policy, they make policy that most people approve. International judges emerge from heterogeneous societies with different values and interests, so when they make policy, their efforts are regarded with suspicion. Many international judges do not come from legalistic cultures and, as a result, are often not even lawyers or judges but politicians who are being given a sinecure—an idea that is unthinkable in much of the West, where lawyers accordingly have trouble taking international courts as seriously as they take their own courts.

Fourth, domestic courts can make policy and assert their power in part because of government safety valves. Bad decisions can often be reversed by legislation, or their consequences softened as a result of discretionary executive enforcement. This is true for the European Court of Justice in the European Union as well. No such safety valves exist at the international level because of the lack of effective enforcement and legislative institutions.

So, while domestic legalism has led to a system of judges with great power, global legalism has led to a system of judges without (or with greatly limited) power.

Human Rights and International Criminal Law

Before World War II, international law almost exclusively concerned the relations between states and ignored the relations between states and individuals—and especially between states and their own citizens. But there were exceptions to this rule, and over time they would expand significantly.

Consider first the relationship between a state and an alien. During the late eighteenth century, the U.S. government understood that it had an international legal obligation to extend normal civil and criminal law protections to British subjects who were lawfully on American territory. If the U.S. government allowed a mob to attack a British subject and refused to give the subject legal process or compensation, then the United States violated its obligations vis-à-vis Britain. Britain, not the victim, had the claim; if it chose not to pursue the claim diplomatically or by threatening retaliation, then the victim of the attack had no further recourse.

At the same time, subjects or citizens of other states generally were not personally responsible for international law violations. During the U.S. Civil War, the British government permitted a British shipyard to build the warship *Alabama* for the Confederacy. The United States accused Britain of violating international law governing neutrality, and subsequently the claim was arbitrated and settled. Throughout, both sides understood that it was pointless to ask whether the particular individuals involved in the incident—the government officials who authorized the operation, the shipyard workers, and others—violated international law or not. None of them could be held personally responsible for violating international law because the relevant law bound states, not individuals. The only question was whether Britain had violated international law.

The main exceptions were for pirates and war criminals. A person who committed piracy was considered a violator of international law, which in practice meant that naval forces or law enforcement agents who captured pirates could try and punish them even though they were not nationals of the prosecuting state or had not committed crimes on the territory of the prosecuting state — traditional requirements for exercising criminal process over someone. And soldiers who committed war crimes, such as executing prisoners, would often be punished by the other side if it captured them.

These practices were the beginning of what we now call international criminal law. In parallel but much more inchoate were the beginnings of what we now call international human rights law. International human rights law has focused on what states can do to their own citizens — although in practice this is easily extended to what states can do to aliens as well. The traditional idea of sovereignty, which is conventionally said to originate with the Peace of Westphalia, which ended the Thirty Years' War in 1648, was that a state controlled what happened on its own territory and, necessarily, had no right to control what happened on the territories of other states. But part of the agreement embodied in the Peace of Westphalia was that, although the government determined the official religion of the state if it wished, it had to respect the rights of members of minority religions (that is, a Catholic state had to protect the rights of Protestants, and vice versa). Thus was established the idea that the government of a sovereign state could not do whatever it wanted to its subjects or citizens, but, as a matter of international law, had to grant them at least some rights.[1]

In the twentieth century, both international criminal law and international human rights law were greatly expanded. International criminal law has come to refer to a set of international crimes, which can be committed by individuals, who then are subject to the jurisdiction of international tribunals and domestic courts under the principle of universal jurisdiction. (Under traditional state practice and principles of international law, a state would not try a national of another state for crimes committed against conationals in that other state.) International human rights law refers to states' obligations to respect certain rights of people irrespective of their nationality.

For global legalists, the rise of individual rights under international law is an exciting development. Domestic legal systems, after all, govern individuals. They also govern political entities, of course, but the regulation of individual behavior is their primary function. An international legal system should have the same function.[2] Indeed, because most people in the world live under domestic legal systems that function poorly, protecting these people would seem to require international involvement. But can international law actually protect individuals in a world still dominated by states?

THE NUREMBERG AND TOKYO TRIBUNALS

Modern international criminal and human rights law has its origins in World War II. The trials of war criminals at Nuremberg, Tokyo, and elsewhere were not the first war crimes trials—several occurred after World War I, for example—but they were novel in other respects. First, they were the first modern effort to try and punish leaders and other important individuals for starting a war—for "crimes against peace" or "aggressive war," as it was called at Nuremberg. Second, the prosecutions involved an effort to expand existing international criminal law, so as (for example) to cover crimes committed during peacetime and to reach soldiers "who were just following orders" and officers or leaders who did not directly order atrocities but anticipated that they would occur and did nothing to stop them. Third, the sheer effort—in terms of the resources devoted to the trials by the victorious nations, especially the United States—had no precedent. After World War I, for example, the victors compelled Germany to promise to try its own war criminals rather than doing it themselves, with the predictable result that the trials were not taken very seriously. After World War II, aside from the Nuremberg trials of major war criminals, there were dozens of trials of other figures, and eventually a massive denazification program. Fourth, and related, there was a self-conscious desire to set precedent and establish a more comprehensive regime of international criminal law than had existed earlier. Fifth, the multinational tribunals at Nuremberg and Tokyo were unprecedented; traditionally, an army might set up a military commission to try a captured enemy soldier suspected of war crimes. The commission would not be international in composition. Finally, the Nuremberg and Tokyo trials were highly legalistic, in the sense of involving, as much as practicable, independent judges, the participation of lawyers on both sides, adherence to procedures, and so forth. Military commissions traditionally used rather summary procedures.

What explains the allied governments' decision to try German and Japanese wrongdoers? The Allies initially hoped that the Nuremberg trial would teach the Germans and their own publics that the German leaders were evil—that there was no possible justification for their behavior. The dual goals were the education of the Germans about their own leadership, so that they could reconcile themselves to a new order where Germany would be ruled by foreign powers or else have greatly reduced international status; and vindication of the political leadership of the allied countries.[3] The trial offered itself as an appropriate instrument for teaching these lessons for several reasons. First, the German leadership clearly behaved worse than the leaders of other countries—the Holocaust was a unique evil. Second, it seemed plausible that ordinary Germans could be persuaded of this view. Third, trials are an excellent instrument of persuasion when defendants are given the chance to speak and defend themselves and procedures are fair; that is, they give no advantage to the prosecution. Similar notions motivated the Tokyo trial.

Beyond this, however, there was a more ambitious goal: to establish that leaders as well as citizens would be subject to international criminal law that would encompass not only traditional war crimes but atrocities committed during peacetime and the decision to go to war in the first place. As noted above, these were innovations for the most part. The Nuremberg and Tokyo trials had not only the backward-looking purpose of meting out punishment to those who deserved it; they had the forward-looking purpose of advancing international criminal law. This included developing the substantive rules, the procedures, and the idea that international tribunals, rather than domestic courts and military commissions, should have jurisdiction of international crimes. Ideally, if individuals in the future knew that they could be punished for the crimes of aggressive war, crimes against humanity, and also ordinary war crimes (also a subject of the Nuremberg trial, but not an innovation), they would be deterred from starting wars or conducting them too brutally. That the crimes were international, and that any tribunals would be international, would increase the likelihood of prosecution and punishment—one cannot avoid them simply by defeating a weak state.

Yet for a very long time, one would have thought that the Nuremberg and Tokyo trials had had no effect whatsoever. It was not until the 1990s that another international criminal tribunal was established. The usual explanation for the disappearance of international criminal law and international criminal tribunals from international relations is the cold war, but one should also note that the legacy of the tribunals was at best ambiguous.

Both tribunals convicted defendants and ordered jailing and executions, but both tribunals had numerous problems, as well. First, many of the charges were based on criminal law that did not exist at the time the acts in question were committed. There was no crime of "aggressive war" (and there still is not); nor were "crimes against humanity" a recognized legal category, though the term had been used a few times before. The prosecutions in Germany were based on the London Charter, a document signed by the United States, the Soviet Union, Britain, and France in 1945. Germany, of course, was not a party to this treaty. So Germany did not consent to its own nationals being subject to trial. As far as international law goes, this was a fatal defect in the legal basis of the trial. The trials were, in essence, administrative proceedings brought against a subject population pursuant to a decree of the victors.

Second, both tribunals were deprived of jurisdiction of crimes committed by the Allies. Thus, the laws that were invented for the trials were not even applied generally. Occasionally defendants were permitted to testify as to the practices of the Allies in order to show that they did not violate a norm of international law, but the *tu quoque* defense was barred. Germans and Japanese could be convicted of acts that, from a moral point of view, might have seemed less questionable than the fire bombing of German and Japanese cities, the atomic bombing of Japanese cities, and various atrocities committed by Allied soldiers, especially the Soviets, who massacred POWs and raped millions of German women. The Soviet leader (Stalin) responsible for the invasions of (that is, "aggressive war" against) Finland and the Baltic states was not subject to trial.

Third, both tribunals had elements of the show trial — that is, the effect of conscious manipulation by their sponsors to achieve certain political ends. The Nuremberg and Tokyo prosecutors sought as defendants representatives of important segments of the population. The German and Japanese publics needed to learn that the rot had spread throughout the military, the bureaucracy, and the industrial elite. A trial of four army generals would not be as effective as a trial of one general, one admiral, one diplomat, and one industrialist. At Nuremberg, Justice Jackson sought to implicate German industry, but when a natural choice—Gustav Krupp—turned out to be too ill to stand trial, Jackson's demand that his son Alfreid be substituted outraged the judges, and they refused.[4] In Japan, the prosecutors made sure not only to charge representatives of each component of the Japanese government but also that there were representatives from different time periods—during the attack on Manchuria as well as the attack on Pearl Harbor.[5] These choices all contributed to a satisfying narrative arc, but they also made the Allies vulnerable to the argument that the trial was intended for propaganda, not to establish the truth.

Why were these problems, rather than just the inevitable compromises that all institutions must make from time to time? The purpose of the trials was to show the world, including the citizens of Germany and Japan, the citizens of the victorious nations, and the governments of other countries, that there would be a new international order, one in which governments would not be permitted to engage in aggressive war, commit war crimes, and commit atrocities against their own citizens such as genocide. The penalty for violation would be criminal prosecution. The flip side of this stance was that nations that did not do any of these things had nothing to fear from the United States and the Soviet Union, or from any other major power.

The legalistic trappings of the trial would show that the victorious powers were not interested in eliminating any person who happened to be a threat to their international ambitions, nor even in exercising the traditional victor's prerogative of taking retribution or revenge. The victorious powers sought to punish only those who had, through their actions, endorsed the notions that aggressive war, genocide, and similar actions were legitimate forms of international action. To persuade the world of their good faith, the victorious powers had to give the defendants an opportunity to be heard, to show that they had not engaged in the actions that, under the new order, would be considered crimes. Otherwise, the world would have no reason to believe that the victors sought to create a new international order that involved some self-restraint on their own ambitions.

The problem was not so much one of victor's justice, but a more basic problem about world order. If the states that were pressing for new norms of international conduct had never complied with them, what reason was there to think that they could be sustainable?

The academic literature considers Nuremberg a success and Tokyo a failure. This might have more to do with the eloquence of the Nuremberg chief prosecutor, Robert Jackson, and the astonishing wickedness of the Nazi regime than anything else. The political theorist Judith Shklar argues that Nuremberg was a success because it advanced international criminal law even if it did not fully comply with legalistic norms itself; the Tokyo trial, she argues, was less successful because the prosecutor, Joseph Keenan, made natural law (that is, moral and quasi-religious) arguments rather than legal arguments.[6] This is surely an ironic criticism given that Jackson's legal arguments were so weak and, inasmuch as he could not admit this, lacking in candor. Jackson's appeal to positive law—such as the London Charter, which the Germans of course were not a party to, and the Kellogg-Briand Pact, which did not create individual criminal liability—were transparent subterfuges. Jackson was either implementing an administrative directive or, like Keenan, appealing to natural law or common morality, though unlike Keenan, not candidly.

The real problem with the Tokyo trial, as Shklar seems to acknowledge, is that the Japanese just could not be regarded as monsters in the same way that the Nazis could. The Japanese wars were not as clearly wars of aggression as the German wars were, or at least, they seemed more continuous with the traditional war-making activities of the Great Powers. Japanese soldiers committed numerous atrocities, but atrocities had long been a part of war, unlike the effort to exterminate an entire ethnic group, as the Nazis tried to do. So the moral argument against the Japanese was not as strong as the moral argument against the Germans.

But these are moral, not legal, categories. If the purpose of Nuremberg was to establish that national leaders could be held criminally responsible for aggressive wars and crimes against humanity, then Tokyo had to occur as well. And if Tokyo had to occur, so did trials of Allied leaders and soldiers who authorized invasions or engaged in atrocities. One can argue back and forth about whether Allied leaders were morally justified in bombing German and Japanese cities, but the Allied leaders were not willing to allow this decision to be made by an independent court under some general legal rule. That this did not happen made it clear that rules against invasions and atrocities were not generally applicable to the world, but would be applied in a discretionary fashion by the most powerful countries. Whether or not this was moral progress, it was opposed to legalism, which requires that the rules apply evenhandedly to all.[7]

THE HUMAN RIGHTS REGIME

Revulsion for the Nazis led to a parallel development: the establishment of the international human rights regime. The origin of the human rights regime can be conveniently dated to the Universal Declaration of Human Rights of 1948. This document was issued by a commission chaired by Eleanor Roosevelt, ratified by the General Assembly, and signed by most nations, though with a number of abstentions. It recognizes rights to life, liberty, security, privacy, property, trial before punishment, education, and equality before the law; and freedom of movement, thought, and religion. It forbids slavery, torture, arbitrary detention, discrimination, and restrictions on migration. It does much else in this vein.

The Universal Declaration of Human Rights was signed with a great deal of fanfare and enthusiasm, as such documents always are. But it was unclear what was supposed to happen next. Normally, when a state enters a treaty, it complies with the treaty in order to avoid offending the treaty partner, which will not comply with its obligations unless the first state obeys the treaty as well. This type of reciprocal logic, which was so important to international law as ordinarily understood, was entirely lacking in the human rights context. If France violated its obligations under a human rights treaty by (say) torturing Algerian natives, no one expected the United States to retaliate by depriving Americans of fair trials. Indeed, governments generally denied that the Universal Declaration of Human Rights was a treaty. But if it was not a treaty, what was it? Perhaps a political document that stated aspirations rather than obligations, but what was the good of that?

This had happened before, of course. The Kellogg-Briand Pact of 1928 purported to outlaw war, was ratified amidst much enthusiastic public celebration and much private government doubt about its legal effect, and had no impact on government behavior as far as anyone could tell. Would the Universal Declaration have the same fate? Anxiety about this possibility led to the creation of bureaucratic machinery, and more paper. Human rights committees and commissions at the UN and elsewhere were set up to monitor human rights compliance around the world and to agitate for stronger international legal obligations. This agitation led to a series of treaties, including the Genocide Convention (1951); the International Convention on the Elimination of All Forms of Racial Discrimination (1965); the International Covenant on Civil and Political Rights (1966); the International Covenant on Economic, Social, and Cultural Rights (ICESCR; 1966); the Convention Against Torture (1987); the Convention on the Rights of the Child (1987); and others. The ICCPR repeats and expands, with greater detail, on the list of "political" rights in the Universal Declaration — rights to political participation, protection against arbitrary criminal punishment, and so forth. The ICESCR repeats and expands on the list of "economic and social" rights in the Universal Declaration — rights to education, work, fair pay, and so forth. The Genocide Convention is a short document that recognizes that genocide is a criminal violation of international law. The other treaties perform similar tasks within the domain set out by their names.

WHY INTERNATIONAL CRIMES AND HUMAN RIGHTS

What accounts for the development of international criminal law and the international human rights regime after World War II? One answer is that the odious nature of the Nazi regime and the enormous destruction of the war persuaded decision makers that international security was connected to human rights. If states could be forced to respect the human rights of their citizens, then aggressive and militaristic regimes could not come into existence or would be immediately shunned and isolated by other countries, so that they would not be able to obtain the power to do harm. I will call this the "security theory of human rights." According to this theory, respect for human rights, compelled if possible by foreign states and international institutions, would enhance global security.

An alternative view is that World War II taught people that the human rights of people living in other countries mattered, were of legitimate concern to foreign states, prevailed over sovereign rights, and thus were an appropriate subject for global regulation. Of course, people cared about the well-being of foreigners prior to World War II, and especially of coethnics and coreligionists living in other countries. But World War II made clear that this kind of altruistic concern, which could motivate episodic interventions like the British humanitarian interventions in the Balkans in the nineteenth century, was not enough. It had to be institutionalized and made systematic; only then could human rights be protected and atrocities be deterred. I will call this the "legalistic theory of human rights." According to this theory, respect for human rights is a value in itself, perhaps an absolute value, to be pursued with as much effort as possible.

Neither of these theories necessarily leads to international criminal law. The idea of international criminal law is essentially the idea of making individuals responsible rather than states. Under classic international law, a state that violates a treaty, such as a human rights treaty, is subject to reprisals from other states, but the government officials who issue the orders or the underlings who carried out the orders are not subject to legal responsibility. International criminal law makes the responsible leaders and followers legally responsible, that is, subject to sanctions like jail time. International criminal law, then, is supposed to enhance the strength of the treaty obligation by making individuals reluctant to give or obey orders that are contrary to international obligations.

The human rights treaties do not (with some exceptions) by themselves create individual criminal liability; states alone have the obligations. This means that states alone can punish other states for failing to comply with the human rights treaties. However, some international human rights obligations, such as the prohibition of torture and genocide, have been criminalized. The reason that criminal sanctions follow more naturally from the legalistic theory than from the security theory is that legalism insists that all people are equally subject to the rules.[8]

Whichever theory is correct—and perhaps both are to some extent—the human rights and international criminal law regimes suffer from a significant defect. As noted above, treaties traditionally are enforced through reciprocity, but reciprocity cannot be the mechanism for enforcement of human rights. When the Rwandan government inflicted genocide on several hundred thousand Tutsis and moderate Hutus, it did not harm any other particular country, and thus no other particular country found it in its interest to retaliate or intervene. To prevent or punish the genocide, third party states must take it on themselves, unilaterally or in a group, to become involved. But a collective action problem severely hinders the response. As a result, even when all other countries agree that a particular government commits atrocities that cannot be justified, the response is likely to be weak. Today's genocide in Sudan confirms this unfortunate fact.

An additional problem is the ugly truth that it is not always correct and desirable to pressure a government to stop violating human rights. To put this point more precisely, governments violate the rights of their citizens because they believe that they should or must. In some cases, repressive measures are thought to be necessary to prevent or end a civil war or insurgency that is far worse than the repression itself or that could lead to a government that is worse than the existing government. Not all civil wars are wars for national liberation. The Taliban government of Afghanistan emerged from a civil war, and no one doubts that if the Shining Path guerillas had prevailed in their insurgency, their government would have been worse than what Peru has today. The United States supports repressive governments in Egypt, Saudi Arabia, and Pakistan, because it fears an Islamic revolution that would yield governments like Iran's in those countries. When Western states pressure weak governments to improve their human rights records, they risk undermining them and preparing the way for civil war. This is not always the case, of course, but it is often enough.

Finally, governments can rarely agree about when a government's human rights violations are egregious enough to warrant collective action, such as economic sanctions or military intervention. This is not purely a matter of honest disagreement; geopolitical rivalries shade governments' evaluations of regimes. During the cold war, the United States preferred to believe that its allies did not violate human rights as much as the Soviets' allies did, or at least that their allies were remediable while the Soviets' were not. Today, everyone recognizes that severe human rights violations occur in Sudan and North Korea, but China overlooks these violations because of its security and economic interests, just as the United States does for Egypt, Saudi Arabia, and Pakistan.

RESULTS: HUMAN RIGHTS

Global legalism is wedded to the idea that when international law is created, states obey it. The human rights treaty regime has been an embarrassment for this idea because it is evident that the treaty regime has either had no effect on the behavior of states or very little. This has not prevented legalists from claiming that the treaties have mattered, a claim that should not be dismissed lightly given the tremendous attention that human rights receive in the media and public debate. The truth, as always, is complex.

A straightforward prediction based on legalistic assumptions is that when a state enters a human rights treaty, it will stop violating human rights or it will not start violating human rights in conditions (such as a new insurgency) where it would in the absence of the treaty obligation. For example, a state that enters the Convention Against Torture will direct its police or military to stop torturing people; if the state did not already tolerate torture, then the treaty will prevent it from doing so if for some reason the temptation to torture increases—as could be the case if a new threat arises or a new government comes to power that does not have the scruples of an older government.

Is this what happens? Yugoslavia signed the Genocide Convention in 1948, yet a genocide occurred in that state in the early 1990s during the Yugoslavian civil war. Cambodia acceded to the Genocide Convention in 1950, yet a genocide occurred in that state in the mid-1970s. Rwanda acceded to the convention in 1975, yet a genocide occurred there in 1994. Sudan acceded to the convention as recently as 2003, yet the government seems to be complicit in genocide today. To be sure, many countries that ratified or acceded to the Genocide Convention have not committed genocides. Sweden ratified the convention in 1952 and has not engaged in genocide since then. But we can be confident that Sweden would not have committed a genocide even if it had not ratified the convention, and the same could be said about almost all the other states that ratified the convention and then refrained from engaging in genocide. Genocide has never been a very attractive policy, and genocides have been exceedingly rare in modern history. The treaty regime has had no observable impact on the propensity of states to engage in genocide.

Genocide is an extreme case, but similar comments can be made about the other human rights treaties. One hundred forty-four states belong to the Convention Against Torture; many of those states, possibly most of them, engage in torture. A recent Human Rights Watch report identifies China, Egypt, Indonesia, Iran, Iraq, Israel, Malaysia, Morocco, Nepal, North Korea, Pakistan, Russia, Syria, Turkey, Uganda, and Uzbekistan.[9] Iran, Iraq, Malaysia, North Korea, Pakistan, and Syria have not ratified the convention; all the others have. Torture is in fact common in many other states—not always as a matter of official policy but often tolerated, especially when it is conducted by security services against insurgents, separatists, or political dissidents, or by hard-to-control local police. The United States, to all appearances, has violated its treaty obligation not to engage in torture; and some European states, by participating in programs that send suspected terrorists to states where they are likely to be tortured, appear to have been complicit.

The ICCPR guarantees political rights of the sort to which Westerners have become accustomed. Its members include such authoritarian states as Algeria (acceded 1989), Belarus (1973), China (1998), Egypt (1982), Iraq (1971), Jordan (1975), North Korea (1981), Russia (as of 1973!), Syria (1969), and Turkmenistan (1997). With 160 parties, nearly all the countries in the world, the ICCPR sweeps in states with all kinds of political systems, many of them decidedly lacking in commitment to liberal rights.

Several scholars have tried to examine more systematically whether states that are parties to human rights treaties are more likely to respect human rights than states that are not parties to human rights treaties. The results are mixed, with some scholars finding no or negative correlation and others finding small positive correlations.[10] Rigorous analysis is difficult because coding human rights violations is an uncertain process. Further, states disagree about what the treaty obligations mean, many states have entered treaties with reservations that limit their own obligations, and there are so many confounding factors. Consider, for example, Hungary, which ratified the ICCPR in 1974. At that time, Hungary was a Communist dictatorship, which would last for another fifteen years. Today, Hungary has a significantly more liberal and democratic system. So over time it has come into compliance with its obligations under the ICCPR, but it is difficult to believe that its ratification of the ICCPR decades earlier was a causal factor. The immediate causes of Hungary's liberalization were the collapse of the Soviet Union, which lost its hold on Hungary; the accompanying loss of faith in the Communist system around the world; and Hungary's desire to integrate with Europe, which demanded as a condition substantial liberal reform. In many cases, the same forces that lead to the overthrow of a dictator and liberalization of the political system also cause the new government to ratify human rights treaties; in these cases, treaty ratification is an effect, not a cause.

188 ‡ CHAPTER EIGHT

Some scholars have argued that human rights treaties made their influence felt in more subtle and indirect, but still real, ways. The Helsinki
Accords of 1975 were an effort by the West and the Soviet bloc to ease
cold war tensions. In return for Western recognition of national borders
in Eastern Europe that the Soviet Union imposed after World War II,
the Soviet Union and its allies agreed to respect human rights, including those cataloged in the Universal Declaration and the various human
rights treaties. The Helsinki Accords did not cause an observable change
in the behavior of the Communist governments, but they did provide some
encouragement to dissidents in the Communist states, who set up various
Helsinki committees and invoked the Helsinki obligations when criticizing their governments for suppressing political dissent. The pressure of
these dissidents, the story continues, contributed to the collapse of the Soviet Union and its satellites.[11]

Maybe. But if this theory is correct, why didn't North Korea's accession
to the ICCPR in 1981 doom its authoritarian government? The Soviet
Union collapsed because, unlike China, it was unable to salvage its economy by adopting market principles. Also contributing to its collapse was
the U.S.-led decades-long policy of containment that isolated the Soviet
Union, prevented it from engaging in colonial expansion, and embroiled
it in ruinous proxy wars. The policy of containment involved, among other
things, supporting dictatorships and insurgencies that countered Soviet
influence, including South Korea, South Vietnam, Pakistan, South Africa,
the Philippines, Guatemala, Honduras, China, the Contras in Nicaragua,
the insurgents in Afghanistan, Franco's Spain, Iran prior to the revolution,
and so on. The trade-off was unavoidable. If the United States isolated
and pressured a dictatorship that violated human rights, then the dictator
would threaten to switch to the Soviet side. If the dictator switched to the
Soviet side, then Soviet power would advance. The Soviet Union was a
greater threat to human rights than any other nation was, so even if the
U.S. government cared about nothing aside from human rights, it would
be a difficult question whether it advanced human rights best by opposing all human rights violations (and thus driving many nations into the
Soviet camp) or by tolerating them with the goal of putting pressure on
the Soviet Union. And, of course, the tradeoff was much more complicated
than this.

It would be surprising, then, if a nation with a history of human rights abuses could bring an end to that abuse merely by entering a human rights treaty. The human rights abuses occurred because the government believed that it had to engage in them in order to stay in power or maintain the peace or defeat an insurgency, or that it had to tolerate them by the military or security services or local police in order to maintain their loyalty. Perhaps the government enters the treaty because of U.S. pressure or because of a desire to express an aspiration, or to reassure political opponents or investors. But it would turn out that the United States and other countries (which in any event rarely concerned themselves about these issues) could not pressure the nation in question to improve its human rights practices because doing so would only weaken a weak state and risk civil war, insurgency, Soviet influence, and the like. At least, the United States could not do so systematically; only, at best, episodically and without any significant carrots or sticks.

There is yet another view, one much more ambitious than the claim that states comply with human rights treaties that they enter. This is the view that human rights norms, or at least the most important human rights norms, have achieved the status of jus cogens—they bind even states that do not consent to human rights treaties, or try to add reservations or understandings that undercut their treaty-based human rights obligations. This view is most popular in Europe, where global constitutionalism has seemed like the next logical step for global legalism.

The jus cogens view is based on a scattering of doctrinal sources, but it is impossible to reconcile it with the realities of international behavior. It is, in fact, mainly a view advanced by Europeans, especially European legal academics. But the world is not Europe. If you look at a list at the top ten most populous states of the world, you will notice that exactly zero of them are European countries. Germany appears at number 13, right after Vietnam, while France appears at number 19, after Iran. The top ten states, which comprise almost 60 percent of the world's population are (in order): China, India, the United States, Indonesia, Brazil, Pakistan, Bangladesh, Nigeria, Russia, and Japan. None of these states, with the increasingly controversial exception of the United States, is a champion of human rights, and several of them are major human rights violators. If we aggregate the European states and treat them as one, then the European

Union ranks third, but still its population accounts for only about 8 percent of the global population. Its views of international law do not supersede those of the rest of the world.

What of the fact that no major nation denies that jus cogens norms exist? In practice, states agree that jus cogens norms exist, they can agree at a high level of abstraction about the content of some of these norms (for example, the prohibition on genocide), but they interpret these norms differently in the application, with the result that state practice does not conform to the official position—or, interpreted differently, the content of jus cogens norms is so minimal in practice as not to make a much of a difference in world affairs.[12]

The postwar human rights treaty regime is best seen, then, as an expression of an increasingly popular view around the world, and especially in the West, that the human rights abuses in other countries are a matter of general concern. Perhaps this reflected moral progress or perhaps it just reflected a lesson of World War II—that the type of regime that commits internal abuses will eventually become a threat to its neighbors. Whatever the case, identification of the goal—the reduction of human rights abuses—was only the beginning. It was then necessary to develop some mechanism or institution that implemented the goal. The traditional means would be diplomatic pressure, but the legalistic mentality insisted on using legalistic means for achieving the political goal. This led to the development of the treaties and the accompanying infrastructure of committees, commissions, and courts. But the legalistic means could not overcome the global collective action problem, here exacerbated by geopolitical rivalries and the fundamental ambiguities about whether human rights are best advanced through systematic isolation or engagement.

A NOTE ON HUMAN RIGHTS COURTS

There are two functional international—actually regional—human rights courts: the European Court of Human Rights and the Inter-American Court of Human Rights. There are also a number of international bodies that have some quasi-judicial power to evaluate states' human rights practices. The Human Rights Council is an institution of the United Nations that has limited power to monitor and review the human rights practices of states. It replaced the UN Commission on Human Rights in 2006, which was dominated by human rights–abusing states and was heavily criticized for focusing on Israel and ignoring most of the rest of the world. The Human Rights Council has, so far, no better a record. There are also various human rights committees connected to the various universal human rights treaties, such as the International Covenant on Civil and Political Rights.

As noted in chapter 7, the ECHR has a full docket and a great deal of respect, and its rulings appear to be obeyed, at least much of the time. The IACHR's record is more mixed; however, it seems to have improved in recent years, possibly in connection with the overall improvement in democracy in Latin America. Neither institution, however, can be said to have had a substantial impact on human rights practices. The ECHR's members are mostly advanced democracies with a strong inclination to respect human rights. A similar pattern appears with respect to the IACHR in Latin America. States are simply too powerful and, at the same time, too subject to inertia, to be responsive to adverse rulings from human rights courts, and this is in part because the states themselves design these courts so that they have limited reach. Thus, global legalists have placed most of their hope for the advance of international criminal law in international criminal courts that enforce international criminal law.

RESULT: INTERNATIONAL CRIMINAL LAW

International criminal law can be thought of as an effort to give the human rights regime teeth. In the case of the worst atrocities, leaders fear not only diplomatic pressure and the other consequences (if any) of violating a human rights treaty; they also must fear that they will eventually be captured, tried, and convicted for their crimes. Of course, leaders will already fear that domestic opponents and domestic insurgents might take revenge against them, whether that revenge takes a legal form or not; international criminal law adds the possibility that foreign prosecutors will bring their often superior resources to bear. Pinochet, for example, was protected from domestic prosecution as a result of various agreements and political temporizing, but when he traveled to the United Kingdom for medical treatment, he was nearly extradited to Spain where a judge had launched criminal proceedings against him. Slobodan Milošević and other leaders of factions in the Yugoslavian civil wars were not vulnerable to prosecution at home, but as a result of international pressure he and others were turned over to the International Criminal Tribunal for the Former Yugoslavia in the Hague, which has spent hundreds of millions of dollars on such prosecutions. The international criminal law regime, then, should deter human rights atrocities at the margin.

As we have seen, however, dictators and their followers have had little to fear from international criminal law. Nuremberg and Tokyo may have stimulated paper developments—the Genocide Convention, for example—but they did not lead to additional international prosecutions. The usual explanation for this failure is the cold war. But although cold war rivalries made international cooperation more difficult, they did not make them impossible—as the human rights treaty regime shows. The problem lay in the basic logic of the international criminal trial.

As we saw before, the designers of the Nuremberg and Tokyo trials refused to give the tribunals jurisdiction over alleged crimes committed by the allies. The natural interpretation of this decision was that international criminal law is not universal but conditional. Some act, X, is an international criminal offense *only if you are not on our side*. The relevant "side," at the time of Nuremberg and Tokyo, was of course that of the Allies.

The Nuremberg prosecutors and judges would not admit this fact, which undermined the legalistic ambition of the tribunal and showed it for what it was—an administrative procedure designed to implement the allies' goal of punishing the worst war criminals in proportion to their crimes, and to make the case for the allies before the world's public. But the tension between the universalistic/legalistic public relations and the particularistic reality was everywhere evident.

Throughout the trial the prosecutors and judges feared that the defendants would argue that (1) the war crimes committed by the Nazis were matched by war crimes committed by the Allies; and (2) Germany's behavior was justified by the Treaty of Versailles and was abetted by the British and the French during the 1930s, who ratified many of the formal violations of the Versailles Treaty by the Germans, and further by Russia, which cooperated with Germany in many ways.[13] Although not many citizens of Allied nations would be receptive to these arguments, German citizens might have been; thus, the trial, like the Versailles Treaty itself, could become a rallying point for unreconstructed Nazis and nationalists in Germany.

Although the defendants did make these arguments, they did not have the expected effect. The Germans at first ignored the trial, regarding it as irrelevant or an exercise in allied propaganda. But then something surprising happened: the Germans began to feel that they were themselves on trial. The trial made clear the vast participation of ordinary citizens in the Nazi extermination machine.

That had never been Jackson's intention. He, like many others, had hoped to prune out Nazism and induce healthy growth in remaining Germany. The idea of German guilt had not appeared in the indictment. It had emerged during the trial.[14]

But a guilty nation was not a nation that could rejoin the world community as a liberal democracy. If there was something wrong with Germans, how could they be given political responsibility? And the notion of German guilt would become particularly difficult for the Americans as it became clear, partway through the trial, and to the premature delight of the defendants, that Germany would be America's ally in the incipient cold war against the Soviet Union.[15] Polling data suggest that the Germans initially thought that the trial was fair, but after a few years there was a dramatic change in attitudes and by the 1950s the dominant view was that the trials were unfair and the convictions were victor's justice.[16]

The Tokyo war crimes tribunal had the opposite but equally unwelcome effect. The Japanese did not feel themselves on trial, or guilty, though they were horrified when they learned about the atrocities committed by their soldiers. But as bad as their soldiers were, they did not seem any worse than the Americans, who had killed hundreds of thousands of civilians through fire bombing and atomic bombing. The trial gave the defendants an opportunity to defend Japan's militarism, an opportunity seized by Hideki Tōjō, and with great success.[17] Tōjō argued that Japan had acted in self-defense against colonial aggression. "Only victor nations sat on the Bench, many of them colonial powers with far longer records of imperialism than Japan — and they allowed the colonies they were intent on regaining no place among the judges."[18] The trial suggested the moral equivalence of the victors and vanquished with respect to aggression, but the victors had a monopoly on hypocrisy.

A great problem for the Tokyo trials was the decision by the United States, made prior to the initiation of the trial, to allow the Japanese emperor to retain his throne. As a result, he could not be on trial, even though he was the one person who had formal—and probably personal—responsibility for all aspects of Japan's aggression. Trying to tie together disparate defendants in a conspiracy when the one person they had in common was absent was a nearly impossible task.[19] The United States had its reasons for immunizing the emperor: American officials believed that a cooperative emperor was their best means for persuading Japan to surrender and then governing it. Here, as at Nuremberg, the need to cooperate with defeated officials and leaders warred with the desire to do justice, and the result was a message with little educative value, at least little that would directly serve the interests of the United States. The trial was widely regarded as a political failure.[20] Japanese did not see the trial as a vindication of the rule of law but as victor's justice. The trial may have contributed to a resurgence of nationalism during the postwar years.[21]

However, nationalism did not reassert itself in all quarters, and one historian argues that the trial—because it was a caricature of justice—contributed to postwar Japanese pacifism. "The crimes revealed by the trial, compounded by the perception that this was a world gone mad with violence and that such crimes against peace and humanity were not unique to Japan, reinforced the deep aversion to militarization and war that had come with defeat."[22] If this was the lesson that the Japanese drew from the trial, it certainly was not the lesson intended by the Americans, who sought Japan as an ally against the Soviet Union, and who not only abandoned further war crimes prosecutions after the Tokyo trial was over but (like in Germany) cooperated with and supported war criminals, including a future prime minister, who could be useful in the cold war.[23]

The cold war and the UN system made it clear that no tribunals would be created, at least in the short term, without the consent of the United States and the Soviet Union, and so leaders could immunize themselves against criminal liability by becoming an ally of either the United States or of the Soviet Union, that is, one of the two great power blocs. There was no other realistic alternative anyway, and so the possibility of a repetition of Nuremberg or Tokyo could not deter any dictator from committing crimes.

Then the cold war ended. The civil war broke out in Yugoslavia in 1991. Wars between Croatia, Serbia, and various factions in Bosnia-Herzegovina resulted in the murder, torture, and displacement of hundreds of thousands of people. Each side sought to consolidate its hold on disputed territory by murdering and expelling civilians who belonged to the ethnic or religious group associated with another side. This was called ethnic cleansing, and it often verged on, or was, genocide. The insertion of peacekeeping troops by the United Nations had little effect, but eventually a combination of diplomacy, economic pressure, and military pressure led to the Dayton resolution of the conflict in Bosnia in 1995. Other conflicts wound down. However, the Serbs had begun using repressive measures against a separatist movement of ethnic Albanians in the Serbian province of Kosovo. In response, NATO launched an air assault on Serbian forces and economic infrastructure, which led to Serbian withdrawal from Kosovo and de facto independence.

The UN could not agree to a forceful military intervention to end the civil war and instead established the International Criminal Tribunal for the Former Yugoslavia, which was given jurisdiction of international crimes committed by participants in the civil war. The tribunal was helpless during the first few years of its operations because the UN, without a major presence on Yugoslavian territory, could not arrest suspects, and none of the warring factions had any interest in turning over war criminals — theirs or captured enemies — to a court in the Hague. But with the winding down of the war, the presence of UN and NATO forces was sufficient to permit police operations; in addition, eventually the various states turned over some war criminals in response to international pressure. As of July 2008, the ICTY had indicted 161 persons and concluded proceedings of 115 of them. Of these, 56 have been sentenced. Many of the defendants were small fry but some, such as Slobodan Milošević, were important figures, though Milošević died during his lengthy trial.

Meanwhile, in 1994, the president of Rwanda, Juvénal Habyarimana, was assassinated, and in the following four months, the Hutu-dominated government unleashed a savage attack on the Tutsi minority and moderate Hutus. Around eight hundred thousand people were murdered before a Tutsi rebel group led by Paul Kagame overthrew the government. The UN did not intervene; UN military forces stationed in Rwanda at the start of the genocide were not given the authority or the means to stop the slaughter. Instead, the UN established another tribunal, modeled on the ICTY, and gave it jurisdiction of international crimes committed in

Rwanda. The International Criminal Tribunal for Rwanda has convicted twenty-eight defendants. The Security Council has ordered the ICTY and the ICTR to wind up business.

Have the ICTY and ICTR been successful? Many thousands of people in the former Yugoslavia and Rwanda committed serious international crimes, and only a tiny fraction of them were tried and convicted. In Bosnia and elsewhere in the former Yugoslavia, most of the others simply went free. In Rwanda, the government installed by Kagame warehoused thousands in jails and subjected them and others to informal (by Western standards) tribal forms of justice — the Gacaca court.

Oddly, the two courts turned out to have opposite effects in the two areas. In Yugoslavia, few wrongdoers were punished by local authorities, as wrongdoers could take refuge with coethnics in Bosnia, or in friendly countries like Serbia, and local institutions in Bosnia after the war were weak. The handful who were captured by or turned over to NATO forces and sent to the Hague were losers of a negative lottery. In Rwanda, the government had ample interest in punishing genocide participants, and the lucky few who found themselves taken to Arusha, where the ICTR trials were held, could depend on fairer procedures and a more comfortable jail cell. The accomplishment of the ICTY was to ensure that a number of major figures were tried along with the many small fry; otherwise, these figures would probably have escaped justice.[24] But the same cannot be said for the ICTR.[25]

Against these ambiguous benefits, one needs to measure the costs. There was a backlash in Serbia against the ICTY; nonetheless, Serbia has been gradually liberalizing. However, Bosnia remains a fractured and dangerous place, and if the trials were intended to advance political integration, they surely failed. In Rwanda, the view seems to be that the court (located in Tanzania) is too remote and far away, and could do little of value for a small, poor country where thousands of people were guilty of participating in a genocide.[26]

The monetary costs have also not been trivial; for example, the ICTY and the ICTR had a joint two-year budget of $545 million in 2006–2007, more than one-eighth of the UN's entire budget.[27] As noted above, through July 2008 the ICTY and the ICTR have convicted only a few dozen defendants. The trials on a per-day basis did not cost much more than the trials in federal court in the United States; the vast expanse and paltry results occurred because the average international trial is so much longer. Most federal criminal trials last only one day and only a trivial percentage last for more than a few weeks. By contrast, the average ICTY trial has lasted about a year.[28]

It has been argued that these figures do not reflect badly on international justice because cases involving mass atrocities are more complex than ordinary domestic criminal cases, and so it is not surprising that they take longer.[29] However, the complexity of the cases was not the whole story. Not every case had to reestablish the facts from the ground up; evidence collected for one case can be used for another; so can an earlier case's factual findings when they bear on a later case. The most likely reason for the length of time is that the courts, by design and in practice, needed to be as fair as possible, fair enough to satisfy, or at least address, the suspicions of the public whose members are being tried. This problem is intimately connected with the whole problem of international justice, when people from different nations have a different sense of what is just, and have trouble overcoming their national prejudices. Courts can operate successfully only when their audience largely agrees on the goals of the criminal law and can trust judges and other court staff. At the international level, these premises are hard to achieve. Instead, judges offer more process, but process by itself cannot satisfy suspicions about the motives of the judges and the states that pick them.[30]

The tribunals provided a measure of justice for victims that might otherwise (at least, in the Balkans, unlike Rwanda, where the government had ample incentive to prosecute the wrongdoers, though inadequate resources) have not happened. But if this is all the trials did, or could do, then it seems doubtful that international criminal law is sustainable as an institution. Unprosecuted wrongs of a serious nature, including unprosecuted international crimes, are an extremely common feature throughout the world — in many countries, because the government commits international crimes (such as torture) or because the government does not have the resources to prosecute international crimes committed by individuals including both ordinary citizens and officials. There is little reason to think that foreign nations would routinely pick up this slack by sponsoring international tribunals. Indeed, during the 1990s and the first decade of the twenty-first century, one can list atrocities in places such as Sudan, North Korea, Egypt, Iran, and many others. If you include relatively routine injustices such as detention without trial, police torture, and the like, the list could be extended to nearly every developing country in the world. With limited exceptions, there has been no serious effort by foreign governments to prosecute these crimes.

The vast investment in international criminal prosecution might therefore seem questionable. Doing justice is important, but what is the rationale for doing justice under such limited conditions? And wouldn't financial and diplomatic resources be better spent on improving security, rebuilding infrastructure, and establishing viable domestic institutions? For global legalists, the advance of the international rule of law must take precedence over these other agendas. For them, the only lesson of the past is that international criminal law must be expanded. The rules must be fleshed out and extended, and the judicial system must be made global in scope, permanent, and independent. This agenda led to the establishment of the International Criminal Court.

THE RECENT PAST AND LIKELY FUTURE OF THE INTERNATIONAL CRIMINAL COURT

The ICC was created by the Statute of Rome, which was opened for signature in 1998 and entered into force on July 1, 2002, when the required number of sixty states ratified it.[31] Under the treaty, the ICC has jurisdiction over war crimes, crimes against humanity, genocide, and, after further negotiations are completed, aggressive war. The ICC would hear cases, for example, of the deliberate targeting of civilians by commanders, the torture and execution of prisoners of war, or the systematic effort to destroy a national, racial, or ethnic group. Until establishment of the ICC, enforcement of the laws of war relied primarily upon domestic legal systems, and states generally have been reluctant to punish their leaders or former leaders for war crimes.[32]

Rather than resolving disputes between states, the Court adjudicates prosecutions of individual defendants. The prosecutions are brought by a special international prosecutor. The ICC exercises its jurisdiction over crimes (1) committed by a national of a state party, or (2) that occur on the territory of a state party when committed by the national of a nonstate party. While focused on individual conduct, the Rome Statute makes an important nod to states. It incorporates the principle of "complementarity," which provides that the court will not hear a case if a state party with jurisdiction investigates or prosecutes the conduct in good faith.[33] If, however, the prosecutor can show that the state has conducted its investigation or prosecution in bad faith, it can bring the case to the ICC.

The court is composed of eighteen permanent judges who are elected by an assembly of the state parties for nonrenewable terms of six or nine years, or renewable three-year terms. They must be nationals of the state parties. The office of the prosecutor is also filled with a person selected by the state parties, for a nonrenewable nine-year term. The state parties have no control over the prosecutor's decision as to what investigations to undertake, what prosecutions to bring, and how to conduct the trial. The prosecutor's decisions on these matters are, however, subject to review by the court itself.

The ICC is independent of the United Nations Security Council. As we saw, recent war crimes tribunals, such as the ad hoc tribunals for the former Yugoslavia and Rwanda, were created by the Security Council. Proponents of the ICC believed, however, that the veto enjoyed by the permanent members of the Security Council (China, France, Great Britain, Russia, and the United States) would undermine the universality of international criminal justice by allowing them to exempt themselves and their allies from the jurisdiction of a new court.[34] While the Security Council may refer cases to the ICC prosecutor, and it may delay prosecutions for renewable twelve-month terms, it may not actually prevent an ICC case from going forward.

However, the ICC, like all other international tribunals, relies on the good will of states. The ICC prosecutor has no independent authority to conduct investigations, gather evidence, interview witnesses, and arrest suspects on the territory of state parties. Instead, the prosecutor must ask state parties to perform these functions for it. In addition, the prosecutor must request that state parties surrender individual defendants for transfer to the seat of the court. A good example of the difficulties on this point is presented by the ICTY's ability to gain jurisdiction over Slobodan Milošević. It was not the ICTY's demands that led to his apprehension and transfer; rather, the United States' military and diplomatic pressure on Serbia, including a threat to withhold half a billion dollars in IMF and U.S. economic aid resulted in his transfer to the ICTY in the Hague.[35] The ICTY did as well as it did because the EU and the United States had an interest in normalizing political conditions in the former Yugoslav territory and believed that prosecuting international criminals served that interest.[36] The ICTR did much more poorly, at least initially, because its mission conflicted with the interest of East African states to which criminal suspects fled, and it had no ability to compel those states to arrest and turn over those people. Its effectiveness was hostage to the political situation among those states.[37] The Rome Statute does not provide for any sanction if a state party obstructs the prosecutor's efforts. This has led some commentators to observe that the ICC prosecutor's institutional weakness could undermine the court.[38]

All of this makes one wonder whether the ICC can be an effective court. Although the Rome Statute is aimed at individual defendants, the ICC's jurisdiction strikes at the heart of state interests. Prosecutions will inevitably raise questions concerning both the legality of a decision by a state to use force and the legality of the tactics used by a state under international law (both jus in bellum and jus ad bello). As Madeline Morris has observed, "In ICC cases in which a state's national is prosecuted for an official act that the state maintains was lawful or that the state maintains did not occur, the lawfulness or the occurrence of that official state act ... would form the very subject matter of the dispute."[39] In addition, states with military forces that operate abroad will fear that soldiers and their commanders, including the highest political authorities responsible for military activities, will be dragged in front of an international court for war crimes prosecution, and be inconvenienced and embarrassed even if not punished. And then, because the definitions of international crimes are so vague, soldiers and officials might find themselves punished for activities that they consider legal and routine.[40] Because of these concerns, the United States not only has withdrawn its signature from the Statute of Rome, but it has launched an aggressive diplomatic campaign to protect American soldiers and civilians from its reach.[41]

The withdrawal of the United States, which can be traced directly to the independence of the court (that is, the lack of an American Security Council veto that could be used to block prosecution of Americans or the nationals of allies) was a blow to the ICC. As the nation that has taken the lead in conducting peacekeeping and humanitarian missions throughout the world, the United States would have been particularly vulnerable to the jurisdiction of the ICC. The other major states that conduct military activities or have strong military concerns have also refused to ratify the Rome Statutes. These states include China, India, Israel, Pakistan, and Russia.[42] Like the United States, these states will pressure state parties not to extradite their nationals to the seat of the ICC if those nationals are found on the state parties' territories. Although not all states will bow to this pressure, those that do will be in violation of their obligations under the Rome Statute; indeed, those that have signed bilateral immunity agreements with the United States arguably are already failing to comply with the Rome Statute.[43]

As time passes and more states put pressure on other states to violate their obligations under the ICC, the only remaining state parties will be states that do not conduct significant military activities on foreign territory. War criminals will appear before the ICC only in those rare cases where they are nationals of a defeated state whose new government seeks to acquire international legitimacy. Operations like those performed by the Yugoslavia and Rwanda tribunals — classic ex post tribunals whose jurisdictions and powers are defined after the events so that the states that establish them may immunize themselves — may in the future be performed by the ICC, but this is just to say that with its wings clipped the ICC will not represent an advance in international adjudication.

Events so far are consistent with this prediction. The ICC has not yet claimed jurisdiction over nationals of a member state who objects to this jurisdiction. Instead, it has been used in an ad hoc fashion to investigate and try international criminals in discrete situations. The governments of Uganda, the Democratic Republic of Congo, and the Central African Republic have requested ICC investigations, and the ICC has complied. In Uganda, further, the government has had second thoughts, as the ICC indictments of leaders of the Lord's Resistance Army have interfered with peace negotiations to end a spectacularly gruesome civil war.[44] The ICC has launched an investigation of international crimes in Sudan at the behest of the Security Council; the Sudanese government, which is complicit in those crimes, has predictably denied that the ICC has jurisdiction.

The legalist responds to these problems by urging the ICC to develop rules that constrain prosecutorial and judicial discretion. The rules would ensure that prosecutions are nonpolitical, which, in this context, would mean broadly in the interest of all or nearly all states.[45] Perhaps, for example, prosecutions would be limited to the worst atrocities. But the states that established the ICC were unable to agree on such limitations, so it seems questionable that the ICC itself would have the authority or inclination to impose them on itself, and, in any event, such self-limitations would be unenforceable. The supporters of the ICC created an institution with considerable discretion precisely because they realized that a rule-bound institution with narrow jurisdiction would not be able to do justice.

Indeed, the ICC is in danger of becoming an International Criminal Court for Africa. As noted, all four of its actions have taken place in Africa, and there are other candidates there as well. Meanwhile, the defenders of the ICC have tried to allay the fears of the United States and other countries that have refused to subject themselves to the jurisdiction of the ICC because of fears of politically motivated prosecutions by noting that under the principle of complementarity, the ICC has no power to investigate international crimes in states that engage in good-faith investigations and prosecutions. If this argument is correct, then the ICC's practical jurisdiction will extend only to African nations and other poor nations with weak institutions. It is only a matter of time before these nations, following the precedent of Serbia, object that they are being picked on by powerful Western nations who are engaging in yet another form of colonial domination.

If this argument is incorrect, then the fears of the powerful states are correct, and they have every reason to refuse to ratify the Rome Statute. Indeed, one suspects that the ICC prosecutor's office will come under pressure from developing nations to show that it is not a tool of colonial oppressors by bringing prosecutions against first-world states. Only such a prosecution could demonstrate that the universalistic pretentions of the Rome Statute are not a sham. Meanwhile, the ICC's prosecutor has received criticism for launching a prosecution of Omar al-Bashir, the president of Sudan. The critics fear that the prosecution will undermine efforts to bring peace to the country and endanger humanitarian workers there.[46] But this is just to say that the prosecutor has failed to display political sensitivity, that is, sensitivity to the interests of powerful states, which is exactly what one would expect from an independent officer.

In sum, there are two causes for concern. On the one hand, where the ICC is potentially effective, it needs to exercise political discretion to determine whether prosecutions and trials will advance or interfere with attempts to settle violent conflicts. On the other hand, if the ICC has such discretion, its targets will be able to accuse it of serving the interests of powerful states unless it brings prosecutions against those states as well. But if it does, it will lose the support of those states.[47]

The ideal of legalism runs aground on the realities of power. If a legalistic institution is created, states will starve it of funds, or ignore it, or work around it, because the institution treats all states as equal although they are not. If the creators of the institution hedge it with restrictions so that it is consistent with the realities of power politics, then it will not be legalistic. There are two recurrent outcomes: first, an institution that frankly is not legalistic or whose legalism is highly limited—this is the UN Security Council; second, an institution that is formally legalistic but it is either ignored or its rules are ignored. This seems the likely fate of the ICC.

All this said, it is too early to pronounce the ICC a failure. If it were, how do we explain that so many states ratified the ICC? Beth Simmons and Allison Danner have argued that authoritarian states with a recent violent past have joined the ICC as a way to credibly commit not to permit atrocities in the future—or, more precisely, to raise the cost of committing future atrocities.[48] The governments of many of these states are anxious to persuade domestic groups, foreign investors, and others that the governments are committed to the rule of law, but because they have weak domestic legal institutions, they cannot persuade anyone of this by simply passing new laws because no one expects them to be enforced. Joining the ICC solves this problem; enforcement now lies in the hands of foreigners with better rule of law values. Simmons and Danner point out that authoritarian states with recent violent pasts have joined the ICC enthusiastically, along with peaceful democracies like Sweden, which face no realistic chance of ever seeing a national brought before the court.

This argument raises two questions. First, if the main advantage of the ICC is to help authoritarian states commit themselves to the rule of law, why have so many people objected to the United States' refusal to join the institution? The United States, whatever its defects, is not an authoritarian state and has adequate domestic judicial institutions. Indeed, there is no particular reason to object to America's efforts to compel its allies to commit not to send Americans to the ICC. And yet these efforts have produced a loud outcry. Here, we see the legalist rejection of the pragmatic goals that

Simmons and Danner attribute to the ICC. Legalists are not interested in giving authoritarian states a means to credibly commit, though they would not object, either. They seek the global rule of law, which means that all states must be treated the same.

Second, as Simmons and Danner acknowledge, the pragmatic goals they attribute to the ICC can be achieved only if in fact the ICC treaty turns out to be enforceable. But is this likely? For it to work as designed, member states must collaborate in turning over criminals. If Simmons and Danner are right that the ICC is meant to be a commitment mechanism, then the authoritarian states that join the institution will not turn over criminals unless compelled by other states — and then one faces, once again, the collective action problem.

Whatever the motivations of authoritarian states, the ICC is seen in Europe as the culmination of international efforts to see to it that perpetrators of significant human rights abuse be subject to judicial process. This legalistic view opposes the American view, which was that the ICC would act only at the behest of the Security Council — a useful instrument for the Great Powers when, as in the Balkans and Rwanda, they believed that a court might help resolve troublesome conflicts. At least in its first few years, the ICC has acted consistently with the narrow American view, which is to say — hardly at all, and then only with the acquiescence of powerful states against weak countries. If this practice should continue, the ICC will share the fate of other courts founded on legalistic ambitions that could not survive the realities of power.

INTERNATIONAL CRIMINAL LAW, HUMAN RIGHTS LAW, AND GLOBAL LEGALISM

On the security theory of human rights law, Western states agreed to human rights treaties that do not significantly curtail their freedom of action and that make clear that they regard certain types of human rights violations presumptive threats to international security. Developing countries have been dragged into this regime, but formal ratification has not resulted in significant improvement in human rights records. Human rights concerns have thus remained as a floating excuse for military intervention that may be actually motivated by other concerns — the interventions in

Kosovo in 1999, Iraq in 2003, and Georgia in 2008, are the salient examples. On this view, the human rights courts, commissions, and committees are marginal institutions that have fleshed out some of the vague provisions of the treaties, and hence have clarified the types of activity that meet with first-world disapproval, but have had no discernable impact on actual practice.

There is a similar security theory of international criminal law. Western states after World War II sought to deter future wars started by aggressive nations like Nazi Germany, but World War I had taught them that punishing such states by requiring them to pay reparations can do more harm than good. Reparations must be paid by the entire population, and they thus can create resentments that in the long term destabilize, rather than improve, international relations. As an experiment, the Allies sought to punish the individuals most responsible for the Nazi regime and its depredations, rather than Germany itself. On the security view, holding individuals rather than states responsible for serious violations of international law can have a useful deterrent effect.

The two security theories offend legalistic notions and, to be sure, the sense of fairness on which those notions are grounded. They either assume that the powerful states responsible for the human rights and criminal law regimes have the interests of the world at heart or that only the interests of those states count. The first assumption is not plausible; the second is inconsistent with widespread intuitions about justice, and would, if accepted, forfeit the voluntary participation of all other states, which would not be party to an order that serves the interests of the few.

From these tensions have arisen the legalistic conceptions of the human rights and international criminal law regimes. Human rights law reflects universal principles of morality, applicable to everyone, everywhere, and it does not matter whether one lives in a powerful state or a weak state. International criminal law also condemns behavior universally recognized as immoral, and individuals who engage in such behavior are subject to trial and punishment. Thus, weak states can voluntarily sign onto this order; they need not be coerced. And everyone owes it his or her loyalty.

The legalistic version is the official ideology; the security version is the actual explanation.[49] This explains the weak or nonexistent enforcement mechanisms for international human rights law, and the selective way in which international criminal prosecutions have occurred. To overcome substantial disagreement among states about what norms are actually universal, negotiators have drafted extremely vague human rights treaties, many of which are mutually inconsistent. The attraction of courts is that they supply, case after case, evidence that states care about human rights and international crimes, and thus serve a reassurance function for global legalism. But, kept weak and constrained, they cannot curb state power.

International Law in Domestic Courts:
ATS Litigation and Climate Change

In chapter 5, I mentioned the dispute between global legalists over domestic and international litigation. For the global legalist, the ideal dispute resolution mechanism for international law violations is the international tribunal, but in practice, the most exciting international litigation is taking place in American domestic courts. This paradox reflects the basic tensions of global legalism: law without government exists at the international level, law normally requires courts to interpret and enforce it, effective courts cannot exist without supporting government institutions, no such institutions exist at the international level. In the absence of effective international courts, the next best thing is the domestic court, which can at least apply the law and enforce it — and maybe advance it.

Alien tort statute litigation has exploded in the United States. When it began in 1980, it seemed unlikely to make much of a mark. In the Filartiga case of that year,[1] the family of the victim of torture in Paraguay brought a case against the police official responsible for the torture under the Alien Tort Statute, which permits aliens to bring suits for torts that violate international law. Although the Alien Tort Statute is more than two hundred years old, no one had brought such a case before — one that relied on modern human rights law. The plaintiffs won, but people like the defendant rarely end up in the United States, where they can come under the jurisdiction of American courts, and almost never have the assets that could pay damages. For a while, this type of litigation was symbolic only.

All this changed when plaintiffs' lawyers realized that they could use the ATS against multinational corporations, which do have substantial assets and can almost always be sued in the United States. Courts have, in some cases, recognized that corporations can be liable on theories of complicity, typically where a corporation engages in business activities in a country, such as building pipelines, and enlists the government to provide security against brigands or insurgents. The local government or military commits human rights violations, and the victims or their relatives bring suit, arguing that the corporation was complicit in those violations. Today, cases arise out of diverse circumstances: against the manufacturer of bulldozers used by the Israeli army in the conflict with Palestinians, producers of defoliants used in the Vietnam War, oil and gas companies caught up in civil strife in Nigeria, corporations that did business in South Africa during the Apartheid era, a mining company in Papua New Guinea that relied on the government to provide security, a produce company in Guatemala which allegedly used a private security company to bust a union, and many more. Meanwhile, litigation against military and civilian officials in foreign governments has continued apace, with lawsuits alleging torture, extrajudicial killings, and other abuses by officials of the governments of Afghanistan, Chile, China, Colombia, El Salvador, Ethiopia, Haiti, Iran, Japan, Nigeria, the Philippines, the United States, and many other countries. Dozens, maybe hundreds of cases, have been filed; and given the amount of bad behavior in the world, the possibilities are endless. ATS litigation has become big business.

As noted above, ATS litigation embodies the paradoxes of global legalism. The effort to vindicate the international rule of law should ideally take place in international tribunals, but because states do not trust international tribunals and so have ensured that they have no power except in narrow settings that states can control and where they have strongly convergent interests, the effort to vindicate the rule of law has ended up in a domestic judicial system — the type of institution that can be independent and powerful precisely because it is rooted in local values and has the support of allied national government institutions. That this type of international law litigation has found a home in American courts owes a lot to serendipity, but it also reflects America's unusual legal, and legalistic, culture. Although a few other nation-states in Europe have taken small steps to prosecute international crimes, in highly limited circumstances, they have not opened up their courts to ATS-style litigation. In the United States, where the courts have traditionally had policy-making powers deriving from the common law, and in addition have unusual independence, and a culture powerfully in favor of litigation prevails, ATS litigation just doesn't strike the discordant note that it would (and does) in Europe and the rest of the world.

In this chapter, I will not dwell on ATS litigation, which has been extensively discussed in the literature. Instead, I focus on an overlapping topic: the legalistic response to the most challenging global problem of our time—climate change. Nearly everyone agrees that any adequate response to this challenge will involve a treaty regime that includes all nations, or certainly all the major nations, of the world. The treaty regime will, in one way or another, require states to cut back on their greenhouse gas emissions. If history is any guide, the burdens of this regime will reflect the relative bargaining positions of the states rather than the principles of international justice. The extremely slow progress on this regime so far probably reflects just this fact—states are bluffing and jockeying for position and engaging in other strategic maneuvers—as well as scientific uncertainty about who exactly will be harmed and by how much.[2] In addition, any treaty regime will suffer from the usual problems of free riding.[3] Frustration about the slow pace of negotiations, and no doubt about their likely outcome, has led people to turn to litigation.

DOMESTIC LITIGATION IN THE UNITED STATES

Litigation has centered in the United States, although there has been some in other countries, as well.[4] This litigation falls into a few different categories.

Nuisance. In February 2008, the governing bodies of the Alaskan town of Kivalina filed suit against Exxon Mobil and other oil and power companies, seeking damages for harm that the town has suffered as a result of global warming. Kivalina sits atop a low-lying barrier reef and is vulnerable to erosion caused by waves and storms. In the past, it had been protected by sea ice, but the ice has melted now, leaving the town exposed to the elements. The town will need to be relocated at a cost between $95 million and $400 million. The plaintiffs argue that, by contributing to the greenhouse gas emissions that have caused global warming, the defendants have committed a tort against Kivalina and should be responsible for damages.[5]

In California, the attorney general, acting on behalf of California's residents, sued six automobile manufacturers, arguing that the greenhouse gas emissions from their automobiles have contributed to erosion, the melting of snowpack, an increase in ozone pollution, and wildfires.[6] In Mississippi, a group of property owners sued a number of greenhouse gas–emitting firms, arguing that their emissions contributed to global warming and hence (they argue) played a factor in the property loss caused by Hurricane Katrina.[7] Eight states have filed suit against a group of large greenhouse gas–emitting utilities and the Tennessee Valley Authority, arguing that their emissions, allegedly 10 percent of carbon dioxide emissions in the United States, have contributed to climate change that has injured people living in those states.[8]

Tort plaintiffs in climate cases face formidable legal obstacles, at least if traditional tort principles are applied without modification. Kivalina can easily prove that Exxon Mobil and the other defendants emitted greenhouse gases, but it cannot easily prove that those emissions actually caused the ice to melt. It is possible that the ice melted as a result of a local atmospheric disturbance unrelated to greenhouse gas emissions; and even if the melting of the ice was caused by atmospheric warming, it might have been caused by emissions that occurred before those complained of. Conceivably, a court could attribute to Exxon Mobil a percentage of the overall responsibility for global warming, but most courts would be reluctant to do this; and it may well be that Exxon Mobil's contribution (as a fraction of the aggregate emissions of ordinary individuals and firms around the world going back decades) was minuscule. Finally, Kivalina would need to prove that Exxon Mobil acted negligently, but it is not at all clear what it would mean to say that emission of greenhouse gases is negligent, as it is something everyone does, all the time, in ordinary life.[9] On doctrinal grounds alone, these tort cases are weak.[10]

Yet in none of the three decided cases mentioned above did the court even reach these questions. In all of the cases, the trial judge invoked the political question doctrine, a controversial and ambiguous doctrine that directs courts not to hear issues that are better addressed through legislation. Below I will discuss why.

Environmental litigation. Litigants have appealed to an array of federal and state environmental statutes, as well. The federal statutes do not specifically address the problem of climate change, and litigants have had to develop ways to bring them to bear on this problem. A number of recently enacted state statutes do address climate change.

The most important federal statute is the Clean Air Act, which directs the EPA to regulate emissions from common sources of air pollution, including automobiles and factories. In 1999, a number of environmental groups urged the EPA to regulate the carbon dioxide emissions of automobiles, arguing that carbon dioxide is a "pollutant" within the meaning of the statute, and that its negative effect on the atmosphere warranted regulation. The EPA ultimately refused. It argued that carbon dioxide is not a "pollutant" and that, given scientific uncertainty and the complexity of global regulation, it could, on policy grounds, refuse to enforce the statute even if its interpretation was incorrect. In *Massachusetts v. EPA*, the Supreme Court rejected these arguments.[11]

Massachusetts v. EPA has implications beyond the regulation of automobile emissions. In *Coke Oven Environmental Task Force v. EPA*, the plaintiffs argued that the EPA's regulation of power plant emissions must take into account the effect of those emissions on climate change.[12] In light of *Massachusetts v. EPA*, it seems likely that the plaintiffs will prevail. However, the significance of the ruling remains unclear. The EPA still retains a great deal of discretion under administrative law principles, and it is possible that it could end up issuing weak regulations or no regulations at all, possibly on the grounds that effective climate regulation, which requires international cooperation, lies outside of the EPA's jurisdictional reach.

Another body of Clean Air Act litigation involves preemption. California and other states have enacted laws that attempt to reduce greenhouse gas emissions within those states. Because the United States has a national market, these laws unavoidably affect business decisions in other states. Businesses have sought to persuade courts that state greenhouse gas laws are preempted by the Clean Air Act. They have had mixed luck so far. In some cases, courts have held that the state regulatory efforts are not preempted; in others, they have held that they are.[13]

Environmental groups have sought to use other statutes as well. They have used the Energy Policy and Conservation Act of 1975, which was enacted in order to encourage energy conservation, to try to force the National Highway Traffic Safety Administration and the Department of Energy to impose stricter energy conservation rules on various manufacturers and to require other agencies to improve their own fuel efficiency.[14] And they have brought suits under the National Environmental Policy Act, which requires federal agencies to issue environmental impact statements, arguing with a great deal of success that agencies have repeatedly failed to report the impact of projects on climate change.[15] These lawsuits cannot compel agencies to abandon projects that have harmful climatic effects but the adverse publicity has apparently led to changes in behavior. Finally, a few cases have been brought under the Endangered Species Act; plaintiffs argue that agencies need to take into account the effects of climate change on endangered species.[16]

Other litigation. Litigation has proceeded along many other fronts. Plaintiffs tried to use the Freedom of Information Act to obtain evidence that the Bush administration has concealed or distorted information about climate change in government reports.[17] And in state courts, plaintiffs have tried to use a range of state statutes in order to compel governments and firms to report the impact of their activities on climate change (such as greenhouse gas emissions) or to refrain from activities that accelerate climate change.[18]

FOREIGN LITIGATION

No other country relies as much as the United States on litigation to resolve problems of policy, but there have been some stirrings in foreign courts. In Argentina, flooding of the town of Santa Fe, which some attributed to climate change, led to an administrative procedure to enforce Article 6(a)(ii) of the United Nations Framework Convention on Climate Change, a provision that requires governments to disclose information on the effects of climate change. It was argued that the national government had violated this provision by failing to disclose relevant information to localities.[19] In Australia, there have been several lawsuits against government agencies for approving power plant construction and coal mine development without taking into account, or failing to properly disclose, their effect on climate change.[20] In Canada, plaintiffs have tried to compel the Canadian government to comply with its obligations in the Kyoto Protocol.[21] In New Zealand, courts have recognized that climate impacts of proposed government projects must be taken into account by regulatory agencies.[22] These cases, and many more like them, are fundamentally different from the litigation in the United States. In the United States, plaintiffs are trying to use tort principles and statutes designed for other problems to force a change in climate policy. In foreign counties, parties are, for the most part, trying to enforce new statutes that reflect changes in climate policy that have been implemented in legislation.

INTERNATIONAL LITIGATION

International courts have limited jurisdictions, and to date, there has been only one attempt to obtain a hearing in an international body on a climate claim. In 2005, a group of Inuits filed a petition with the IACHR. The Inuits argued that the United States had violated international human rights norms by emitting excessive greenhouse gases into the atmosphere and had damaged the environment in which they lived. The commission initially declined to accept the petition, but proceedings are continuing.[23] The weakness of international courts and the very limited compass of international environmental law[24] suggests that this approach does not have much of a future.

This brings us back to Alien Tort Statute cases—a form of foreign litigation in domestic courts. If a plausible claim can be made that the emission of greenhouse gases violates human rights, and that these human rights are embodied in treaty or customary international law, then American courts may award damages to victims.[25]

Whether victims of global warming pursue human rights claims in American courts on the basis of the ATS or instead find another forum that provides better legal options or greater political visibility, we should distinguish the legal basis of their claims and the normative basis of this type of litigation. For if the legal basis is weak[26] but the normative basis is strong, governments should be encouraged to strengthen the law; and if the legal basis is strong but the normative basis is weak, governments should be encouraged to weaken the law. In this chapter, I will focus on normative issues, and address the legal questions only to the extent that doing so is unavoidable. My argument is that the claim that individuals have an international human right of some sort that is violated by the emission of greenhouse gases, and that such a right should be vindicated in human rights litigation, is not normatively attractive. To keep the discussion simple, I will use ATS litigation as my running example.[27]

INTERNATIONAL LITIGATION: PROBLEMS

From the perspective of litigation strategy, the appeal of the international human rights approach is easy to understand. International litigation against states might pressure governments to adopt more environmentally friendly policies; domestic litigation against multinational corporations might pressure them to reduce their greenhouse gas emissions. Litigation can generate press attention, mobilize public interest groups, galvanize ordinary citizens, and, ultimately, gain compensation for victims. At a minimum, it creates pressure that might generate wiser policy, as governments may finally change policy and enter treaties in order to reduce the risk of liability and the public relations costs of litigation. These and similar reasons seem to back the recent scholarship advocating international human rights litigation on account of global warming.[28] But litigation can also create pressure that generates bad policy. Putting aside possible indirect political effects, and assuming that political progress on global warming will continue to be slow, the question for scholars is whether this litigation, if successful, is likely to have beneficial effects on people's lives.

As we saw earlier, true international litigation — involving an international forum — is almost nonexistent, and in the foreseeable future is likely to stay that way. So the only plausible type of international litigation worth discussing is Alien Tort Statute litigation, which is actually a hybrid of national and international litigation. It takes place in American courts, but it involves international law. For the purpose of discussion, we will focus on ATS litigation.

Assumptions. To keep the discussion manageable, we make several simplifying assumptions.

First, in answering the question, we will focus on corporations rather than other potential defendants, such as foreign states and foreign government officials. States are highly unlikely to be found liable in ATS litigation, at least under current law, because of foreign sovereign immunity.[29] Foreign government officials may be found liable; however, they are unlikely to have assets in the United States. Foreign corporations can be held liable — especially if they have acted in complicity with states — and these corporations may have assets in the United States.[30] American corporations are, of course, vulnerable. Thus, if greenhouse gas–related human rights litigation is to succeed, it will need to target corporations — domestic, foreign, multinational — and it will also be necessary that the prospect of litigation and damages will deter corporations from offering their services to foreign states and officials. If none of these assumptions is correct, human rights litigation based on the ATS will have no impact on global warming.

Second, we will assume that the proper level of liability for corporations is equal to the value of the negative external effects of their activities on climate change. As climate change is not an intrinsic harm, but is a harm only insofar as it has a negative impact on human beings, the relevant negative external effects are those that are net of any beneficial effects from global warming such as enhanced agricultural productivity in northern latitudes. It necessarily follows that the awards should not be maximal (all that we say applies to injunctions as well): corporations should not be forced to shut down factories unless the climate costs of their activities exceed the value they produce in the form of consumer surplus and returns to shareholders. Thus, we put aside the unlikely possibility that the optimal global warming policy involves shutting down all of industry or in other ways effecting a radical transformation of economic activity around the world.[31]

Third, throughout the discussion, we will assume that the problems of causation can be overcome, though we have doubts on this score. Certainly, it would be impossible for a victim of global warming to show that one particular corporation or factory caused his injury. Any theory would need to allocate liability on the basis of market share or some other proxy for degree of responsibility, and although American courts sometimes do this,[32] the difficulties of using such theories for global warming are considerable. Suppose that it can be shown that over a certain period, global warming increases the probability of flooding in some coastal region by X percent. A flood during that period causes the destruction of $100 million of property, but there is no way to prove that the flood would not have occurred if the corporate defendants in question had not emitted excessive greenhouse gases. One might imagine arguing that (1) $100 million multiplied by X should be paid (2) by all firms (and indeed individuals) who contribute to the X percent increase in the probability of flooding through their greenhouse gas emissions, allocated according to their share of responsibility. However, even if courts accept this logic (which seems unlikely), they are likely to demand a great deal of evidence for the X percent figure — and science will probably fail to meet that demand. And science is also unlikely to be able to allocate responsibility among all the possible greenhouse gas emitters around the world—corporations, individuals, governments, and others. If these and similar calculations cannot be performed, either courts will deny liability, in which case the whole international human rights approach will fail, or will assign liability in an arbitrary fashion, with the result that many greenhouse gas emitters will be excessively deterred (because their activities in fact have no causal effect on the flooding) and others will be insufficiently deterred. These formidable problems throw into doubt the enterprise, but we will put them aside for now.

Fourth, we assume that progress with global warming depends on litigation succeeding against corporations around the world and not just in America. As noted above, a healthy climate is a public good; if one state drastically reduces its greenhouse gas emissions and other states do not, then the greenhouse gas problem will not be solved. This is true even for the biggest greenhouse gas emitter, the United States. If factories are shut down in the United States while climate-based environmental regulations remain lax in other countries, then the slack in supply will be taken up by new factories constructed in foreign countries with weaker regulation. This was one of the reasons, described above, for why domestic tort litigation against corporations in the United States could not by itself make progress with global warming. International litigation, since it would target foreign as well as domestic corporations and thus apply a consistent liability standard around the world, holds out more hope on this score, at least on first sight.

The costs and benefits. Let us now consider some relevant costs and benefits of international human rights litigation directed at corporations.

On the benefits side, the argument is simple. Nearly everyone agrees that global warming is a serious problem and that the only way to address it is by reducing greenhouse gas emissions. A treaty regime that requires states to tax or otherwise restrict greenhouse gas emissions would be optimal, but such a treaty regime is far away. In the meantime, any regulatory or legal activity that increases the cost of activities that involve the release of greenhouse gases can only have a beneficial effect. Human rights litigation would do just this. Though far from ideal, it would cause large corporations to reduce their greenhouse gas emissions at the margin to avoid the potentially large liability that would result from a successful ATS suit, and possibly to avoid the public relations embarrassment of such litigation. Awards would compensate impoverished victims of global warming around the world, permitting them to rebuild their lives on higher ground.

Unfortunately, the story is not so simple. To see why, we need to fill in some of the details about how an ATS lawsuit might proceed. Suppose that ATS litigation against multinational greenhouse gas–emitting corporations results in large awards of damages. In reaching this outcome, courts would need to make numerous judgments about liability and harm along the way. For example, they would need to decide whether only negligent emissions of greenhouse gases can create liability or whether a standard of strict liability should be applied. In the former case, some judgment would need to be reached about what counts as due care in this context. Can corporations evade liability if they can show that the costs of reducing emissions exceed the benefits in terms of reducing the impact on climate change? Or if they did not know or anticipate the dangers of global warming at the time they built greenhouse gas–emitting factories? Further, courts would face difficult valuation problems that are familiar from environmental regulation and litigation. One question, for example, would be whether the destruction of a glacier as the result of rising temperatures should be considered a compensable harm because people care about the glacier and its ecosystem or not because people are not harmed in a pecuniary or physical sense. Another question is how to value the loss of life caused by flooding and other natural disasters, the loss of life resulting from an increase in the prevalence of tropical diseases if such is the case, reductions in healthiness and well-being resulting from the same, and second-order harms caused by loss of consortium, the deaths and injuries of children, and so forth. Courts have a great deal of discretion to decide these questions in the American tort system, even though many of these questions are clearly policy questions that are normally — even in the United States, but more so in other countries — resolved by governments, which can balance the values and interests of different people.

In principle, the discretion of American courts would be constrained by international law. The ATS permits a remedy only if the act in question is an international law violation as well as a tort. But international human rights are extremely vague, and the relevant rights in hypothetical global warming litigation—rights to life and health—are at the extreme point of vagueness. Possibly these rights would exclude "existence value" harms like the one discussed above, but possibly not. Possibly these rights could be monetized so that a cost-benefit comparison could be done, but possibly not. Courts would thus need to make the trade-offs between economic activity, which generates wealth, jobs, and funds for desirable government programs, such as health care and environmental protection, on the one hand, and "life" and "health" on the other. Of course, courts could avoid making substantial policy judgments by understanding life and health rights in the narrowest possible way. This would reduce liability to a minimum and not interfere much with the activity of firms, and thus not with the regulatory choices of governments. But this would also mean that no progress would be made with global warming.[33]

The upshot is that even if courts could and were willing to, handle these complexities, and further, if they did so in a way that permitted substantial progress with global warming, then they would implicitly be making climate change policy both for the United States and for the world—for the United States, because defendants that are American companies would need to bring their greenhouse gas emissions into line with the policies chosen by American courts, and for the rest of the world, because defendants that are foreign companies or multinationals would need to bring their greenhouse gas emissions from factories in foreign countries into line with the policies chosen by courts if they want to maintain access to the American market.[34] The two types of defendants raise slightly different considerations, so they should be addressed separately.

The case for American courts regulating American companies through the ATS is stronger than the case for American courts imposing their policy views on foreign countries through the ATS, but the case is still weak. The reasons are familiar from the literature on the comparative advantages of courts and agencies for regulation.[35] Regulatory bodies are superior when victims are dispersed and their losses are relatively small; when centralized enforcement permits the development of expertise oriented toward the problem at hand; and when judgment-proofness is a potential problem. So we prefer the EPA to a system of national pollution regulation created by courts pursuant to common law nuisance law because most victims of pollution are not injured enough for lawsuits to be worthwhile; the EPA has better information than victims about the effects of pollution; and polluters will not be deterred adequately if expected liability exceeds their ability to pay, whereas they can be adequately deterred by inspections and fines. Agencies or legislatures also can take into account the interests of everyone rather than just those who go to the trouble of litigating; they can design programs such as emissions trading that are beyond the powers of courts. And fee-consuming lawyers are cut out of the picture. Nonetheless, human rights litigation is appealing just because Congress and the EPA refuse to act; so the argument that regulation by agency is superior to regulation by court cannot be a decisive objection to litigation. The best argument for encouraging courts to address the problem of global warming is that this problem has not been adequately addressed by the political branches; bad judicial regulation might be better than no regulation at all.

The more significant problem is that American courts would be making climate policy not just for the United States but for the world — at least to the extent that other governments benefit from, and need, multinational corporations that keep assets in the United States.[36] If foreign corporations need access to the American market, then they must comply with American law. If they do not comply with American law, then assets they bring to the United States can be seized by plaintiffs. If an American court directs them to reduce greenhouse gas emissions, then they must shut down at least some of their factories, including factories located overseas, or otherwise adopt controls or abandon the American market.

In the former case, American law effectively supersedes the less restrictive law that prevails in the foreign state. If, say, China does not regulate greenhouse gas emissions, and an American court orders a Chinese corporation to pay an award based on greenhouse gas emissions emitted in China that probabilistically contributed to flooding in Madagascar, then the corporation, to maintain access to American markets, must comply. To avoid further liability, the Chinese corporation would need to bring its Chinese operations into compliance with the tort standard used by the American court. If, for example, the court holds that a certain level of emissions is negligent, the Chinese corporation would need to reduce the emissions of its Chinese factories. The more lax Chinese environmental law would not permit it to escape this outcome.

In the latter case, American courts would be, in effect, setting up a regime of sanctions under which American markets would be effectively closed to foreign corporations that do not comply with the emissions standards set up by the courts. Sanctions are traditionally created by Congress and the president, because they are a matter of policy, and, more important in the present context, are extremely sensitive, as they can provoke economic retaliation by foreign countries. Although nominally directed at foreign corporations, these sanctions would effectively be a challenge to the economic, environmental, and development policies of other nations on the ground that those policies are insufficiently sensitive to the dangers of climate change.[37]

This would be odd. There is no reason to think that American courts could or should develop greenhouse gas policy for Australia, Ecuador, Sweden, and Chad. Each country has its own needs and interests. Some countries are not badly affected by climate change but are deeply concerned about economic development, without which most of their citizens will remain forever impoverished; others are or will be affected.[38] Some countries may be worried that to avoid further liability corporations will shut down factories that supply jobs to many citizens, with the result that social unrest will occur.[39] Even on a very simple view of the world that all that really matters is climate policy, American judicial determination of that policy is likely to have bad effects, simply because American courts, unlike governments, have no idea whether liability rules that make sense for American firms will make sense for foreign firms. And, of course, governments care about other things besides climate policy — security, culture, economic activity, the social welfare system, and so on — and must balance concerns about the climate with concerns about these other factors. Restrictive greenhouse gas rules created by American courts could not possibly take account of this type of legitimate local variation. American courts that have addressed the issue have so far agreed and dismissed the cases on "political question" grounds, meaning that courts do not have the capacity to solve the problem, which is best left to the government.[40]

Foreign states object when American courts try to control activities on their territory, and so we would have to expect a reaction from affected individuals, groups, and states if this ATS litigation were to succeed. As noted above, a simple way for multinational corporations to avoid paying damages in ATS litigation is to remove attachable assets from the United States. This would be extremely costly, of course; in essence, corporations would have to give up the U.S. market. But at the margin, some corporations will do this so that they can operate greenhouse gas–emitting factories in foreign countries without paying damages to victims in American court. Many corporations would continue to be able to serve the American market by manufacturing goods abroad and exporting them. So the net effect of ATS litigation would be to cause corporations and their assets to migrate to other countries, although some corporations would remain and reduce their emissions at the margin in order to preserve access to the U.S. market.[41] But as other firms withdraw assets or migrate abroad, ATS liability awards would have less and less effect on the activities of corporations around the world and eventually would do little or nothing to solve the problem of global warming. It would serve as a tax on doing business in the United States, one that, because of the collective nature of the climate problem, would have little effect on global warming. And we would have to expect some American industry to move overseas in order to avoid this tax.

Another possibility is that foreign corporations would persuade their home governments to give them subsidies that offset their ATS liability. This seems a plausible expectation for countries where corporations have a lot of political influence, and where governments fear social unrest caused by short-term unemployment resulting from the shutting down of greenhouse gas-emitting factories. Thus, ATS awards would essentially be payments from the taxpayers of poor countries, to victims, many of whom could be relatively wealthy — such as owners of houses in low-lying coastal plains.

This is not just a problem with poor countries. Alien tort statute litigation creates tension between the United States and foreign states that object to the application of American-style litigation, with its high awards, on their corporations. South Africa, for example, objected to ATS litigation alleging that foreign corporations were complicit in Apartheid.[42] ATS litigation against foreign corporations that contribute to greenhouse gas emissions is likely to produce similar tensions. Given that even European countries have been slow to address the problem of global warming, we can assume that European governments would be reluctant to impose significant costs on domestic corporations. If so, they are not likely to approve of American litigation that has the same effect.

If all this is true, then we should expect a backlash in foreign countries against ATS liability, at least if the latter is substantial enough to have significant impact on the activities of corporations that emit greenhouse gases.

Foreign countries might retaliate against the United States by reducing their willingness to cooperate along other dimensions of international relations of significance to Americans and the American government—trade and security, for example.[43] Even more troublesome, foreign countries can nullify the effect of ATS litigation by reducing their own greenhouse gas controls. If the political economy in any given foreign country is such that corporations will be subject to only limited regulation, then ATS litigation that results in a greater de facto degree of regulation would likely be met with a relaxing of controls.

The problem can be summarized as follows. If ATS litigation results in significant liability, then either massive evasion will occur as corporations withdraw from the United States and foreign countries immunize corporations that do substantial business on their territory, or—even worse, but highly unlikely—massive evasion will *not* occur and American courts will draw up global environmental policy that makes sense to the judges but does not reflect the needs and interests of people living all over the world. In the first case, ATS litigation could well impose costs on Americans without creating any global benefits. In the second case, ATS litigation could harm foreigners more than it helps them. To be sure, these negative effects are not inevitable. Courts might turn out to be good policymakers, other nations could end up acquiescing in this policy, and corporations might find it cheaper to comply with judicial policy than withdrawing from the American market. All this could be true, but it is unlikely to be true.

Distributional implications. Supposing ATS litigation on the basis of global warming succeeds, it will have distributional implications that may not be desirable. Much depends on how plaintiffs' lawyers design the litigation and how courts determine the contours of the tort claims, so the discussion is necessarily speculative—even more so than the cost-benefit discussion above.

The victims of global warming are dispersed throughout the world. In the near future, at least, they will be concentrated in poor countries in low-lying islands and coastal regions, where rising sea levels result in more frequent floods, erosion, and the destruction of property. Other victims will include farmers whose land can no longer support traditional crops because of climatic changes, people who become vulnerable to diseases that migrate north, and people who rely on glaciers for their water supply.[44]

Many people will be affected only in marginal ways—perhaps food prices will be higher than they would otherwise be, or air conditioning bills will be higher, or more storms will result in more damage and higher insurance bills.[45]

We could imagine suits being brought on behalf of all these people. Although, in the near term, probably the suits will be brought on behalf of the worst-off victims in the poorest countries, suits will be brought on behalf of wealthier victims if the first type of lawsuit succeeds. If, for example, it can be shown that global warming–influenced flooding wiped out an impoverished village in Bangladesh, then it can be shown that global warming–influenced flooding wiped out middle-class homes in Bangladesh. Conventional tort remedies, which are used in ATS cases, imply that the middle-class victims would be entitled to higher awards than the impoverished victims—for the simple reason that the middle-class victim has valuable assets that can be destroyed, whereas the impoverished victim does not. This means that plaintiffs' lawyers will migrate toward the middle class and the relatively wealthy. In these ways, both the incentives of lawyers and the principles of the law imply that the litigation will redistribute wealth from multinational corporations to middle-class or relatively wealthy victims. Corporations will pass on the costs to their customers. As the costs of products increase, the poor around the world will be hit hardest. An energy corporation that raises prices to finance ATS awards will pass the cost on to consumers, and higher energy bills will be felt more keenly by the poor—even the very poor who must commute on buses, for example—than by the relatively wealthy.

This outcome is not a certitude, but it seems likely for two reasons. First, the American tort system, through which human rights litigation must flow, takes the distribution of wealth as given, and rarely tries to redistribute. Second, the American tort system favors large claims over small claims, because plaintiffs must incur the high risks and fixed costs of litigation itself. When plaintiffs are scattered around the world, the task falls to entrepreneurial plaintiffs' lawyers, who have strong economic incentives to aggregate a few large claims rather than millions of small claims. And when they do aggregate many small claims, experience has shown that administrative costs are high and the risks of corruption and abuse are substantial.[46] Victims often end up receiving a small portion of their claim, the rest going to lawyers and administrative expenses.[47]

On the other side, if the tort awards are reasonably accurate, corporations respond by reducing greenhouse gas emissions, and as a result climate change proceeds at a slower pace, millions of people around the world will benefit, and most of these people will be poor. However, these particular beneficiaries are not poor people living today but poor people who will be alive in the future. The reason is that that an enormous stock of greenhouse gas emissions has built up in the atmosphere, and so progress against climate change can occur only after this stock has been reduced, which will take many years, even if corporations radically reduce their emissions.[48] The effect of litigation today would be to benefit poor victims today very little or not at all, or even make them worse off as many would have to pay higher prices; wealthier victims would probably do better; and poor and wealthier people in the distant future will be made better off, if all goes well and litigation does not suppress economic growth by more than it helps the climate. And "poor" people in the distant future are likely to be better off than poor people today, at least if historical trends continue, and global warming is moderate rather than catastrophic.[49] Such a distributional outcome is morally questionable at best.

CLIMATE LEGALISM

In the United States, litigation drives policy to a greater extent than it does in other countries. Consider how tort litigation has driven policy toward the consumption of tobacco products, for example, or how constitutional litigation has driven policy on schools, prisons, and abortion. That litigation can be effective for changing policy cannot be denied; that litigation leads to better policy than can be achieved through politics is hotly contested.[50]

Critics of what is sometimes called "regulation by litigation" argue, with much justice, that regulation ought to proceed from the deliberations of elected officials or from the agencies that they establish for that purpose. Elected officials have legitimacy and a sense of what the public demands. Agencies have expertise. Judges are generalists who lack expertise, sensitivity to public concerns, and democratic legitimacy. Lacking expertise, judges must defer to the lawyers who argue before them, and these lawyers have a strong interest in serving their clients (victims and industry) but not necessarily the public at large, including future victims of the activity in question. And lawyers charge enormous fees while judges set up cumbersome administrative mechanisms.[51]

Regulation by litigation has its defenders, but whatever its merits in the form of domestic litigation in the United States, the idea that it can be extended so as to address international concerns is most implausible. No other country has the American system, and indeed, other countries view it with distaste. So if global climate regulation by litigation is to proceed, it will almost certainly take the form of domestic litigation in the American courts. But American courts have neither the capacity nor the legal authority to regulate beyond American borders, so there is, as a practical matter, no way for them to constrain businesses in China, India, Russia, and Spain. A successful tort action against American firms that emit greenhouse gas emissions would just drive industry to foreign countries and could have little effect on the overall problem.

It is characteristic of global legalism to ignore such practical concerns. For the legalist, vindication of international legal rights is a good in itself, or at least is presumptively good, and a very heavy burden of proof is put on those who raise doubts.

America versus Europe

———— ▸ CONCLUSION ◂ ————

As I noted in the preface, Europeans and Americans view international law differently. Characterizing this conflict is difficult because, of course, there is a diverse array of views on both sides with much overlap, and — I believe — many American scholars have largely come to agree with the European scholars, albeit in the peculiar idiom of American legal scholarship. The American establishment — including liberals in the press and in political leadership — have not thrown in their lot with the Europeans, but there is some movement in this direction. Meanwhile, it is unclear that European governments agree with their own scholars.

Let us, then, make some distinctions with the understanding that they are not far from caricature. On one side are the American government, the elites, and the general public, which think of international law in instrumental terms. International law consists of agreements and norms that reflect the mutual interest of states involved, and can and ought to be changed as the interests of states change. This view of international law harks back to the old positivist tradition of international law that existed in Europe, as well as the United States. International law is just a form of international cooperation and has no particular moral valence beyond any other form of cooperation — and certainly does not consist of rules that constrain sovereigns. This instrumental view of international law shows up every other day in editorials in the popular press, popular foreign policy journals like *Foreign Affairs*, and government documents. The liberal-conservative divide is essentially an empirical one, albeit with people's empirical judgments no doubt influenced by their normative beliefs. Liberals worry more than conservatives that violation of international law today may weaken valuable international structures tomorrow, but liberals, like conservatives, put America's interests first.

On the other side are European academics and commentators, possibly the European public, and—somewhat less clearly—European governments, which refuse to think of international law in purely instrumental terms.[1] While acknowledging that many treaties reflect instrumental goals, these global legalists believe that instrumental thinking about international law can only erode global confidence in it, and that the core of international law is "constitutional" in the following sense. Certain norms—basic human rights norms—cannot be violated under any circumstances. The charter of the United Nations is also higher law, to which all other international law (except the human rights norms) is subordinated. As to mainly American fears that this conception leads to rule by international elites and the devaluation of democracy, Europeans offer certain accommodations—a commitment to transparency, the involvement of NGOs in policymaking, and so forth—but not the still-impossible-to-imagine global democracy.

American legal academics find themselves drawn to this European view, in no small part because the European commitment to human rights is popular among liberal American academics. But they are made uneasy by Europe's cavalier dismissal of democracy, as it appears in American eyes.[2] Americans simply do not share Europeans' fears about democracy; in the United States, the people remain the source of all political authority as a matter of public discourse. Even constitutional limits on democracy are attributed to the people—"We the People." So in American legal scholarship, the move toward global constitutionalism is more hesitant and circumspect. Rather than appealing to universal moral norms or, less so, the rule of the elites, Americans either assume that more international law must advance American interests or appeal to "transnational legal process," the idea that, somehow, domestic and international litigation will paper over the democratic deficit. For if Americans love democracy, they also love litigation, and they are willing to allow judges to make policy as long as they do not veer too far from the political center.

This may explain why international adjudication—the rule of judges—has done so much better than other institutionalized forms of international cooperation: it may be the only common ground for Americans and Euro-

peans in the debate over global constitutionalism. Legalism has always had
its best opportunity to flourish when people cannot overcome their differences through politics. Unfortunately, legalism itself depends on deep
agreement about norms and on highly developed institutions. It turns out
that American legalism does not extend very far from its shores: international courts are not the same thing as American courts, which are staffed
by Americans who share American values and interests. And so while
the international tribunal is, for Americans, the least disfavored of international institutions that are not controlled by the United States, it never
has received much support from the United States. Their reputation to
the contrary, European countries have also lost whatever enthusiasm they
have had for international courts—putting aside regional courts that advance European cooperation and the International Criminal Court, which,
by design, is unlikely ever to try a European defendant.

What will happen next? The United States will continue to resist efforts to constrain itself in the snarls of international legal norms, believing that it needs freedom of action in order to protect its interests and
advance liberty and democracy around the world. Europe will continue
to argue that international law serves American as well as global interests in the promotion of human rights and international security. Their
debates will continue, as they have for so long, to ignore the views and
interests of rising powers such as China, Russia, India, and Brazil. But
before long, these countries, too, will be able to advance their views about
international law—views that will no doubt serve their interests, as well.[3]
Indeed, they already have. Russia has quickly learned that pliable human
rights language and the precedents of Kosovo and Iraq can be turned to its
advantage; its legal justification for the attack on Georgia and occupation
of South Ossetia is no better or worse than the justification for the invasion
of Kosovo. China has asserted its sovereign right to trade with Sudan and
other human rights–abusing nations in Africa. And developing nations
as a group have registered their opposition to a climate pact that puts any
burden on them. Only those who have lost sight of the geopolitical interests of nations and have mistaken the legalistic rhetoric of Europe and the
United States for reality can be surprised by these events. Those people
will continue to be unprepared to address such events as they occur.

NOTES

PREFACE

1 Jack L. Goldsmith & Eric A. Posner, The Limits of International Law (Oxford, 2005).

2 For a discussion of the controversy, see Peter Hilpold, *Humanitarian Intervention: Is There a Need for a Legal Reappraisal?*, 12 Eur. J. Int'l L. 437 (2001).

3 See Michael J. Glennon, Limits of Law, Prerogatives of Power: Interventionism After Kosovo (Palgrave, 2001).

4 There is a definite asymmetry between liberal and conservative arguments in the popular press. When criticizing, say, the treatment of detainees at Guantanamo Bay, liberals cite international law as an independent reason for shutting down the camp. When criticizing, for example, violations of trade treaties, conservatives usually cite the benefits of free trade and do not attach any weight to the treaty regime itself.

5 For a careful exegesis of U.S. international lawbreaking, see John F. Murphy, The United States and the Rule of Law in International Affairs (Cambridge, 2004).

6 See, e.g., Martti Koskenniemi, *International Law in Europe: Between Tradition and Renewal*, 16 Eur. J. Int'l L. 113 (2005). Koskenniemi himself does not defend this approach. See also Sabrina Safrin, *The Un-Exceptionalism of U.S. Exceptionalism*, 41 Vand. J. Trans'l L. 1307 (2008).

7 See Robert O. Keohane, After Hegemony: Cooperation and Discord in World Political Economy (1984).

8 Goldsmith & Posner, supra note 1.

CHAPTER ONE

1 The idea goes back many centuries but received essential clarification from Paul Samuelson. See Paul Samuelson, *The Pure Theory of Public Expenditure*, 26 Rev. Econ. & Statistics 387 (1954). There have been countless elaborations since then, including many discussions of the global version. See, e.g., Mancur Olson, The Logic of Collective Action: Public Goods and the Theory of Groups (1965); Russell Hardin, Collective Action (1982); Todd Sandler, Global Collective Action (2004); Scott Barrett, Why Cooperate? The Incentive to Supply Global Collective Goods (2007).

2   Not all global problems are collective action problems; some are coordination problems, which can be challenging but are solvable. See Barrett, supra note 1; Goldsmith
& Posner, supra preface note 1.

3   For an excellent overview, see Richard H. Steinberg, *Power and Cooperation in International Environmental Law*, in Research Handbook in International Economic Law
(Andrew T. Guzman & Alan O. Sykes eds., 2007).

4   See my discussion in Eric A. Posner, *International Law: A Welfarist Approach*, 73 U. Chi.
L. Rev. 487 (2006).

5   Alexander Wendt, *Why a World State Is Inevitable*, 9 Eur. J. Int'l Rel. 491 (2003); see
also Daniel Deudney, Bounding Power: Republican Security Theory from the Polis to
the Global Village (Princeton, 2006).

6   Norman Angell, The Great Illusion (G.P. Putnam's Sons, 3rd rev. & enlarged ed.
1912).

7   See Francis Fukuyama, *The End of History?* The Nat'l Interest (Summer 1989). The
essay was later expanded into a book. See Francis Fukuyama, The End of History and
the Last Man (1992).

8   See, e.g., Bruce Russett, Grasping the Democratic Peace (1994).

9   See James D. Fearon, *Domestic Political Audiences and the Escalation of International
Disputes*, 88 Am. Pol. Sci. Rev. 57 (1994).

10 Todd Sandler & Keith Hartley, *Economics of Alliances: The Lessons for Collective Action*,
39 J. Econ. Lit. 869 (2001).

11 Probably the two greatest influences on the development of global legalism among
American academics are Louis Henkin and Harold Koh. See Louis Henkin, How Nations Behave (2d ed. 1979); *Harold Koh, Why Do Nations Obey International Law?* 106
Yale L. J. 2599 (1997). However, I do not claim that either scholar would defend every
element of global legalism as I describe it. Global legalism is not a precise set of doc-
trines or methodological commitments; it is better described as a general attitude about
the nature of international law, and global legalists frequently disagree about particu-
lars. One can find this attitude in virtually any article or book written by an American
international law scholar, where the standard assumption is that if a global problem
exists, the solution is more law, and little or no attention is given to whether states have
an interest in creating and supporting the proposed legal solution. For a very recent example, see Antonia Chayes, *How American Treaty Behavior Threatens National Security*,
33 Int'l Security, 45 (2008). To be sure, there are some critics and dissenters, but they
are in a small minority. For a historical discussion of the tension between "formalist"
(that is, legalist) and "realist" (that is, skeptical) scholars in the United States, see Marti
Koskenniemi, The Gentle Civilizers of Nations: The Rise and Fall of International
Law 1870–1960 ch. 6 (Cambridge, 2001). Koskenniemi seems to think that American
legal scholars tend to be "realists." However, in my view, the legalists have today the
upper hand.

As for political scientists who write about international relations, I do not believe
that any major scholar is a global legalist. See, for example, Legalization and World
Politics (Judith Goldstein et al. eds., 2001), which lays down a descriptive research

agenda that rejects the common assumptions of legalists (e.g., p. 4). This research has
its roots in international relations scholarship that uses the rational choice methodology; see, e.g., Robert Keohane, After Hegemony (1984); David A. Lake, Entangling
Relations: American Foreign Policy in its Century (Princeton, 1999); Oran R. Young,
Governance in World Affairs (1999). Global legalism is mostly confined to law schools,
the media, and politics. A few philosophers, however, might be called legalists because
they assume that legal institutions can solve international problems without trying to
explain how they would do so. See, e.g., Brian Barry, *Statism and Nationalism: A Cosmopolitan Critique*, in NOMOS XLI: Global Justice 12, 39 (Ian Shapiro and Lea Brilmayer
eds., 1999); Jonathan Glover, *State Terrorism*, in Violence, Terrorism, and Justice 256,
272 (R.G. Frey and Christopher W. Morris eds., Cambridge 1991).

12 Alexis de Tocqueville, Democracy in America 251–58 (Harvey C. Mansfield & Delba
Winthrop trans. and eds., 1992).

13 Id. at 257.

14 Cf. David Luban, *The* Noblesse Oblige *Tradition in the Practice of Law*, 41 Vand. L.
Rev. 717 (1988).

15 See, e.g., Mark Tushnet, Taking the Constitution Away from the Courts (Princeton,
1999); Jeremy Waldron, Law and Disagreement (Oxford, 1999); Larry D. Kramer, The
People Themselves: Popular Constitutionalism and Judicial Review (Oxford, 2004);
Adrian Vermeule, Law and the Limits of Reasons (Oxford, forthcoming 2008).

16 David Hackett Fisher, Albion's Seed: Four British Folkways in America (Oxford,
1989).

17 See Judith Shklar, Legalism: Law, Morals, and Political Trials (2d ed. 1986). For a
related definition of "judicialization," see C. Neal Tate, *Why the Expansion of Judicial Powers?* in The Global Expansion of Judicial Power 28 (C. Neal Tate & Torbjörn
Vallinder eds., 1995), who emphasizes (1) the extent to which policymaking occurs
in courts; and (2) the extent to which quasi-judicial rules and procedures dominate
decision-making in policymaking bodies other than courts.

18 Not only in the United States, but in Britain as well. See R.W. Kostal, A Jurisprudence
of Power: Victorian Empire and the Rule of Law 478 (2005). By contrast, civil law
judges enjoy considerably less prestige; they are regarded as bureaucrats. The prestige
must be the result of two factors unique to the common law system: the independence
of judges and their acknowledged power to make policy. In the civil law system, judges
are more akin to bureaucrats who follow orders. To be sure, the contrast can be over-
drawn; we are talking about the reputation of judges, whatever it is they actually do
when they make decisions.

19 See, e.g., Walter K. Olson, The Litigation Explosion: What Happened When American Unleashed the Lawsuit (1991); Robert A. Kagan, Adversarial Legalism (2001);
Thomas F. Burke, Lawyers, Lawsuits, and Legal Rights: The Battle Over Litigation
in American Society (2002).

20 For a general discussion, see Tate, supra note 17, at 28–33.

21 John Ferejohn, *Judicializing Politics, Politicizing Law*, 65 Law & Contemp. Probs. 41
(2002); Tonja Jacobi, Explaining American Litigiousness: A Product of Politics, Not

Just Law Northwestern Law School Working Paper 2007-012 (2007), http://www.law .northwestern.edu/searlecenter/papers/Jacobi_Causes_of_Litigiousness.pdf.

22 See Ran Hirschl, Towards Juristocracy: The Origins and Consequences of the New Constitutionalism (2004).

23 See Jeffrey A. Segal & Harold J. Spaeth, The Supreme Court and the Attitudinal Model (1993).

24 In an interesting article, Jonathan Zasloff makes a related argument that what he calls "classical legal thought" played an important role in American foreign policy during the first half of the twentieth century, thanks in large part to the influential role of lawyers such as Elihu Root in the development of foreign policy. Zasloff blames classical legal thinking for America's disastrous turn from realism during the interwar period, which resulted in excessive faith on international law, a faith that was due to central tenets of classical legal thought: the importance of public sentiment rather than the state for enforcing the law; the power of spontaneous legal evolution, and emphasis on legal expertise rather than politics for resolving social disagreements. See Jonathan Zasloff, *Law and the Shaping of American Foreign Policy*, 78 N.Y.U. L. Rev. 239 (2003).

25 Hirschl, supra note 22; The Global Expansion of Judicial Power (C. Neal Tate & Torbjörn Vallinder eds. 1995).

26 See Alec Stone Sweet, Governing with Judges: Constitutional Politics in Europe (2000).

27 See Andrew Moravcsik, The Origins of Human Rights Regimes: Democratic Delegation in Postwar Europe, 54 Int'l Org. 217 (2000), for such an interpretation of the human rights regime.

28 See Mary Ann Glendon, Rights Talk: The Impoverishment of Political Discourse (1991).

29 See Waldron, supra note 15.

30 See Vermeule, supra note 15.

31 See Walter Olson, supra note 19; Kagan, supra note 19.

32 See Ernst-Joachim Mestmäcker, *On the Legitimacy of European Law*, 58 RabelsZ 615 (1994).

33 E.g., Goldstein et al., supra note 11.

34 Goldsmith & Posner, supra preface note 1.

35 See Koh, supra note 11.

36 On the relationship between Nuremberg and legalism, see Shklar, supra note 17.

CHAPTER TWO

1 William Ian Miller, Bloodtaking and Peacemaking: Feud, Law, and Society in Saga Iceland (Chicago, 1990).

2 Robert Ellickson, Order Without Law: How Neighbors Settle Disputes (1991). Ellickson's work has a parallel in the political science literature on governance of commons. See, e.g., Elinor Ostrom, Governing the Commons: The Evolution of Institutions for Collective Action (New York, 1990), 207. I discuss these issues in Eric A. Posner, Law and Social Norms (Harvard, 2000).

3   The Security Council has, in recent years, engaged in quasi-legislative activity, but its efforts remain limited and sporadic. See, e.g., Munir Akram & Syed Haider Shah, *The Legislative Powers of the United Nations Security Council*, in Towards World Constitutionalism: Issues in the Legal Ordering of the World Community (Ronald St. John Macdonald & Douglas M. Johnston eds., Martinus Nijhoff, 2005).

4   For data, see Thomas J. Miles & Eric A. Posner, Which States Enter into Treaties, and Why? Working Paper (2008), http://papers.ssrn.com/sol3/papers.cfm?abstract_id =1211177. See also Robert A. Denemark & Matthew J. Hoffman, *Just Scraps of Paper? The Dynamics of Multilateral Treaty-Making*, 43 Cooperation & Conflict 185 (2008).

5   See Goldsmith & Posner, supra preface note 1.

6   See, e.g, Tom R. Tyler, Why People Obey the Law (Princeton, 1990); Eric A. Posner, *Law and Social Norms: The Case of Tax Compliance*, 86 Va. L. Rev. 1781 (2000) (discussing literature on tax compliance).

7   See Goldsmith & Posner, supra preface note 1.

8   There are also rational-actor accounts that involve substate institutions or groups.

9   See, e.g., Thomas M. Franck, The Power of Legitimacy Among Nations (Oxford, 1990).

10 See Edwin Brochard, *War, Neutrality and Non-Belligerency*, 35 Amer. J. Int'l L. 618 (1941).

11 This effort often comes under the name of international or global or world constitutionalism. See, e.g., Ernst-Ulrich Petersmann, Constitutional Functions and Constitutional Problems of International Economic Law (1991); Mattias Kumm, *The Legitimacy of International Law: A Constitutionalist Framework of Analysis*, 14 Eur. J. Int'l L. 907 (2004); Erika de Wet, *The Emergence of International and Regional Value Systems as a Manifestation of the Emerging International Constitutional Order*, 19 Lieden J. Int'l L. 611 (2006). Many excellent essays on this topic can be found in Towards World Constitutionalism: Issues in the Legal Ordering of the World Community (Ronald St. John Macdonald & Douglas M. Johnston eds., 2006). For other perspectives, see Jed Rubenfeld, *Unilateralism and Constitutionalism*, 79 N.Y.U. L. Rev. 1971 (2004); Stephen Gardbaum, *Human Rights as International Constitutional Rights*, 19 Eur. J. Int'l L. 749 (2008).

12 As Anne Peters notes, "the US posture of international law exceptionalism threatens international constitutional principles." See Anne Peters, *Compensatory Constitutionalism: The Function and Potential of Fundamental Internal Norms and Structures*, 19 Leiden J. Int'l L. 579, 605 (2006). The puzzle then is how one can claim a constitutional system when the "sole superpower," as she puts it, does not obey its rules. And, of course, the United States is not the only state that has broken the laws or failed to ratify the treaties, she mentions. Consider, for example, the frequent violations of the UN charter prohibition on the use of force by many different countries. See Michael J. Glennon, Limits of Law, Prerogatives of Power: Interventionism After Kosovo (Palgrave, 2001). On European violations of international law, see Safrin, supra preface note 6.

13 For an example of this type of thinking, see Alexander Orakhelashvili, *The Impact of Peremptory Norms on the Interpretation and Application of United Nations Security*

Council Resolutions, 16 Eur. J. Int'l L. 59 (2005). Orakhelashvili argues that jus cogens norms bind the Security Council, simultaneously claiming that jus cogens norms are, by definition, peremptory and, in establishing their existence, relies on the decisions of international tribunals and other organizations set up by states to do their bidding. And for skepticism, see Martti Koskenniemi, *International Law in Europe: Between Tradition and Renewal*, 16 Eur. J. Int'l L. 113 (2005). There have been more theoretically oriented arguments that are similar to the arguments I criticize in chapter 3. See, e.g., Niels Petersen, Rational Choice or Deliberation? — Customary International Law Between Coordination and Constitutionalization, Max Planck Institute for Research on Collective Goods, Bonn, 2008/28.

14 See, e.g., Thomas Franck, *The Emerging Right to Democratic Governance*, 86 Amer. J. Int'l L. 46 (1992).

15 Independent International Kosovo Commission, The Kosovo Report 186 (2000); W. Michael Reisman, *Kosovo's Antinomies*, 93 Am. J. Int'l L. 860, 862 (1999).

16 Richard A. Falk, *What Future for the UN Charter System of War Prevention?* 97 Amer. J. Int'l L. 590 (2003).

17 See Bardo Fassbinder, *The Meaning of International Constitutional Law*, in Towards World Constitutionalism, supra note 3, at 837, 841.

18 See, e.g., Antonio Augusto Cançado Trindade, The Relevance of International Adjudication Revisited: Reflection on the Need and Quest for International Compulsory Jurisdiction, in *Towards World Constitutionalism*, supra note 3, at 515; Anne Peters, *International Dispute Settlement: A Network of Cooperational Duties*, 14 Eur. J. Int'l L. 1 (2003).

CHAPTER THREE

1 In political science, this approach is associated with "liberal theory"; see, e.g., Andrew Moravcsik, *Taking Preferences Seriously: A Liberal Theory of International Politics*, 51 Int'l Org. 513 (1997).

2 See, for example, Anne-Marie Slaughter, The New World Order (2004); Abram Chayes & Antonia Handler Chayes, The New Sovereignty: Compliance With International Regulatory Agreements (Harvard, 1995); Kal Raustiala, *The Architecture of International Cooperation: Transgovernmental Networks and the Future of International Law*, 43 Va. J. Int'l L. 1 (2002); Ryan Goodman & Derek Jinks, *How to Influence States: Socialization and International Human Rights Law*, 54 Duke L.J. 621 (2004).

3 For economic models and some evidence, see, e.g., Kenneth M. Kletzer & Brian D. Wright, *Sovereign Debt as Intertemporal Barter*, 90 Amer. Econ. Rev. 621 (2000); James Conklin, *The Theory of Sovereign Debt and Spain under Philip II*, 106 J. Pol. Econ. 483 (1998).

4 See Harold Hongju Koh, *Bringing International Law Home*, 35 Hous. L. Rev. 623 (1998); Harold Hongju Koh, *Why Do Nations Obey International Law?* 106 Yale L. J. 2599, 2645–56 (1997) (book review); Harold Hongju Koh, *Transnational Legal Process*, 75 Neb. L. Rev. 181 (1996). For an application of these ideas, see William S. Dodge, *The*

Helms-Burton Act and Transnational Legal Process, 20 Hastings Int'l & Comp. L. Rev. 713 (1997); Christopher J. Borgen, Transnational Tribunals and the Transmission of Norms: The Hegemony of Process, (2008) (unpublished manuscript) http://ssrn.com/abstract=793485.

5   Slaughter, supra note 2. See also Raustiala, supra note 2.

6   By "nonstate actors," I mean to refer to the standard cast of characters: interest groups, NGOs, politicians, individuals, governmental units, international organizations, and so forth. Thus, the term includes the people who control the state, such as a president or prime minister, because they are individuals rather than the state itself.

7   Louis Henkin, Constitutionalism, Democracy and Foreign Affairs (1990). Chayes & Chayes, supra note 2, at 3–9.

8   A.J.P. Taylor, The Struggle for Mastery in Europe (1963).

9   See, e.g., Oona A. Hathaway, *Between Power and Principle: A Political Theory of International Law*, 72 U. Chi. L. Rev. 469 (2005).

10   See Goldwater v. Carter, 444 U.S. 996 (1979) and Kucinich v. Bush, 236 F.Supp.2d 1 (D.C. Cir. 2002); Louis Henkin, Foreign Affairs and the U.S. Constitution 214 (2d. ed. 1996). For criticism of this view, see Derek Jinks & David Sloss, *Is the President Bound by the Geneva Conventions?* 90 Cornell L. Rev. 97 (2004).

11   A self-executing treaty is a treaty that, by its terms, has the force of domestic law. A non–self-executing treaty creates an international legal obligation but no domestic legal obligation. See Marjorie M. Whiteman, 14 Digest of International Law 304 (U.S. Dept. of State, 1970).

12   See Restatement (Third) of Foreign Relations Law, § 115(1)(a) (1987). It was precisely this concern that treaties could not bind the government that led Louis Henkin to criticize the last-in-time rule and argue that treaties should prevail over statutes; see Louis Henkin, How Nations Behave: Law and Foreign Policy (Columbia, 2d ed. 1979), at 63–64.

13   On this, see Robert D. Putnam, *Diplomacy and Domestic Politics: The Logic of Two-Level Games*, 42 Int'l. Org. 427 (1988). Again, it's not clear that there is a legal ban, but there is likely a political hurdle.

14   The Paquete Habana, 175 U.S. 677 (1900).

15   Id. at 700.

16   See Henkin, supra note 12, at 63–64.

17   For an early judicial statement, see Taylor v. Morton, 23 F. Cas. 784 (C.C.D. Mass. 1855). To be sure, courts have been somewhat more aggressive in some countries (like Israel, but only since about 2002) than others. Usually, however, courts leave the government the right to repudiate its international obligations as long it does so explicitly.

18   As in the Sosa case; see Sosa v. Alvarez-Machain, 542 U.S. 692 (2004). The U.S. government was not the defendant because of sovereign immunity, but the United States filed a brief supporting the defendants.

19   There is some debate about what the proper interpretation of the constitution is on this issue, however. Compare Henkin, supra note 12, at 222, and Jinks & Sloss, supra note 10, at 56–64.

20 See Hamdan v. Rumsfeld, 548 U.S. 557 (2006). In the subsequent statute, the Military Commissions Act, Congress limited the right of defendants to take advantage of common Article 3 but did accept that it was applicable in the conflict with Al-Qaeda. Some commentators do think that the act violated common Article 3.

21 Slaughter, supra note 2, at 65–100.

22 Slaughter probably has in mind a case in which one state has better law than the other, and judges from the other state, learning about this law, harmonize their own domestic law with it, so that judges from the first state become more willing to enforce judgments from the second state. Maybe this happens, maybe not. But one should note that even if it does, it is not clear that this would count as "cooperation" in a normatively meaningful sense. Perhaps, the second state's "bad" law is suited to local conditions—perhaps limited resources preclude the kind of procedural protections that are routine in the first state—so that changing the law makes the second state worse off rather than producing joint gains.

23 See Karen Alter, Establishing the Supremacy of European Law: The Making of an International Rule of Law in Europe (Oxford, 2001).

24 See, e.g., Chayes & Chayes, supra note 2, at 112–53.

25 They might also be tried by domestic courts martial or civilian courts; but only if the government decides to enforce international law domestically, which returns us to the first theory.

26 But as the post–World War II experience shows, eventually other considerations will come into play; after a few years the prosecutions will end and prisoners will be released. See Ann Tusa & John Tusa, The Nuremberg Trials (Atheneum, 1984) (Germany); Meirion Harries & Susie Harries, Sheathing the Sword (Hamish Hamilton Ltd., 1987) (Japan).

27 War crimes prosecutions have taken place in the United States in recent years, mainly in connection with the war in Iraq, but these have been exceedingly rare.

28 See From Nuremberg to the Hague (Philippe Sands ed., Cambridge, 2003).

29 See Jack L. Goldsmith, The Self-Defeating International Criminal Court, 70 U. Chi. L. Rev. 89 (2003).

30 See, e.g., Clifford Krauss, Britain Arrests Pinochet to Face Charges by Spain, N.Y. Times, Oct. 18, 1998, at A1. Belgium's war crimes law, which allowed suits by aliens against aliens, was cut back in deference to American objections. Craig S. Smith, Belgium Plans to Amend Law on War Crimes, N.Y. Times, June 23, 2003, at A9.

31 See, e.g., Christopher Hitchens, The Trial of Henry Kissinger (Verso, 2001).

32 E.g., Filartiga v. Pena-Irala, 630 F.2d 876 (2d Cir. 1980).

33 Or, at least officials will feel guilty for violating their duty when international law itself is fair. See Thomas Franck, supra chap. 2 note 9.

34 There are many versions of this argument in the literature; one discussion can be found in Goodman & Jinks, supra note 2.

35 Tom R. Tyler, Why People Obey the Law (Princeton, 1990).

36 See Eric A. Posner, Do States Have a Moral Obligation to Obey International Law? 55 Stan. L. Rev. 1901 (2003).

37 For a discussion of these points, see John O. McGinnis & Ilya Somin, *Should International Law be Part of Our Law?* 59 Stan. L. Rev. 1175 (2007).

38 For a discussion of the tax compliance literature, see Eric A. Posner, *Law and Social Norms: The Case of Tax Compliance*, 86 Va. L. Rev. 1781 (2000).

39 Tyler, supra note 35.

40 Cf. Franck, supra chap. 2 note 9.

41 Koh, *Transnational Legal Process*, supra note 4, at 204.

42 E.g., Slaughter, supra note 2; Raustiala, supra note 2.

43 Koh, *Bringing International Law Home*, supra note 4, at 647.

44 See Kyle Bagwell & Robert W. Staiger, The Economics of the World Trading System 30–32 (2002); Gene M. Grossman & Elhanan Helpman, Interest Groups and Trade Policy (2002).

45 See, e.g., Koh, *Transnational Legal Process*, supra note 4, at 207; Chayes & Chayes supra note 2, at 250–70; Slaughter, supra note 2.

46 See the International Committee of the Red Cross Web site, available at http://www .icrc.org/Web/eng/siteeng0.nsf/html/faq?OpenDocument. The Red Cross has special status because the Geneva Conventions themselves recognize it as a monitoring body.

47 Their activities are discussed on their Web sites. See http://www.amnesty.org/; http://www.hrw.org/; and http://www.freedomhouse.org/.

48 For example, there are NGOs that advocate family planning and the right to abortion and NGOs that oppose abortion.

49 The Second Optional Protocol to the International Convention on Civil and Political Rights bans the death penalty (Art. 1[1]); many treaties ban the juvenile death penalty, including the ICCPR (Art. 6[5]) and the Convention on the Rights of the Child (Art. 37[a]).

50 The results are available at Roper poll, http://www.pipa.org/OnlineReports/Globalization/notes/90.html (accessed July 23, 2004). Question asked: "As you may know, there is an organization called the 'World Court' that tries to settle international disputes peacefully among countries that accept its jurisdiction. If the World Court finds that actions by the United States have violated international law, should the U.S. accept the Court's decisions, or should it feel free to ignore the Court's decisions if it disagrees with them?"

51 Chicago Council on Foreign Relations, American Public Opinion and Foreign Policy 24, fig. 3-4 (2002), http://www.worldviews.org/detailreports/usreport.pdf.

52 Id. at 35, fig.4-7.

53 Program on International Policy Attitudes, Americans on Globalization: A Study of US Public Attitudes (March 28, 2000), http://www.pipa.org/OnlineReports/Globalization/4.html.

54 Chicago Council on Foreign Relations, supra note 51, at 19, fig. 2-2.

55 Richard Bernstein, *U.N. Assembly Adopts Measure "Deeply Deploring" Invasion of Isle*, N.Y. Times, November 3, 1983, at A21.

56 Neil A. Lewis, *The U.S. and Panama: Legal Issues; Scholars Say Arrest of Noriega Has Little Justification in Law*, N.Y. Times, January 10, 1990, at A12.

57 One survey found 80 percent of Europeans supporting the use of force to "uphold international law." Chicago Council on Foreign Relations, European Public Opinion & Foreign Policy 20, fig.3-2 (2002). However, I have not found polling data analogous to the American data discussed above, so I have been unable to determine whether Europeans have similar attitudes.

58 Treaty Between the United States of America and the Union of Soviet Socialist Republics on the Limitation of Anti-Ballistic Missile Systems, May 26, 1972, U.S.–USSR, art. 5, http://www.state.gov/www/global/arms/treaties/abmpage.html.

59 Koh, *Transnational Legal Process*, supra note 4, at 195.

60 Id.

61 Charles L. Glaser & Steve Fetter, N*ational Missile Defense and the Future of U.S. Nuclear Weapons Policy*, 26 Int'l Security 40 (2001).

62 Clinton did not abandon SDI altogether. See William J. Broad, *From Fantasy to Fact: Space-based Laser Nearly Ready to Fly*, N.Y. Times, Dec. 6, 1994, at C1.

63 See John C. Yoo, *Politics as Law? The Anti-Ballistic Missile Treaty, the Separation of Powers, and Treaty Interpretation*, 89 Calif. L. Rev. 851, 902–3 (2000).

64 See Stephen J. Hadley, *A Call to Deploy*, 23 Wash. Q. 95 (2000) (arguing that missile defense can be effective against rogue states). But see Glaser & Fetter, supra note 61, at 62 (generally unfavorable toward missile defense, but arguing that it might have small role for damage limitation purposes)

65 David E. Sanger & Elisabeth Bumiller, *U.S. to Pull Out of ABM Treaty, Clearing Path for Antimissile Tests*, N.Y. Times, Dec. 12, 2001, at A1 (noting muted European/Russian reaction to withdrawal); Michael Wines, *Moscow Miffed Over Missile Shield but Others Merely Shrug*, N.Y. Times, Dec. 19, 2002, at A18 (describing the indifference of most nations to the shield).

66 Stephen A. Holmes, U.S. Gives Mexico Abduction Pledge, N.Y. Times, June 22, 1993, at A11.

67 United States v. Alvarez-Machain, 504 U.S. 655 (1992).

68 He ultimately lost; see Sosa v. Alvarez-Machain, 542 U.S. 692 (2004).

69 See Koh, *Transnational Legal Process*, supra note 4, at 195–96.

70 Robert Pear, *Justice Dept. Scrambles to Explain Abduction Plot*, N.Y. Times, May 27, 1990, at A24. Tim Golden, *U.S. Tries to Quiet Storm Abroad Over High Court's Right-to-Kidnap Ruling*, N.Y. Times, June 17, 1992, at A8.

71 For some examples, see Richard Clarke, Against All Enemies (Free Press, 2004).

72 This is reflected in the Hague Conventions of 1899 and 1907 and in subsequent weapons treaties.

73 Koh, *Bringing International Law Home*, supra note 4, at 656–57.

74 Id. at 662.

75 Id. at 662–63.

76 See *U.S. Promises "Safer" Landmines*, BBC News, February 27, 2004, http://news.bbc.co.uk/2/hi/americas/3491826.stm.

77 See 1997 Mine Ban Treaty — Non-signatorites (last modified July 2, 2003), http://www.icbl.org/treaty/nonsign.php3.

78 For details, see the country reports, http://www.icbl.org/lm/ and http://www.mine action.org/index.cfm. For a pessimistic (but early) report, see Steven Lee Myers, *Diana's Dubious Legacy; Land-Mine Ban Has Trouble Getting Off the Ground*, N.Y. Times, September 5, 1999, at D3.

79 According to a 2004 report by Human Rights Watch, 26 percent of treaty parties have passed required national legislation under the treaty. See Human Rights Watch, Landmine Monitor Fact Sheet (2004), http://www.icbl.org/content/download/20111/387737/file/art9_feb_2004.pdf.

80 For details, see Kenneth Roberts, *Bullying and Bargaining: The United States, Nicaragua, and Conflict Resolution in Central America*, 15 Int'l Security 67 (1990); Holly Sklar, Washington's War on Nicaragua (1988); Thomas Walker, Nicaragua: Living in the Shadow of the Eagle 25–76 (4th ed. 2003); Cynthia Arnson, Crossroads: Congress, the President, and Central America 1976–1993 (2nd ed. 1993).

81 Koh, *Bringing International Law Home*, supra note 4, at 645.

82 Kathryn Roth & Richard Sobel, Chronology of Events and Public Opinion, in Public Opinion in U.S. Foreign Policy: The Controversy over Contra Aid 22 (Richard Sobel ed., 1993).

83 Id. at 23. Two other polls that year found that 33 percent of Americans "approved" of the policy and 43 to 48 percent "disapproved" of it.

84 Id. at 24–27.

85 See Richard Sobel, Public Opinion about U.S. Intervention in Nicaragua: A Polling Introduction, in Public Opinion in U.S. Foreign Policy, supra note 82, at 49–56.

86 Id. at 65–66.

87 Arnold H. Lubasch, *Lawsuit Dismissed on Ship that Struck Mine*, N.Y. Times, Dec. 12, 1986, at A16.

88 See Bernard Weinraub, *U.S. Limits Role in Court at Hague*, N.Y. Times, Oct. 5, 1985, at A5.

89 See Richard Sobel, *Contra Aid Fundamentals: Exploring the Intricacies and the Issues*, 110 Pol. Sci. Q. 287 (1995). There was some expression of concern in Congress about the ICJ hearing prior to its final decision; Congressman Barnes criticized the Reagan administration for trying to avoid ICJ jurisdiction. But his main concern seemed to have been the administration's refusal to consult with or inform Congress about its plans to mine the harbors. See The Mining of Nicaraguan Ports and Harbors, Hearing and Markup before the Committee on Foreign Affairs, House of Representatives, 98th Cong., 2d Sess., April 11, 1984, at pp. 1–8. See also U.S. Decision to Withdraw from the International Court of Justice, Hearing before the Subcommittee on Human Rights and International Organizations of the Committee on Foreign Relations, House of Representatives, 99th Cong., 1st Sess., October 30, 1985. Bills deploring the withdrawal from the ICJ were introduced in the House (with 58 cosponsors) and the Senate (with eight cosponsors) but never voted on. HR 2695, a bill seeking to end support for all international organizations until the administration re-consented to compulsory jurisdiction in the ICJ, was voted on and defeated 21–74. See also Weinraub, supra note 88, at A5 (describing congressional reaction to withdrawal as "subdued").

90 Sobel, *Contra Aid Fundamentals*, supra note 89.

91 See Ellen L. Lutz & Kathryn Sikkink, *International Human Rights Law and Practice in Latin America*, 54 Int'l Org. 633 (2000); see also Joel E. Oestreich, Power and Principle: Human Rights Programming in International Organizations (Georgetown, 2007). For a discussion, see Goldsmith & Posner, supra preface note 1, at ch. 4.

92 Chaim D. Kaufmann & Robert A. Pape, *Explaining Costly International Moral Action*, 53 Int'l Org. 631 (1999).

93 See Eric Neumayer, *Do International Human Rights Treaties Improve Respect for Human Rights?* 49 J. of Conflict Resol. 925, 950–51 (2005); Emilie M. Hafner-Burton & Kiyoteru Tsutsui, *Human Rights in a Globalizing World: The Paradox of Empty Promises*, 110 Am. J. Soc. 1373, 1395–1402 (2005); Oona A. Hathaway, *Do Human Rights Treaties Make a Difference?* 111 Yale L. J. 1935, 1998 (2002); Linda Camp Keith, *The United Nations International Covenant on Civil and Political Rights: Does it Make a Difference in Human Rights Behavior?* 36 J. Peace Res. 95 (1999); Todd Landman, Protecting Human Rights: A Comparative Study (2005); Emilie M. Hafner-Burton & James Ron, Can the Human Rights Movement Achieve its Goals? 12–17 (2008) (unpublished manuscript) http://www.princeton.edu/~ehafner/pdfs/achieve_goals. pdf); Emilie M. Hafner-Burton, *Right or Robust? The Sensitive Nature of Repression to Globalization*, 42 J. Peace Res. 679 (2005); Emilie M. Hafner-Burton & Kiyoteru Tsutsui, *Justice Lost! The Failure of International Human Rights Law To Matter Where Needed Most*, 44 J. Peace Res. 407 (2007). Some of these studies find that human rights practices improve when the state is transitional, but here the most likely explanation for the correlation is that the desire of the public and elites to Westernize after being under the yoke of an authoritarian regime explains both the decision to enter human rights treaties and the improvement in human rights practices. See also Sonia Cardenas, Conflict and Compliance: State Responses to International Human Rights Pressure (University of Pennsylvania, 2007).

94 Robert H. Ferrell, Peace in Their Time: The Origins of the Kellogg-Briand Pact 17–18, 26 (W. W. Norton & Company, 1969).

95 Id. at 18.

96 Id. at 22–33, 124. Ferrell discusses many other players, passim.

97 Koh, *Bringing International Law Home*, supra note 4, at 662.

98 Id.

99 Hans Morgenthau, *The Twilight of International Morality*, 58 Ethics 79 (1948).

100 Kenneth Waltz, Theory of International Politics (Addison-Wesley, 1979).

101 The democratic peace theory — according to which democracies are more likely to go to war with authoritarian states than they are with each other, or than authoritarian states are with other authoritarian states — is one example. Charles Lipson, Reliable Partners: How Democracies Have Made a Separate Peace (Princeton, 2003); Michael W. Doyle, *Kant, Liberal Legacies, and Foreign Affairs: Parts I and II*, 12 Phil. Pub. Aff. 205, 323 (1983); Bruce Russett, The Fact of Democratic Peace, in Debating the Democratic Peace, at 58 (Michael E. Brown, Sean M. Lynn-Jones & Steven E. Miller eds., MIT, 1996). For an effort to extend this theory to general international

relations, see Anne-Marie Slaughter, *A Liberal Theory of International Law*, 94 Amer. Soc. Int'l L. Proc. 240 (2000); and for a critique, see Jose E. Alvarez, *Interliberal Law: Comment*, 94 Amer. Soc. Int'l L. Proc. 249 (2000).

102 See John Mearsheimer, The Tragedy of Great Power Politics (W.W. Norton, 2001).

103 See Goldsmith & Posner, supra preface note 1.

104 Koh's contribution is methodological: he stresses the role of nonstate actors. But he does not provide a theory, that is, a model of the behavior of nonstate actors that provides predictions about when states comply with international law.

105 "As governmental and nongovernmental transnational actors repeatedly interact within the transnational legal process, they generate and interpret international norms and then seek to internalize those norms domestically. To the extent that those norms are successfully internalized, they become future determinants of why nations obey." Koh, *Why Do Nations*, supra note 4, at 2651.

106 Raustiala, supra note 2, at 26–49.

107 This is an example of what he calls "capacity-building." Mexico "wants" to comply with environmental norms—indeed, has its own environmental law that it does not enforce vigorously—but does not have the bureaucratic capacity to do so. The United States helps build up this capacity by supplying expertise and other resources. See Raustiala, supra note 2, at 79–81.

108 Restatement (Third) of Foreign Relations § 702 (1987).

109 Application of the Convention on the Prevention and Punishment of the Crime of Genocide (Bosn. & Herz. v. Yugoslavia.) 1996 ICJ 25 (July 11).

110 Part of the confusion here comes from disagreement about what counts as a source of law; in part, norms seem to be considered jus cogens only because states say they are or because international organizations say they are; in that sense, positivism seems to be playing a role. But I prefer to avoid these murky waters.

111 An alternative interpretation of IL(R) is that, regardless of what states do, human rights abuses violate international law.

112 See the discussion of their argument above; see also Thomas Risse & Kathryn Sikkink, The Socialization of International Human Rights Norms into Domestic Practices: Introduction, in The Power of Human Rights: International Norms and Domestic Change, at 1 (Thomas Risse, Steve Ropp, & Kathryn Sikkink eds., Cambridge, 1999); Margaret E. Keck & Kathryn Sikkink, Activists Beyond Borders: Advocacy Networks in International Politics (Cornell, 1998).

113 See Goodman & Jinks, supra note 2, at 18, citing Francisco Ramirez et al., *The Changing Logic of Political Citizenship: Cross-national Acquisition of Women's Suffrage Rights, 1890–1990*, 62 Amer. Soc. Rev. 735 (1997).

114 See Keohane, supra chap. 1 note 11.

CHAPTER FOUR

1 This point is different from, though related to, the more familiar point that globalization weakens the power of states to regulate their populations. See, e.g., Susan Strange,

the Retreat of the State: The Diffusion of Power in the World Economy (Cambridge, 1996); and for trenchant criticism of this argument, see Daniel W. Drezner, All Politics Is Global: Explaining International Regulatory Regimes (Princeton, 2007).

2 Alberto Alesina & Enrico Spolaore, The Size of Nations (MIT, 2003). See also Robert D. Cooter, The Strategic Constitution, ch. 5 (Princeton, 2000), for a useful discussion.

3 The classic work is Charles Tilly, Coercion, Capital and European States, AD 990–1990 (Cambridge, 1990). More recent work in the political scientist literature takes an "institutionalist" approach similar to that of the Alesina/Spolaore model. For a discussion, see Hendrik Spruyt, *The Origins, Development, and Possible Decline of the Modern State*, 5 Ann. Rev. Polit. Sci. 127 (2002).

4 Consider the analogy to Coase's theory of the firm. See Ronald H. Coase, *The Nature of the Firm*, 4 Economica 386 (1937). See also David A. Lake, Entangling Relations: American Foreign Policy in its Century (Princeton, 1999).

5 Alesina & Spolaore, supra note 2.

6 Alesina & Spolaore acknowledge this but claim that the era was in fact protectionist (supra note 2, at 188–90); even if true, the number of states, according to their theory, should have declined, but that did not happen either. Alesina & Spolaore instead argue that protectionism led to colonial expansion.

7 See Thomas Miles & Eric A. Posner, Which States Enter Treaties, and Why: A Transaction Costs Approach (unpublished manuscript) (2007).

8 See American Nongovernmental Organizations Coalition for the ICC, Bilateral Immunity Agreements (listing the numerous countries that are concluding bilateral immunity agreements), http://www.amicc.org/usinfo/administration_policy_BIAs.html #countries.

9 See Alesina & Spolaore, supra note 2, for a discussion.

CHAPTER FIVE

1 American Servicemembers' Protection Act of 2002, 22 U.S.C.A. § 7427(a) (2008).

2 543 U.S. 551 (2005).

3 http://www.govtrack.us/congress/bill.xpd?bill=hr110-372.

4 See, e.g., International Delegation (Darren G. Hawkins et al. eds., Cambridge, 2006).

5 See e.g., Curtis A. Bradley, *International Delegations, the Structural Constitution, and Non-Self-Execution*, 55 Stan. L. Rev. 1557 (2003).

6 See, e.g, Jeremy A. Rabkin, Law without Nations? Why Constitutional Government Requires Sovereign States (Princeton, 2007).

7 Paquete Habana, 175 U.S. 677, 700 (1900).

8 See, e.g., Louis Henkin, Foreign Affairs and the United States Constitution (Oxford, 2d ed. 1996).

9 For a representative example of this view, see Derek Jinks & Neal Kumar Katyal, *Disregarding Foreign Relations Law*, 116 Yale L. J. 1230 (2007).

10 Robert E. Scott & Paul B. Stephan, The Limits of Leviathan (Cambridge, 2006).

11 See Rabkin, supra note 6.

12 See Eric A. Posner & Adrian Vermeule, *Interring the Nondelegation Doctrine*, 69 U. Chi. L. Rev. 1721 (2002).

13 For a sample of the debate about international delegation and its democratic pedigree, see Jack Goldsmith & Stephen Krasner, *The Limits of Idealism*, Daedalus, Winter 2003, at 47; Diane F. Orentlicher, *Whose Justice? Reconciling Universal Jurisdiction with Democratic Principles*, 92 Geo. L. J. 1059 (2004).

14 NAFTA Ch 11, § B, Art. 1115.

15 Jinks & Katyal, supra note 9.

16 Mingtai Fire & Marine Ins. Co. v. United Parcel Serv., 177 F.3d 1142 (9th Cir. 1999).

17 Tom Ginsburg, Svitlana Chernykh & Zachary Elkins, *Commitment and Diffusion: Why Constitutions Incorporate International Law*, 2008 U. Ill. L. Rev. 201, 204–6 (2008).

18 There is a great deal of variation across states and some states — the Netherlands and Germany, for example — are more open to international law than others. See The Role of Domestic Courts in Treaty Enforcement: A Comparative Study (David Sloss & Derek Jinks eds., Cambridge University Press, forthcoming).

19 See, e.g., James J. Sheehan, Where Have All the Soldiers Gone? The Transformation of Modern Europe (Houghton Mifflin, 2008).

20 See Karen Alter, *The European Union's Legal System and Domestic Policy: Spillover or Backlash?* 54 Int'l Org. 489 (2000).

21 See Kadi and Al Barakaat International Foundation v Council and Commission, Eur. Ct. J., C-402/05 P and C-415/05 P (2008). See generally Magdalena Licková, *European Exceptionalism in International Law*, 19 Eur. J. Int'l L. 463, 482–84 (2008).

22 See Laurence R. Helfer, *Overlegalizing Human Rights: International Relations Theory and the Commonwealth Caribbean Backlash Against Human Rights Regimes*, 102 Colum. L. Rev. 1832 (2002).

23 For other work suggesting that legalization will not occur except when integration is at high level, here involving an empirical analysis of regional trade pacts, see James McCall Smith, *The Politics of Dispute Settlement Design: Explaining Legalism in Regional Trade Pacts*, 54 Int'l Org. 137 (2000).

24 See Eric A. Posner & Cass R. Sunstein, *Chevronizing Foreign Relations Law*, 116 Yale L. J. 1170 (2007).

25 See Eric A. Posner & Cass R. Sunstein, *Law of Other States*, 59 Stan. L. Rev. 131 (2006).

26 Slaughter, supra chap. 3 note 2.

27 Eyal Benvenisti, *Reclaiming Democracy: The Strategic Uses of Foreign and International Law by National Courts*, 102 Amer. J. Int'l Law 241 (2008).

28 See Posner & Sunstein, *The Law of Other States*, supra note 25.

29 Sandra Day O'Connor, Assoc. Justice, U.S. Supreme Court, Remarks at the Southern Center for International Studies (Oct. 28, 2003) http://www.southerncenter.org/OConnor_transcript.pdf.

30 Cf. Roger P. Alford, *In Search of a Theory for Comparative Constitutionalism*, 52 UCLA L. Rev. 639 (2005). Alford similarly doubts that democratic failure theory justifies reliance on foreign law for constitutional interpretation.

31 Some countries, such as Spain, have statutes that grant such jurisdiction, known as universal jurisdiction, though this remains rare.

32 E.g., Sosa v. Alvarez-Machain, supra chap. 3 note 18.

33 For a recent survey, see Internationalized Criminal Courts and Tribunals (Cesare P.R. Romano et al. eds., Oxford 2004).

34 This has been recognized by many commentators, at least implicitly; see, e.g., Luigi Condorelli & Théo Boutruche, *Internationalized Criminal Courts and Tribunals: Are They Necessary?* in Internationalized Criminal Courts, supra note 33, at 427.

PART II

1 For a representative example of this view, see Andreas L. Paulus, *From Neglect to Defiance? The United States and International Adjudication*, 15 Eur. J. Int'l L. 783 (2004).

CHAPTER SIX

1 See generally, J. G. Merrills, International Dispute Settlement (3d ed. Cambridge, 1998).

2 See id. at 88; see also Christine Gray & Benedict Kingsbury, Inter-State Arbitration Since 1945: Overview and Evaluation, in International Courts for the Twenty-First Century 55, 63–68 (Mark W. Janis ed., Martinus Nijhoff, 1992).

3 See Treaty of Amity, Commerce, and Navigation, Nov. 19, 1794, U.S.-Gr. Brit., 8 Stat. 116, T.S. No. 105 (signed at London, approved by Senate June 24, 1795, ratified by United States, Aug. 14, 1795).

4 See, e.g., David D. Caron, *The Nature of the Iran–United States Claims Tribunal and the Evolving Structure of International Dispute Resolution*, 84 Amer. J. Int'l L. 104 (1990).

5 See generally Martin Shapiro, Courts: A Comparative and Political Analysis (Chicago, 1986).

6 Cf. Merrills, supra note 1, at 168–69.

7 See generally Project on International Courts and Tribunals, http://www.pca-cpa.org/.

8 Ian Brownlie, Principles of Public International Law 710 (4th ed. Oxford, 1990). Prior to 1998, of the 25 cases considered by the Court, 21 were disposed of within its first 30 years, and then only 4 cases were brought to the PCA thereafter, with the last one in 1970. William E. Butler, *The Hague Permanent Court of Arbitration*, in International Courts for the Twenty-First Century, in International Courts for the Twenty-First Century 43, 43–44 (Mark W. Janis ed., Springer, 1992). For the post-1998 history, see below.

9 See Statute of the Permanent Court of International Justice, http://www.worldcourts .com/pcij/eng/documents/1920.12.16_statute.htm.

10 See International Court of Justice, http://www.icj-cij.org.

11 See European Court of Justice, http://www.curia.eu.int.

12 See European Court of Human Rights http://www.echr.coe.int.

13 See, Inter-American Court of Human Rights, http://www.corteidh.or.cr.

14 UN Convention on the Law of the Sea, concluded on December 10, 1982, entered into force November 16, 1994, 21 I.L.M. 1261 (1982).

15 See, e.g., Security Council Resolution on Establishing an International Tribunal for the Prosecution of Persons Responsible for Serious Violations of International Humanitarian Law Committed in the Territory of the Former Yugoslavia, 32 ILM 1203 (1993); U.N. Sec. Res. 955, Establishing the International Tribunal for Rwanda, 33 ILM 1598 (1994).

16 Rome Statute of the International Criminal Court, http://www.un.org/law/icc/statute/romefra.htm.

17 The fragmented development of international courts worries some international legal scholars, who favor a unitary international legal system, but not others. See, e.g., Jonathan Charney, *Is International Law Threatened by Multiple International Tribunals?* 271 Recueil. Des. Cours. 101 (1998); Michael Reisman, *The Supervisory Jurisdiction of the International Court of Justice: International Arbitration and International Adjudication*, 258 Recuil. Des. Cours. 9 (1996); Robert Jennings, *The Role of the International Court of Justice in the Development of International Environment Protection Law*, 1 Recueil. Des. Cours. 240 (1992); Philip Jessup, *Do New Problems Need New Courts?* 65 Proc. Amer. Soc. Int'l Law 261 (1971).

18 Such "ad hoc chambers" were used in cases involving Canada and the United States (1981); Burkino Faso and Mali (1985), El Salvador and Honduras (1986), and the U.S. and Italy (1987). See Shabtai Rosenne, The World Court: What Is It and How it Works 56–58 (Terry D. Gill ed., 2003).

19 Avena and Other Mexican Nationals (Mex. v. U.S.), 43 I.L.M. 581 (Mar. 31, 2004).

20 The actual nomination procedure is more indirect.

21 China did not have a judge from 1967 to 1985.

22 The data set I analyze ends in 2004. In subsequent footnotes, I extend the analysis to August 2008 where I have been able to do so.

23 Events of 2005 through mid-2008 are consistent with this conclusion. Only one contentious case began in 2005, three in 2006, zero in 2007, and four as of August 2008.

24 The trend holds up regardless of whether one counts the *Yugoslavia v. Nato* case as one or many. In the seven cases from 2005 to mid-2008, a major power was the applicant in zero cases, and a respondent in three of the cases, just under half.

25 I limit myself to these cases because in many instances, the invocation of compulsory jurisdiction is clearly spurious (for example, when Yugoslavia filed a proceeding against the U.S. in 1999, which had withdrawn from compulsory jurisdiction fourteen years earlier).

26 An account of optional clause litigation, published in 1987, argued that there was only one case after 1951 in which the optional clause alone clearly provided the basis for jurisdiction, the applicant prevailed, and the respondent complied with the judgment (Temple of Preah Vihear). Two other cases provided weak evidence that compulsory jurisdiction mattered, but no case after 1961. See Gary L. Scott & Craig L. Carr, *The ICJ and Compulsory Jurisdiction: The Case for Closing the Clause*, 81 Am. J. Int'l L. 57 (1987). My review of post-1987 cases reveals none in which the optional clause was

successfully invoked, the respondent lost the case, and the respondent complied with the judgment.

27 My sources for this information are the ICJ yearbooks and the ICJ Web site. These sources provide no information after 1994, and it is not clear whether that is because there have been no treaties with ICJ clauses since then, or because the ICJ stopped collecting and reporting this information. Note that the treaties under consideration are limited to those registered with the UN.

28 Focusing just on multilateral treaties, the numbers are 2.8, 2.0, and 1.3. One might argue that reason for this annual decline is that the earlier treaties were more important and the later treaties were less important, but this seems unlikely, especially given the large number of new states from the 1960s on.

29 Based on my search of the Westlaw U.S. treaty database.

30 Many new treaties since the ICJ's founding have conferred jurisdiction on it in the case of disputes (often through optional protocols), thus increasing the number of international legal disputes that could be potentially resolved by the ICJ without the consent of one party, but apparently not having this effect.

31 Tom Ginsburg & Richard H. McAdams, *Adjudicating in Anarchy: An Expressive Theory of International Dispute Resolution*, 45 Wm & Mary L. Rev. 1229 (2004). There are two other partial sources (Jonathan I. Charney, Disputes Implicating the Institutional Credibility of the Court: Problems of Non-Appearance, Non-Participation, and Non-Performance in International Law at a Crossroads 288 [Lori Fisler Damrosch ed., 1987]; Colter Paulson, *Compliance with Final Judgments at the International Court of Justice Since 1987*, 98 Am. J. Int'l L. 434 [2004]), which are roughly but not fully consistent with Ginsburg and McAdams. For an apparently more optimistic account of the record of compliance with ICJ decisions, see Constanze Schulte, Compliance with Decisions of the International Court of Justice (Oxford, 2004). However, the author defines compliance in an unpersuasively broad fashion.

32 Even here, however, one might argue that simultaneous diplomatic pressures, rather than the ICJ judgment itself, drive compliance. However, I will assume otherwise.

33 E.g., Edward McWhinney, Judicial Settlement of International Disputes (Martinus Nijhoff, 1991); Rosenne, supra note 18. Skeptics of the ICJ include Chayes & Chayes, supra chap. 3 note 2; Michael Reisman, Metamorphoses: Judge Shigeru Oda and the International Court of Justice in Canadian Yearbook in International Law 198 (1995).

34 See Eric A. Posner & Miguel de Figueiredo, *Is the International Court of Justice Biased?* 34 J. Legal Stud. 599 (2005). We ran numerous regressions and tried to control for all plausible variables, with and without judge and case fixed effects. The relationships described in the text are fairly robust, but because of multicolinearity, some of the variables would lose statistical significance when tested with the others. Among the variables mentioned, the wealth variable was the most robust against alternative specifications; regime type was less robust.

35 See Centre for International Courts and Tribunals, Selecting International Judges: Principle, Process and Politics (University College London, 2008).

36 Erik Voeten has recently found national bias in the voting of ECHR judges. See Erik Voeten, The Impartiality of International Judges: Evidence from the European Court of Human Rights, paper presented at the annual meeting of the Midwest Political Science Association, Apr 12, 2007, available at SSRN: http://ssrn.com/abstract=705363.

37 For some of the history, see McWhinney, supra note 33, at 16–23, 92–93.

38 McWhinney, supra note 33.

39 See McWhinney, supra note 33, who celebrates this development. A more critical view is expressed by Reisman, Metamorphoses, supra note 33.

40 Rosenne, supra note 18, at 45–46.

41 Id.

CHAPTER SEVEN

1 For a useful summary of these courts, see The Project on International Courts and Tribunals, The International Judiciary in Context, http://www.pict-pcti.org/publications/synoptic_chart/Synop_C4.pdf.

2 On this topic, see Symposium: The Proliferation of International Courts and Tribunals: Piecing Together the Puzzle, 31 N.Y.U. J. Int'l L. & Pol. 679 (1999).

3 American Convention on Human Rights, Nov. 22, 1969, 1144 UNTS 123 (entered into force July 18, 1978).

4 See Statute of the Inter-American Court on Human Rights, O.A.S. Res. 448 (IX-0/79).

5 OAS Res XXX (1948).

6 Inter-American Commission of Human Rights, http://www.cidh.oas.org/what.htm; Philippe Sands, Ruth Mackenzie, & Yuval Shany (eds.), Manual on International Courts and Tribunals (Butterworths, 1999), at 217.

7 American Convention, arts. 67 & 68.

8 IACHR Statute arts. 4–6.

9 American Convention arts. 61–64.

10 See Sands et al., supra note 6, at 217. I counted 55 from the annual reports, but trust the figure given in From Nuremburg to the Hague more than my own effort. See, e.g., 1999 Annual Report of the Inter-American Court of Human Rights, OEA/SerL/V/III.47, doc. 6 (2000).

11 David Harris, Regional Protection of Human Rights: The Inter-American Achievement, in The Inter-American System of Human Rights 2 (David Harris & Stephen Livingstone eds., 1998).

12 Id.

13 Tom Farer, The Rise of the Inter-American Human Rights Regime: No Longer a Unicorn, Not Yet an Ox, in The Inter-American System of Human Rights, supra note 11, at 31, 33–34.

14 See Harris, supra note 11, at 25 & n. 131; Dinah Shelton, Reparations in the Inter-American System, in The Inter-American System of Human Rights, supra note 11, at 151, 158.

15 Available at http://www.cidh.org/annualrep/2007eng/Chap.3g.htm.

16 For discussions, see William J. Davey, The WTO Dispute Settlement System, in Trade, Environment and the Millennium 119–42 (Gary P. Sampson & Bradness Chambers eds., 2d ed. United Nations University Press, 2001); Ernst-Ulrich Petersmann, The GATT/WTO Dispute Settlement System: International Law, International Organizations and Dispute Settlement (Martinus Nijhoff, 1997).

17 Netherlands Measures of Suspension of Obligations to the United States, Basic Instruments & Selected Documents, Article XXIII, Supp. 32 (1952).

18 That the WTO system, at least in design, represents a "triumph" of legalist thinking over "pragmatic" thinking is not seriously in dispute. See G. Richard Shell, *Trade Legalism and International Relations Theory: An Analysis of the World Trade Organization*, 44 Duke L. J. 829 (1995).

19 Eric A. Posner & John C. Yoo, *Judicial Independence in International Tribunals*, 93 Calif. L. Rev. 1 (2005). See also Marc L. Busch & Eric Reinhardt, Transatlantic Trade Conflicts and GATT/WTO Dispute Settlement, in Transatlantic Economic Disputes: The EU, the U.S. and the WTO 465, 482–83 (Ernst-Ulrich Petersmann & Mark A. Pollack eds., 2004); Marc L. Busch & Eric Reinhardt, The Evolution of GATT/WTO Dispute Settlement, in Trade Policy Research 143 (John M. Curtis & Dan Ciuriak eds., 2003); Karen J. Alter, *Resolving or Exacerbating Dispute? The WTO's New Dispute Resolution System*, 79 Inter. Aff. 783 (2003).

20 I relied on the following studies: Busch & Reinhardt, Evolution, supra note 19, at 151; Edward D. Mansfield & Eric Reinhardt, *Multilateral Determinants of Regionalism: The Effects of GATT/WTO on the Formation of Preferential Trading Agreements*, 57 Inter. Org. 829 (2003); Eric Reinhardt, Aggressive Multilateralism: The Determinants of GATT/WTO Dispute Initiations, 1948–1998 (2000). See also Marc L. Busch & Eric Reinhardt, Testing International Trade Law: Empirical Studies of GATT/WTO Dispute Settlement, in The Political Economy of International Trade Law: Essays in Honor of Robert Hudec 457 (D.M. Kennedy & J.D. Southwick eds., 2002); Busch & Reinhardt, *Transatlantic Trade Conflicts*, supra note 19; Todd Allee, Legal Incentives and Domestic Rewards: The Selection of Trade Disputes for GATT/WTO Dispute Resolution (Dept. of Political Science, Univ. of Illinois 2003) (unpublished manuscript); Marc L. Busch & Eric Reinhardt, *Developing Countries and GATT/WTO Dispute Settlement*, 37 J. World Trade 719, 725 table 1 (2003); Eric Reinhardt, *Adjudication Without Enforcement in GATT Disputes*, 45 J. Conflict Res. 174, 177 (2001).

21 Chad P. Bown, *On the Economic Success of GATT/WTO Dispute Settlement*, 86 Rev. Econ. Stat. 811 (2004).

22 Chad P. Bown & Bernard M. Hoekman, *WTO Dispute Settlement and the Missing Development Country Cases: Engaging the Private Sector*, 8 J. Int'l Econ. L. 861 (2005); Chad P. Bown & Bernard M. Hoekman, *Developing Countries and Enforcement of Trade Agreements: Why Dispute Settlement Is Not Enough*, Centre for Economic Policy Research, Discussion Paper No. 6459, Sept. 2007.

23 Convention for the Protection of Human Rights and Fundamental Freedoms, Sept. 3, 1953, 213 U.N.T.S. 221. For secondary literature on the Convention see in particular Francis Jacobs & Robin White, The European Convention on Human Rights (3d ed.

2002); P. van Dijk & G.J.H. van Hoof, Theory and Practice of the European Convention on Human Rights (3d ed. 1998); J.G. Merrills & A.H. Robertson, Human Rights in Europe. A study of the European Convention on Human Rights (4th ed. 2001).

24 This new institutional machinery is based on the provisions of Protocol No. 11 of the European Convention on Human Rights. For details of these changes, see Merrills & Robertson, supra note 23, at 297–325.

25 Registrar of the European Court of Human Rights, The European Court of Human Rights: Historical Background, Organization, and Procedure (2003), http://www.echr .coe.int/Eng/Edocs/HistoricalBackground.htm.

26 Currently, however, the seats of judges in respect of Azerbaijan, Armenia, and Bosnia and Herzegovina are vacant.

27 Registrar of the European Court of Human Rights, Survey of Activities 2002, http://www.echr.coe.int/Eng/Edocs/2002SURVEY.pdf.

28 http://www.echr.coe.int/NR/rdonlyres/1378B206-4F40-4873-BF32-3BEA8FC 4465B/0/Stats2007.pdf.

29 Swedish Engine Drivers Union Case, 20 Eur. Ct. H.R. (1976).

30 Ireland v. United Kingdom, 25 Eur. Ct. H.R. (ser. A) at 72 (1978).

31 Alex Stone Sweet & Thomas L. Brunell, Constructing a Supranational Constitution: Dispute Resolution and Governance in the European Community, 92 Amer. Pol. Sci. Rev. 63, 65 (1998).

32 See Andrew Drzemczewski & Jens Meyer-Ladewig, *Principal Characteristics of the New ECHR Control Mechanism, as Established by Protocol No. 11, Signed on 11 May 1994*, 15 Hum. Rts. L. J. 81, 82–83 (1993) (citing examples of compliance); Jörg Polaciewicz & Valérie Jacob-Foltzer, *The European Human Rights Convention in Domestic Law: The Impact of the Strasbourg Case-Law in States Where Direct Effect Is Given to the Convention*, 12 Hum. Rts. L.J. 65 (1991) (same); Andrew Moravcsik, *Explaining International Human Rights Regimes: Liberal Theory and Western Europe*, 1 Eur. J. Int'l Relations 157, 171 (1995). For more formal efforts to measure compliance, see Christopher Zorn & Steven R. Van Winkle, Explaining Compliance with the European Court of Human Rights (2000) (unpublished manuscript); Christopher Zorn & Steven R. Van Winkle, Government Responses to the European Courts of Human Rights (2001) (unpublished manuscript). We find the data more ambiguous than they do. The first paper has a regression in which the dependent variable is whether a person brings a claim for compensation against a state; not whether a state complies or not. The second paper's regression measures states' choices among responses to a finding of noncompliance — administrative, legislative, judicial, or constitutional — but not whether the response was adequate rather than merely formal.

33 The ECHR provides some statistical data on its caseload and judgments but does not attempt to measure compliance. For a discussion of the difficulty of measuring compliance, see Hathaway, supra chap. 3 note 93, at 1935.

34 Its Freedom House scores have declined from 3 for political rights and 4 for civil rights in 1996 and 1997, to 6 and 5, respectively, for every year since 2005; they are measured on a seven point scale where 1 is best and 7 is worst. See Freedom House, Free-

dom in the World, Historical Data (2008), http://www.freedomhouse.org/template
.cfm?page=15.

35 A number of books discuss the organization and functioning of the European Court of
Justice. See, in particular, Richard Plender, European Courts Practice and Procedure
(2d ed. Sweet & Maxwell, 2000, loose leaf); Anthony Arnull, The European Union and
its Court of Justice (1999); The European Court of Justice (Gráinne de Burca & J.H.H.
Weiler eds., 2001).

36 For useful discussions of the role of the ECJ, see De Burca & J.J.H. Weiler, The European Court of Justice (2002); Anne-Marie Slaughter et al., The European Courts and
National Courts—Doctrine and Jurisprudence: Legal Change in its Social Context
(1998).

37 The court is assisted by eight advocates general. Their role is to present reasoned opinions on the cases brought before the court. Article 222 TEC (Treaty establishing the
European Community).

38 L. Neville Brown & Tom Kennedy, The Court of Justice of the European Communities
19–21 (5th ed. Sweet & Maxwell, 2000).

39 Id. at 115.

40 In 1989, the Communities created a Court of First Instance, composed also of fifteen
judges, one each from each member state, appointed to six-year terms by unanimous
approval of the member states. The CFI hears cases that arise in the original jurisdiction of the ECJ in the staff, coal and steel, competition, and certain trademark cases.
Since 1994, all cases against the Community by individuals are first heard in the CFI.
The European Council decides which classes of cases should be transferred to the
CFI. The ECJ sits as an appellate body over cases first heard in the CFI.

41 See the statistics concerning the judicial work of the European Court of Justice of the
Annual Report 2002, http://www.curia.eu.int/en/instit/presentationfr/rapport.htm.

42 Stacy Nyikos, The European Court of Justice and National Courts: Strategic Interaction within the EU Judicial Process, http://law.wustl.edu/igls/Conconfpapers/
Nyikos.pdf.

43 See, e.g., Hjalte Rasmussen, The European Court of Justice (1998).

44 Garrett, *The Politics of Legal Integration in the European Union*, 49 Int'l Org. 171, 177
(1995).

45 Signed in 1958 in Rome as amended by the treaty establishing the European Community (EC Treaty).

46 For a brief history of the Internal Market initiatives, see Jonas Tallberg, European
Governance and Supranational Institutions 34 (Routledge, 2003).

47 Charmasson v. Minister for Economic Affairs and Finance, Case 48/74, ECR 1383
(1983) (banana quota); Commission v. France, Case 232/78, ECR 2729 (sheep meat
case).

48 Garrett, Kelemen, *Schulz, The ECJ, National Governments, and Legal Integration in the
European Union*, 52 Int'l Org. 149 (1998).

49 Tallberg, supra note 47, at 34.

50 European Commission, First Annual Report to the European Parliament on Commission Monitoring of the Application of Community Law (1983). COM (84) 191 final 11.4.1984, pp. 27–30.

51 European Commission, Communication from the Commission on Implementation of the Legal Acts Required to Build the Single Market, quoted in id. at 52–53.

52 There are two primary sources for ECJ compliance data. The first is the Annual Reports of the Commission on the Monitoring of the Application of Community Law. These reports are available at http://europa.eu.int/comm/secretariat_general/sgb/droit_com/index_en.htm. The second source of data is provided by the European University Institute's Robert Schuman Centre for Advanced Studies. Their compliance data is available at http://www.iue.it/RSCAS/Research/Tools/ComplianceDB/. The European Commission's annual report lists 105 judgments of the Court of Justice that have not been implemented. Of these judgments, 53 were issued within a year prior to the Annual Report. Of the other 52 judgments, 24 were from 2000, while the other 28 were from years dating back to 1991. While France, Greece, and Italy account for about one-half of the noncompliance, virtually all of the EU members have failed to comply with at least 1 ECJ judgment, and a majority of the EU members have failed to comply with at least 5 judgments.

53 Brown & Kennedy, supra note 39, at 115.

54 David W.K. Andersen & Marie Demetriou, References to the European Court (2d ed. 2002).

55 See Tallberg, supra note 47, at 98–99.

56 Stone Sweet & Brunell, supra note 31, at 63, 65.

57 Martin J. Shapiro & Alex Stone, *The New Constitutional Politics*, 26 Comp. Pol. Stud. 397 (1994); Joseph Weiler, *The Transformation of Europe*, 100 Yale L.J. 2403 (1991).

58 Harm Schepel & Erhard Blankenburg, *Mobilizing the European Court of Justice*, in The European Court of Justice 29 (Gráinne de Búrca & J.H.H. Weiler eds., Oxford 2002).

59 Alter, supra note 19, at 217–21.

60 International relations scholars have different views about the high member state compliance with the ECJ. Some of these scholars view the ECJ's decisions as consistent with member state interests and have argued that the ECJ promotes these interests (or, in some arguments, the interests of France and Germany) by solving monitoring and incomplete contracting problems for the member states. See Geoffrey Garrett, *International Cooperation & Institutional Choice*, 46 Int'l Org. 533 (1992); Geoffrey Garrett & Barry R. Weingast, *Ideas, Interests, and Institutions: Constructing the European Community's Internal Market*, in Ideas and Foreign Policy 173 (Judith Goldstein & Robert Keohane eds. 1993). The justices of the ECJ, subject as they are to renewable terms, wish to increase their power through the expansion of EC law but will not issue decisions that deviate from the strong preferences of the most powerful member states.

Other scholars argue that EC institutions have a more active role. See Walter Mattli & Anne-Marie Slaughter, *Revisiting the European Court of Justice*, 52 Int'l Org. 177 (1998); Martin Shapiro, *The Politics of Legal Integration in the European Union*, in Euro-Politics:

Institutions and Policymaking in the New European Community 123 (A. Sbragia ed., 1991); Weiler, supra note 58, at 2403. These scholars see an alliance of sorts between the ECJ, the national judiciaries, and private parties that benefit from supranational EC rules; this group is the driving force behind the expansion in the ECJ's power and jurisdiction. The ECJ's decisions are not necessarily consistent with the interests of the member states, but the member states have been unwilling to contain its expansion of authority. See also Karen Alter, Establishing the Supremacy of European Law (2001).

61 The court's Web site has this information: http://www.itlos.org/start2_en.html.

62 The following discussion is an application of agency theory to the problem of international adjudication. For more comprehensive discussions, see Posner & Yoo, supra note 19; Eric A. Posner & John C. Yoo, *Reply to Helfer and Slaughter*, 93 Cal. L. Rev. 957 (2005). For other rational choice approaches, see Ginsburg & McAdams, supra chap. 6 note 31; Andrew T. Guzman, International Tribunals: A Rational Choice Approach (2008), http://papers.ssrn.com/s013/papers.cfm?abstract_id=1117613.

63 Efforts to measure the quality of judicial systems, while crude, confirm conventional wisdom to this effect. The World Bank has developed a rule of law measure from approximately –2.5 to 2.5 (higher is better). OECD countries average 1.51. Most of the rest of the world is considerably lower (sub-Saharan Africa has a score of –0.75; Middle East and North Africa, –0.04; South Asia, –0.46; East Asia, 0.15; Latin America, –0.52; Eastern Europe and Baltics, 0.08; Former Soviet Union, –0.89; Caribbean, 0.43). All data are from 2007. See World Bank, Governance Matters 2008, http://info .worldbank.org/governance/wgi/index.asp.

64 See, e.g., *The Proliferation of International Tribunals: Piecing together the Puzzle*, 31 N.Y.U. J. Int'l L. & Pol. 679 (1999).

65 See http://www.pict-pcti.org/publications/synoptic_chart/Synop_C4.pdf.

66 See, e.g., Jenny S. Martinez, *Towards an International Judicial System*, 56 Stan. L. Rev. 429 (2003); Anne-Marie Slaughter, *A Global Community of Courts*, 44 Harv. Int'l L. J. 191 (2003).

67 Many scholars seem to recognize this fact, and the focus in the literature now is how courts can take account of conflicting jurisdictions. See, e.g., Yuval Shany, The Competing Jurisdictions of International Courts and Tribunals (Oxford, 2003); Chester Brown, A Common Law of International Adjudication (Oxford, 2007); Jenny Martinez, *Towards an International Judicial System*, 56 Stan. L. Rev. 429 (2003). For others, competition among tribunals may itself lead to good outcomes. See Jacob Katz Cogan, *Competition and Control in International Adjudication*, 48 Va. J. Int'l L. 411 (2008).

68 A.M. Stuyt, Survey of International Arbitrations 1794–1989 (3d ed. 1990).

69 The Great Powers include Britain, France, Italy after 1870, Japan after 1904, Prussia (Germany after 1870), and Russia. Conventionally, the United States is excluded before 1898, but since the United States was a major maritime power throughout the nineteenth century, it seems appropriate to include it. See Norman Rich, Great Power Diplomacy 1814–1914, at 213–23 (McGraw-Hill, 1992).

70 Jackson H. Ralston, International Arbitration from Athens to Locarno (Stanford, 1929).

71 Raymond claims that democracies choose arbitration more often than mediation, because arbitration is more legalistic, and democracies care more for the rule of law. See Gregory A. Raymond, *Democracies, Disputes and Third-Party Intermediaries*, 38 J. Conflict Res. 24 (1994). His regression, which uses the Stuyt database, does show that pairs of democracies are more likely to use arbitration (that is, "commissions") than mediation (that is, "heads of state"), but not that democracies are more likely to use either of these procedures than an alternative like diplomacy or war. In addition, he interprets the head of state cases as not involving legal judgments; this appears to be wrong. The one party cases seem to be formal arbitrations.

72 http://www.pca-cpa.org/showpage.asp?pag_id=1029.

73 See Daniel W. Drezner, Regime Proliferation and World Politics: Is There Viscosity in Global Governance (2007) (unpublished manuscript), http://mershoncenter .osu.edu/events/Archived%20Events/06-07events/january07/Viscosity%20of% 20Global%20Governance.pdf; Eyal Benvenisti & George Downs, *The Empire's New Clothes: Political Economy and the Fragmentation of International Law*, 60 Stan. L. Rev. 595 (2007).

CHAPTER EIGHT

1 See Stephen D. Krasner, Sovereignty: Organized Hypocrisy (Princeton, 1999), for a recent discussion of the meaning of sovereignty.

2 For one of many examples of this view, see Mark A. Drumbl, Atrocity, Punishment, and International Law (Cambridge, 2007).

3 Richard H. Minear, Victors' Justice: The Tokyo War Crimes Trial 13–14 (2001).

4 Ann Tusa & John Tusa, supra chap. 3 note 26, at 138–39.

5 Solis Horwitz, The Tokyo Trial, in International Conciliation, No. 457, pp. 473, 495–97 (1950).

6 See Judith Shklar, supra chap. 1 note 17.

7 Many scholars writing today try to reconcile a commitment to international legalism with a sense of the practical realities of the state system. See, e.g., Mark Osiel, *The Banality of Good: Aligning Incentives Against Mass Atrocity*, 105 Colum. L. Rev. 1751 (2005).

8 For a discussion of the relationship between legalism and international criminal adjudication, see Gary Jonathan Bass, Stay the Hand of Vengeance: The Politics of War Crimes Tribunals (Princeton, 2000).

9 Human Rights Watch, Torture Worldwide (2005), hrw.org/english/docs/2005/04/27/china10549.htm.

10 Eric Neumayer, Do International Human Rights Treaties Improve Respect for Human Rights?, 49 J. of Conflict Resolution 925, 950–51 (2005); Emilie M. Hafner-Burton & Kiyoteru Tsutsui, *Human Rights in a Globalizing World: The Paradox of Empty Promises*, 110 Am. J. of Soc. 1373, 1395–1402 (2005); Hathaway, supra chap. 3 note 93, at 1935, 1998; Linda Camp Keith, *The United Nations International Covenant on Civil and Political Rights: Does it Make a Difference in Human Rights Behavior?* 36 J. of Peace Res. 95, (1999); Todd Landman, Protecting Human Rights: A Comparative Study

(Georgetown, 2005); Emilie M. Hafner-Burton & James Ron, Can the Human Rights Movement Achieve its Goals? 12–17 (2008) (unpublished manuscript), http://www .princeton.edu/~ehafner/pdfs/achieve_goals.pdf; Emilie M. Hafner-Burton, *Right or Robust?: The Sensitive Nature of Repression to Globalization*, 42 J. Peace Res. 679 (2005); Emilie M. Hafner-Burton & Kiyoteru Tsutsui, *Justice Lost! The Failure of International Human Rights Law To Matter Where Needed Most*, 44 J. Peace Res. 407 (2007).

11 For this argument, see Daniel C. Thomas, The Helsinki Effect: International Norms, Human Rights, and the Demise of Communism (Princeton, 2001).

12 Cf. Andrews L. Paulus, Jus Cogens *in Time of Hegemony and Fragmentation: An Attempt at a Re-appraisal*, 74 Nordic J. Int'l L. 297 (2005). Paulus' view is sympathetic but largely skeptical: "Thus, *jus cogens* is as empty or full as consensus on these basic principles in the international community." Id. at 333.

13 Tusa & Tusa, supra chap. 3 note 26, at 260, 304.

14 Id. at 223.

15 Churchill's "iron curtain" speech at Fulton, Missouri, was the turning point. See Tusa & Tusa, supra chap. 3 note 26, at 201.

16 See Public Opinion in Occupied Germany: The OMGUS Surveys, 1945–49, pp. 93, 121, 138 (Anna J. Merritt & Richard L. Merritt eds., 1970); Public Opinion in Semi-sovereign Germany: The HICOG Surveys, 1949–1955, p. 101 (Anna J. Merritt & Richard L. Merritt eds., Urbana, 1980); and see generally Richard L. Merritt, Democracy Imposed: U.S. Occupation Policy and the German Public, 1945–49, pp. 160–73 (1995). The trials did not have measurable impact on American public opinion. See William J. Bosch, Judgment on Nuremberg: American Attitudes Toward the Major German War-Crime Trials 87–116 (University of North Carolina, 1970).

17 Harries & Harries, supra chap. 3 note 26, at 163.

18 Id. at 175; see also John W. Dower, Embracing Defeat: Japan in the Wake of World War II (W.W. Norton, 1999), at 471.

19 Dower, supra, at 460.

20 Harries & Harries, supra chap. 3 note 26, at 175–76. See also Osiel, supra note 7, at 181 & n. 43 (citing sources).

21 Dower, supra, at 444.

22 Id. at 474. For a general discussion of Japanese attitudes about the Tokyo trail, along with a comparison to German attitudes about the Nuremberg trial, see Ian Buruma, The Wages of Guilt 159–68 (1994).

23 Id. at 525–26.

24 See, e.g., James Meernik, *Victor's Justice or the Law?* 47 J. Conflict Res. 140 (2003), who finds evidence that the ICTY was not biased by improper political factors.

25 Ku & Nzelibe have made the broader point that because the type of leader likely to be tried by an international court will usually suffer a worse fate at the hands of political opponents, the introduction of international courts may actually increase the incentive to commit atrocities in order to obtain or stay in power. See Julian Ku & Jide Nzelibe, *Do International Criminal Tribunals Deter or Exacerbate Humanitarian Atrocities*, 84 Wash. & Lee L. Rev. 777 (2006). See also Jack Snyder & Leslie Vinjamuri, *Trials*

and Errors: Principle and Pragmatism in Strategies for International Justice, 28 Int'l Sec. 5 (2003), which expresses skepticism about the deterrent effect of international courts. For a model in which international courts can have deterrent effect despite their lack of enforcement power, see Michael J. Gilligan, *Is Enforcement Necessary for Effectiveness? A Model of the International Criminal Regime*, 60 Int'l Org. 935 (2006). Gilligan argues that, at the margin, states that would have give former dictators asylum will decline to do so when the court is available and the dictator voluntarily steps down to avoid being violently deposed; thus, the ex ante cost of committing atrocities rises. Finally, for a favorable assessment of the ICTY and ICTR, see, for example, Payam Akhavan, *Beyond Impunity: Can International Criminal Justice Prevent Future Atrocities?* 95 Am. J. Int'l L. 7 (2001).

26 For this and other criticisms, see José E. Alvarez, *Crimes of States/Crimes of Hate: Lessons from Rwanda*, 24 Yale J. Int'l L. 365 (1999).

27 See David Wippman, *The Costs of International Justice*, 100 Am. J. Int'l L. 861 (2006).

28 Id. at 873–74.

29 Id. at 880.

30 In an insightful article, the authors argue that the ICTY has promoted the image of legal liberalism while acquiescing in the interests of powerful states that seek to rein in its work by shifting resources from investigation to the trials. As a result, the trials can be held out as exemplars of legal liberalism, while few people are actually convicted. See John Hagan, Ron Levi, & Gabrielle Ferrales, *Swaying the Hand of Justice: The Internal and External Dynamics of Regime Change at the International Criminal Tribunal for the Former Yugoslavia*, 31 L. & Soc. Inquiry 585 (2006).

31 See Rome Statute of the International Criminal Court, http://www.un.org/law/icc/statute/romefra.htm. A useful reference work is William A. Schabas, An Introduction to the International Criminal Court (2001).

32 Steven R. Ratner & Jason S. Abrams, Accountability for Human Rights Atrocities in International Law 160, 168 (2001).

33 Rome Statute, art. 17(1)(a).

34 Jack L. Goldsmith, *The Self-Defeating International Criminal Court*, 70 U. Chi. L. Rev. 89, 90 (2003).

35 Id. at 93.

36 See Rod Rastan, *Testing Co-Operation: The International Criminal Court and National Authorities*, 21 Leiden J. Int'l L. 431 (2008).

37 See Steven D. Roper & Lilian A. Barria, *State Co-Operation and International Criminal Court Bargaining Influence in the Arrest and the Surrender of Suspects*, 21 Leiden J. Int'l L. 457 (2008).

38 See Alison Danner, *Navigating Law and Politics*, 55 Stan. L. Rev. 1633, 1648–49 (2003); Leila Sadat & Richard Carden, *The New International Criminal Court*, 88 Geo. L. J. 381, 415 (2000). For an account of the ICC's activities so far, and its reliance on the uncertain good will of other states, see Roper & Barria, supra note 37.

39 Madeline Morris, *High Crimes and Misconceptions: The ICC and Non-Party States*, 64 L. & Contemp. Probs. 13, 21 (2001).

40 See Goldsmith, supra note 34; Ruth Wedgwood, *The Irresolution of Rome*, 64 L. & Contemp. Probs. 193, 194 (2001)

41 See Human Rights Watch, Bilateral Immunity Agreements (2003), http://www.hrw .org/campaigns/icc/docs/bilateralagreements.pdf.

42 Human Rights Watch, Rome State Ratifications, http://www.hrw.org/campaigns/ icc/ratifications.htm.

43 Human Rights Watch, Bilateral Immunity Agreements, supra note 41.

44 See Jeffrey Gettleman & Alexis Okeowo, *Rebels Delay Landmark Peace Deal In Uganda*, N.Y. Times, April 11, 2008, at A10.

45 See, e.g., Alexander K.A. Greenawalt, *Justice Without Politics? Prosecutorial Discretion and the International Criminal Court*, 39 N.Y.U. J. Int'l Law & Politics 583 (2007).

46 See David Pallister, *Human Rights: Growing Clamour To Remove The Hague Prosecutor Who Wants Sudanese President Arrested*, Guardian (UK), Aug. 18, 2008, http://www .guardian.co.uk/world/2008/aug/18/humanrights.sudan.

47 There is confusion in the literature about this issue. The problem with the ICC is not that it lacks enforcement power. Cf. Michael J. Gilligan, *Is Enforcement Necessary for Effectiveness? A Model of the International Criminal Regime*, 60 Int'l Org. 935 (2006). The WTO also lacks enforcement power, and it seems to be an effective institution. And even if the ICC did have enforcement power, states could undermine it by starving it of funds. The question is whether the ICC will actually act in a manner that states approve of. This is an agency problem, not an enforcement problem.

48 Beth Simmons & Alison Danner, *Credible Commitments and the International Criminal Court* (2007) (unpublished manuscript).

49 For a shrewd evaluation of international criminal justice efforts and their relationship to the interests of states, see Frédéric Mégret, *The Politics of International Criminal Justice*, 13 Eur. J. Int'l L. 1261 (2002).

CHAPTER NINE

1 Filartiga v. Pena-Irala, 630 F.2d 876 (2d Cir. 1980).

2 See Eric A. Posner & Cass R. Sunstein, *Climate Change Justice*, 96 Geo. L. J. 1565 (2008).

3 The major problem is that of collective action. A healthy climate is a public good, and so states have an incentive not to cooperate in producing it. See Goldsmith & Posner, supra preface note 1. Aggravating this problem, it appears that some states have little to fear from global warming, whereas others—especially poor nations and low-lying island nations—have much to fear. See William D. Nordhaus & Joseph Boyer, Warming the World: Economic Models of Global Warming 95–98 (2000). With conflicting interests, nations are even less likely to cooperate. However, other environmental treaties, such as the Montreal Protocol, have been successful, and one cannot exclude on first principles the possibility that nations might be able to reach agreement on the climate as well. For a discussion of these issues, see Richard H. Steinberg, Power and Cooperation in International Environmental Law, in Research Handbook In International Economic

Law (Andrew T. Guzman & Alan O. Sykes eds., Edward Elgar, 2008); Scott Barrett, Environment and Statecraft: The Strategy of Environmental Treaty-Making (Oxford, 2003).

4   In the following, I rely on several very helpful surveys, including Justin R. Pidot, Global Warming in the Courts: An Overview of Current Litigation and Common Legal Issues (2006), http:// www.law.georgetown.edu/gelpi/current_research/documents/ GWL_Report.pdf; BNA, Daily Environment Rep., Climate Change Litigation, vol. 10, no. 63 (April 2007); Todd O. Maiden & Eric M. McLaughlin, *Climate Change Litigation: Trends and Developments*, Daily Environment, April 3, 2007; David Hunter & James Salzman, *Negligence In The Air: The Duty Of Care In Climate Change Litigation*, 155 U. Pa. L. Rev. 1741 (2007); Michael B. Gerrard, *Survey of Climate Change Litigation*, N. Y. L. J. 1 (September 28, 2007).

5   Native Village of Kivalina and City of Kivalina v. ExxonMobil et al., Complaint, United States District Court, Northern District of California (Feb. 26, 2008), http:// www.adn.com/static/adn/pdfs/Kivalina%20Complaint%20-%20Final.pdf.

6   People of the State of California, ex rel. Bill Lockyer, Attorney General v. General Motor Corp., et al, No. 06-cv-05755 (N.D. Cal. filed Sept. 20, 2006).

7   Comer v. Murphy Oil, USA, et al., No. 05-cv-00436-LTSRHW (S.D. Miss., filed Sept. 20, 2005).

8   Connecticut v. Am. Elec. Power Co., 406 F. Supp. 2d 265 (S.D.N.Y. 2005).

9   The complaint also charges that Exxon deliberately misled the public by advancing scientific claims about global warming that it knew to be false. This claim also raises difficult questions of causation and harm.

10 For the contrary view, see Jonathan Zasloff, *The Judicial Carbon Tax: Reconstructing Public Nuisance and Climate Change* (2008) (unpublished manuscript), http://papers .ssrn.com/sol3/papers.cfm?abstract_id=1113143.

11 549 U.S. 497 (2007).

12 No. 06–1131, 2006 U.S. App. LEXIS 23499, at *1–4 (D.C. Cir. Sept. 13, 2006); these are "new source" rules and do not apply to existing power plants.

13 Compare Central Valley Chrysler-Jeep, Inc. v. Goldstone, 2007 WL 4372878 (E.D. Cal. Dec. 11, 2007). (no preemption); Green Mountain Chrysler Plymouth Dodge Jeep v. Crombie, 508 F. Supp. 2d 295 (D. Vt. 2007) (no preemption); and Engine Mfrs. Ass'n v. S. Coast Air Quality Maint. Dist., 498 F.3d 1031 (9th Cir. 2007) (allowing for some preemption).

14 See Ctr. for Biological Diversity v. Nat'l Highway Traffic Safety Admin., 508 F.3d 508 (9th Cir. 2007); State of New York v. Bodman, No. 1:05-cv-07807 (S.D.N.Y. filed Sept. 7, 2005, consolidated with Natural Resources Defense Council v. Bodman, No. 05-cv-07808 (S.D.N.Y. filed Sept. 7, 2005); Center for Biological Diversity v. DOE, 419 F. Supp. 2d 1166, 1169–70 (N.D. Cal. 2006); Natural Resources Defense Council v. Mineta, 2005 WL 1075355 (S.D.N.Y. 2005); NRDC v. Abraham, 355 F.3d 179 (2d Cir. 2004); Center for Biological Diversity v. Abraham, 218 F. Supp. 2d 1143 (N.D. Cal. 2002):

15 See Center for Biological Diversity v. NHTSA, 508 F.3d 508 (9h Cir.); Montana Environmental Information Center v. Johanns, No. 1:2007CV01311 (D. D.C., filed July 23,

2007); Mayo Found. v. STB, 472 F.3d 545 (8th Cir. 2006); Friends of the Earth v. Watson [previously Mosbacher], 2005 U.S. Dist. LEXIS 42335 35 ELR 20179 (N.D. Cal. 2005); Senville v. Peters, 327 F. Supp. 2d 335 (D. Vt. 2004); Mid States Coalition for Progress v. Surface Transportation Board, 345 F.3d 520 (8th Cir. 2003); Border Power Working Group v. Dept. of Energy, 260 F. Supp. 2d 997 (S.D. Cal. 2003); City of Los Angeles v. National Highway Traffic Safety Administration, 912 F.2d 478 (D.C. Cir. 1990). State law versions of NEPA have also resulted in litigation; see BNA supra at 9–10.

16 See Natural Resources Defense Council v. Kempthorne, 2007 WL 1577896 (E.D. Cal. May 25, 2007); Center for Biological Diversity v. Norton, No. 3–05–05191 (N.D. Cal filed Dec. 15, 2005).

17 Citizens for Responsibility and Ethics in Washington v. Council on Environmental Quality, No. 1:07CV00365 (D.D.C. filed Feb. 20, 2007).

18 See, e.g., Okeson v. City of Seattle 159 Wash.2d 436, 150 P.3d 556; In Re Quantification of Environmental Costs, 578 NW 2d 4794 (1998); Utsey v. Coos County, 32 P.3d 933 (Or. Ct. App. 2001).

19 http://www.climatelaw.org/cases/country/argentina/accion/.

20 Australian Climate Justice Program et al. v. HRL Ltd, cite (2007); Gray v The Minister for Planning and Others, [2006] NSWLEC 720; Wildlife Preservation Society of Queensland v. Minister for the Environment and Heritage, [2006] FCA 736; Australian Conservation Foundation v Minister for Planning, [2004] VCAT 2029; Australian Conservation Foundation v. Latrobe City Council, No P 2257/2004.

21 Friends of the Earth v. Minister of Environment, Court file No T-1683-07; Friends of the Earth v. Minister of Environment (2007).

22 Meridian Energy Ltd v Wellington City Council, W31/07 (2007); Greenpeace New Zealand Incorporated v. Northland Regional Council and Mighty River Power Limited, CIV 2006-404-004617 (2006); Genesis Power Limited v. Energy Efficiency and Conservation Authority, No A 148/2005; Environmental Defence Society v. Auckland Regional Council, No A 183/2002; Environmental Defence Society and Taranaki Energy Watch v. Taranaki Regional Council and Stratford Power Limited, No A 184/2002

23 U.S. and Canadian Inuits v. United States, Inter-American Commission on Human Rights (2006); Donald M. Goldberg & Martin Wagner, *Petitioning for Adverse Impacts of Global Warming in the Inter-American Human Rights System*, in Climate Change Five Years After Kyoto 191 (Velme I. Grover ed., 2004).

24 For a discussion, see Roda Verheyen, Climate Change Damage and International Law: Prevention Duties and State Responsibility chs. 4–5 (2005).

25 For the argument, see Rosemary Reed, *Rising Seas and Disappearing Islands: Can Island Inhabitants Seek Redress Under the Alien Tort Claims Act?* 11 Pac. Rim L. & Pol'y J. 399 (2002).

26 See Armin Rosencranz & Richard Campbell, *Foreign Environmental and Human Rights Suits Against U.S. Corporations in U.S. Courts*, 18 Stan. Envtl L.J. 145 (1999).

27 Many of the points I will make are specific to ATS litigation, but others are more general.

28 See Hari M. Osofsky, *The Geography of Climate Change Litigation: Implications for Transnational Regulatory Governance*, 83 Wash. U. L.Q. 1788, 1855 (2005); Michael R. Anderson, *Human Rights Approaches to Environmental Protection: An Overview*, in Human Rights Approaches to Environmental Protection [hereafter, Human Rights Approaches] 1, 21–22 (Alan E. Boyle & Michael R. Anderson eds., 1996). Anderson also surveys the disadvantages. Id., 22–23. For other criticisms of the international human rights approach to environmental protection, see J.G. Merrills, *Environmental Protection and Human Rights: Conceptual Aspects*, in Human Rights Approaches 25; Alan Boyle, *The Role of International Human Rights Law in the Protection of the Environment*, in Human Rights Approaches 43. Other relevant essays can be found in Human Rights and the Environment (Lyuba Zarsky ed., 2002); see also Donald M. Goldberg & Martin Wagner, *Petitioning for Adverse Impacts of Global Warming in the Inter-American Human Rights System*, in Climate Change: Five Years After Kyoto, ed. (Velma I. Grover ed., 2004).

29 See Foreign Sovereign Immunity Act, 28 U.S.C. § 1604.

30 See John Doe I v. Unocal Corp., 963 F. Supp. 880 (C.D. Cal. 1997); National Coalition Gov't of the Union of Burma v. Unocal, Inc., 176 F.R.D. 329 (C.D. Cal. 1997).

31 The Stern Review, for example, estimates that the cost of a reasonable response to global warming would be about one percent of global GDP per year. See Stern Review: The Economics of Climate Change, Executive Summary xiii (2006), http://www.hm -treasury.gov.uk/independent_reviews/stern_review_economics_climate_change/ sternreview_summary.cfm. This estimate is on the high end; Nordhaus's estimate is significantly lower. See Nordhaus & Boyer, supra note 3. The difference is mainly attributable to the fact that the Stern Review does not discount future costs and benefits, whereas Nordhaus does. See William D. Nordhaus, The Stern Review on the Economics of Climate Change (2006), http://nordhaus.econ.yale.edu/SternReviewD2.pdf. The point for present purposes is that even the pessimistic estimate, if converted into a liability rule, implies that liability would not be so high as to drive most firms out of business.

32 See, e.g., Michael Saks & Peter Blanck, *Justice Improved: The Unrecognized Benefits of Aggregation and Sampling in the Trial of Mass Torts*, 44 Stan. L. Rev. 815 (1992).

33 This would also be the case if the state action requirement were interpreted strictly, so that, for example, corporations could be liable only insofar as their greenhouse gas emissions were directed or encouraged by a state. This would drastically limit the scope of liability so that the litigation would be ineffectual.

34 A rather odd qualification is that the level of emissions would be somewhat less than the global optimum, because the well-being of only aliens—not Americans!—could be taken into account.

35 There is a large body of literature on this topic. For an early discussion of the basic tradeoffs between litigation and regulation, see Steven Shavell, *Liability for Harm Ver-*

sus Regulation and Safety, 13 J. Legal Stud. 357 (1984); in the context of environmental litigation, see Anderson, supra note 28, at 22–23.

36 Judges have long expressed skepticism about their own ability to predict and evaluate the foreign relations implications of their own decisions in cases involving the interests of foreign states, and so they often defer to the advice of the executive branch. See Posner & Sunstein, supra chap. 5 note 24, at 1170.

37 See Gary Clyde Hufbauer & Barbara Oegg, *Beyond the Nation-State: Privatization of Economic Sanctions*, 10 Middle East Pol'y 126, 133–34 (2003).

38 On the geographically diverse effects of climate change, see Stern Review, Pt. 2, p. 75, http://www.hm-treasury.gov.uk/media/9A2/97/Chapter_3__Global_Impacts.pdf; Nordhaus & Boyer, supra note 3, at 159–60.

39 This is even clearer in the hypothetical world where foreign governments or states were held liable for having inadequate greenhouse gas emission laws — surely ironic for American courts to hold foreign governments liable for failing to implement controls that the American government itself fails to implement. But this would be the effect of holding foreign corporations liable, as discussed in the text.

40 See, e.g., People of State of California v. General Motors Corp., Slip Copy, 2007 WL 2726871, *8, N.D.Cal., 2007.

41 ATS litigation like this would be similar to ordinary government sanctions on countries that engage in bad behavior, the difference being that the political branches, not the courts, decide when to impose sanctions. Sanction regimes are often ineffective, and their effectiveness is highly dependent on specific conditions being satisfied — for example, they are more likely to work on friends than enemies. See Gary C. Hufbauer et al., Economic Sanctions Reconsidered: History and Current Policy (2nd ed. 1990).

42 See Sosa v. Alvarez-Machain, 542 U.S. 692, 733 n.21 (2004).

43 See Curtis Bradley, *The Costs of International Human Rights Litigation*, 2 Chi. J. Int'l L. 457, 460–62 (2001); Hufbauer & Oegg, supra note 37.

44 See Stern Review, supra note 31.

45 For a discussions, see Stern Review, supra note 31; William D. Nordhaus & Joseph Boyer, Warming the World: Economic Models of Global Warming (2003).

46 See *The Asbestos-Fraud Express*, Wall St. J., June 2, 2006, at A18.

47 W. Kip Viscusi, Regulation through Litigation (AEI Press, 2002).

48 Stern Review, supra note 31, at Part I, 11–12.

49 See Thomas C. Schelling, *Intergenerational Discounting*, 23 Energy Pol'y 395 (1995).

50 Viscusi, supra note 47.

51 See the essays in Viscusi, supra note 47.

CONCLUSION

1 The significant exception is Koskenniemi, who acknowledges the instrumentalism of the European governments though he does not defend it; see, e.g., Martti Koskenniemi, *International Law in Europe: Between Tradition and Renewal*, 16 Eur. J. Int'l L. 113 (2005).

2   To avoid misunderstanding, I should point out that some Europeans think of "democracy" as encompassing what Americans would generally think of policy outcomes required by constitutional constraints and dismiss the American version of democracy as purely procedural. So they do not think that global constitutionalism necessarily sacrifices democratic principles, whereas most Americans would.

3   As I write these words in the summer of 2008, Russia invades Georgia. The measure of one's shock is, I suspect, proportional to one's commitment to global legalism. There is nothing new about states violating the UN Charter's prohibition on the use of force. See, e.g., Michael J. Glennon, Limits of Law, Prerogatives of Power: Interventionism After Kosovo (Palgrave, 2001).

INDEX